Covering Muslims

Covering Muslims

American Newspapers in Comparative Perspective

ERIK BLEICH
A. MAURITS VAN DER VEEN

OXFORD
UNIVERSITY PRESS

OXFORD
UNIVERSITY PRESS

Oxford University Press is a department of the University of Oxford. It furthers the University's objective of excellence in research, scholarship, and education by publishing worldwide. Oxford is a registered trade mark of Oxford University Press in the UK and certain other countries.

Published in the United States of America by Oxford University Press
198 Madison Avenue, New York, NY 10016, United States of America.

© Oxford University Press 2022

CIP data is on file at the Library of Congress
ISBN 978–0–19–761172–2 (pbk.)
ISBN 978–0–19–761171–5 (hbk.)

DOI: 10.1093/oso/9780197611715.001.0001

1 3 5 7 9 8 6 4 2

Paperback printed by LSC Communications, United States of America
Hardback printed by Bridgeport National Bindery, Inc., United States of America

For Jennifer and Helen

Contents

Preface

Is the media's coverage of Muslims and Islam as negative as critics claim? And if so, why? We address these questions in this book because of our long-standing shared interest in understanding how people construct "others," in particular marginalized groups in North American and European countries. Here, we provide more thorough and systematic answers than had previously been possible, by taking advantage of the increasing availability of newspapers in digitized form and of computational approaches that enable scholars to analyze greater quantities of texts than any team of researchers could possibly read and code by hand.

The spark for the book came from a discussion we had in 2012. Erik had begun analyzing newspaper headlines about Muslims, hoping to learn more about the framing of Muslims as a minority group in a post-9/11 world. Meanwhile, Maurits had been working on applying computational text analysis to study the framing of foreigners in Europe, and was confident that such tools could allow Erik to expand his analysis to full newspaper articles. We quickly realized that the tone of articles was the dominant feature of coverage, given its dramatic negativity.

Because existing approaches to the measurement of tone (generally referred to as "sentiment analysis") had significant limitations, we spent the following years developing and fine-tuning our own approach. Our ultimate aim was to construct a method that would reliably indicate not just whether a newspaper article is positive or negative, but also how positive or negative it is—a crucial question too infrequently addressed in the literature. We wanted to compare tone across topics, time periods, and even countries, so we needed a way to benchmark our measures. And we wanted to look within the articles to understand the words and topics most commonly associated with Muslims in the press.

With his background in computer science, Maurits developed python notebooks and code files that allowed deep and varied dives into our newspaper articles, often responding to Erik's requests for new types of analyses. Erik worked with his lab students at Middlebury College to help streamline the system and make it more accessible to nonspecialists; Maurits continued to explore new dimensions of data analysis with his lab at William & Mary. We owe a particular debt of gratitude to our students, who inspired us to develop applications of our methods that apply to a wide variety of topics of interest to a broad readership.

Once we had our system in place, we were able to answer the key questions that had drawn us to this topic: Is it really true that coverage of Muslims is more negative than one would expect? How much more negative is it than coverage of comparable groups? And is it possible to pinpoint the topics associated with both the most negative and the least negative coverage, so we can better understand *why* it is so negative and also offer prescriptions for how the media might produce more balanced coverage?

Preliminary answers to these questions, presented at academic conferences, were invariably met with further questions. Struck by the potential for systematic analysis offered by our computational approach, discussants, fellow panelists, and audience members would ask various questions: "What about comparing coverage to this or that other group?" "Can you identify how much of a difference 9/11 made?" "Is the United States coverage unique compared to other countries?" These seemed to us questions better answered in a comprehensive account in book form than in separate articles.

Writing a book is generally a solitary enterprise. Co-authoring made it far less so. The ability to bounce ideas off each other, to pass drafts back and forth repeatedly, and simply to check in regularly on the other person not only made the writing process less daunting, it also greatly improved the final product. This is without a doubt a better book than either of us would have written on our own. Having first worked together on a project almost three decades ago in graduate school, it has been very rewarding to renew our collaboration in recent years, and now to have this book to show for it.

The title of our book, *Covering Muslims*, is a conscious echo of Edward Said's *Covering Islam*, which first appeared in 1981. Said's book used qualitative, interpretive methods to critique the media for its pervasive negative tone. Forty years later, our quantitative analyses do little to challenge Said's conclusions, underscoring the long-standing nature of this problem. Our book's cover features an image by the Barcelona-based contemporary collage artist and illustrator Max-o-matic (Máximo Tuja). It is an image that appears alongside a 2016 newspaper article in our dataset: "The Life of Marshall Hodgson," by Lydia Kiesling in the *New York Times Magazine*. Not only does the image directly depict the process of writing about Muslims and Islam, the article it accompanies is also one of a small subset of articles in our dataset that focus on culture rather than current affairs, noting that Hodgson as a scholar viewed "Islam as a global creative force that propelled numerous achievements in science, art and politics." The tone of such articles is much less negative than the overall average for our corpus; their presence in the dataset goes some way toward meeting Said's call for the media to help dispel "the myths and stereotypes of Orientalism," something he notes Hodgson also tried to do before his untimely death in 1968.

As is always the case with a large, multiyear research project, we have incurred many debts along the way. Thanks are due to our many interlocutors at academic conferences in recent years. In particular, Sara Wallace Goodman was the first to suggest that this project should be a book; Pepper Culpepper regularly served as a sounding board, and along the way became interested in applying computational approaches in his own research; we turned to Stuart Soroka for advice numerous times, and he was always generous with his feedback; David McBride, our wonderful editor at OUP, pushed us to look beyond the Anglophone North to understand newspaper coverage of Muslims in the Global South.

When the first draft of the manuscript was complete, William & Mary helped us organize a book workshop. Scheduled to take place in Williamsburg, Virginia, in April 2020, the COVID-19 pandemic forced us to conduct it over Zoom instead. The participants in the workshop gamely sat in front of a computer all day, in several different time zones, and provided truly invaluable comments and suggestions that have made this a far better book. We owe them particular thanks for spurring us to revisions that greatly strengthened the manuscript. They are Claire Adida, Hajo Boomgaarden, Sharan Grewal, S. P. Harish, Nazita Lajevardi, Jaime Settle, and Fiona Shen-Bayh.

Because our project has been incubating for a long time, we have also communicated with many colleagues and presented our work at a number of institutions. We would like to thank Will Allen, Chris Bail, Ken Benoit, Scott Blinder, Amber Boydstun, Jeff Carpenter, Claes de Vreese, Randall Hansen, Marc Helbling, Amaney Jamal, Simon Kuper, David Laitin, Michèle Lamont, David Leal, Rahsaan Maxwell, Rochelle Terman, Kjerstin Thorson, Josh Tucker, and Joost van Spanje. For hosting our invited talks, we thank colleagues at Michigan State University, the University of Amsterdam, the University of British Columbia, the University of Massachusetts at Amherst, the Computer Science Department at William & Mary, and the Economics Department at Middlebury College. We also thank the journal *Politics, Groups, and Identities* for permission to update and adapt our 2021 article as a portion of our analysis in chapter 3. We are especially grateful to the administrators at Middlebury College and William & Mary who have fully supported our work over the years.

Finally, our partners Jennifer Bleich and Helen Murphy have served as sounding boards for our project along the way, and graciously took care of family business during our frequent and lengthy online discussions and when we were away presenting our work. For all this, and for so much more, this book is dedicated to them.

1

Media coverage of Muslims

Introduction and overview

> *Just once I want CNN to be like, "Now we are going to Mohammed in
> Iran." They go to some guy who's like, "Hello, I am Mohammed and I'm
> just baking a cookie. I swear to God. No bombs, no flags, nothing. Back
> to you, Bob." That would be the whole news piece. They're never going
> to do that. Even if they ever did that, they would follow it up with an-
> other news piece. This just in: A cookie bomb just exploded.*
> —Maz Jobrani, *The Axis of Evil Comedy Tour*[1]

Muslims have long been a stigmatized group in the United States. One of the
earliest articles mentioning Muslims in the *New York Times*, for example, was
an 1858 story headlined "Another Mussulman Outrage in Syria." It described
the murder of "an English lady of extreme benevolence" by two men heard
"cursing the Christians, and threatening death to anyone whom Allah threw
in their way."[2] This thread of suspicion is hardly a historical artifact. In the
contemporary era, even prior to the 9/11 attacks, Muslims were frequently
mentioned in connection with controversial topics like the Nation of Islam,
"Black Muslim" criminality, and foreign conflict zones like Iran, Lebanon,
Afghanistan, and Iraq. In the living memory of most Americans, Muslims
and Islam have regularly been associated with both internal and external
threats.

American Muslims understand this. They overwhelmingly and accurately
believe that they face significant discrimination, and that most Americans
do not see Islam as fully belonging in the United States. A 2017 survey revealed that 50% of all US respondents feel Islam is not part of mainstream

---

[1] YouTube, https://www.youtube.com/watch?v=718bxd8ojBY, 1:48–2:12, accessed August 1, 2020.
[2] *New York Times*, November 1, 1858.

Covering Muslims. Erik Bleich and A. Maurits van der Veen, Oxford University Press. © Oxford University Press 2022.
DOI: 10.1093/oso/9780197611715.003.0001

American society, that over 40% think there is a "natural conflict" between Islam and democracy, and that Islam encourages violence more than other faiths (Pew Research Center and Lipka 2017). This skepticism and outright hostility translate into concrete effects. The New America think tank and the Council on American-Islamic Relations (CAIR) have documented a wide variety of anti-Muslim activities in the United States, including vandalism against mosques, anti-Muslim statements by politicians and public figures, proposals for "anti-sharia" legislation, and verbal and physical assaults against Muslim Americans (New America, n.d.; CAIR, n.d.).

Scholars, too, argue that Muslims are an especially demonized outgroup in the United States. Kalkan, Layman, and Uslaner (2009, 2), for example, explain that Americans view Muslims not only as religious minorities, but also as cultural minorities "defined by behaviors or values that many find unusual or offensive." For Lajevardi (2020, 12), Muslim Americans are often viewed not just as a religious group, but also as a racialized one for whom "external markers such as dress, skin color, accent, and language" identify them to some as "a threat to American culture and national security." And Oskooii, Dana, and Barreto (2019, 4) argue that "unfavorable views toward Muslim Americans" are rooted partly in the "specific characterization of Muslims and Arabs as culturally inferior, opposed to democratic norms, and a rising challenge to the modern Christian world." Such suspicions affect not only Muslims within the United States, but also those wanting to come to the country. Comparing American respondents' willingness to have their country grant citizenship to legal immigrants who are Christian or Muslim, Creighton and Jamal (2015, 90) show that Muslims are an "outgroup subject to distinct intolerance."

Intensely negative attitudes toward Muslim immigrants and their descendants also exist outside of the United States. In the European context, for example, Zolberg and Long (1999) and Alba (2005) argue that religion functions as a "bright line" between Muslims and non-Muslims that constitutes a significant division within societies. Experimental studies and survey data both support the notion that Muslims and Islam are viewed with substantial skepticism in Europe: between 23 and 41% of European country respondents agreed that "Muslims want to impose their religious law on everyone else" (Pew Research Center 2018; see also Adida, Laitin, and Valfort 2016; Helbling and Traunmüller 2018), even though a comprehensive overview of global Muslim attitudes concludes that Muslims are "neither extraordinarily religious nor inclined to favor mixing religion and politics" (Fish

2011, 64). Detrimental perceptions and actions toward Muslims have also been documented in countries such as Canada, Australia, and New Zealand (Poynting and Perry 2007; Miller 2017; Shaver et al. 2017).

Many people living in Western liberal democracies view Muslims with such wariness that scholars have developed the term "Islamophobia" to denote sweeping forms of unwarranted hostility toward them (Allen 2010; Bleich 2011; Esposito and Kalin 2011; Helbling 2012). For social scientific purposes, Islamophobia involves "indiscriminate negative attitudes or emotions directed at Islam or Muslims" (Bleich 2011, 1585). In its starkest form, Islamophobia thus involves anger, fear, hatred, or suspicion of Islam or Muslims as a whole. It is often measured through questionnaires designed to detect animus along a variety of dimensions (Lee et al. 2013; Hopkins and Shook 2017). This has allowed researchers to test its consistency across countries (Uenal et al. 2021) and to link it at the individual level to outcomes such as voting, policy preferences, or psychological distress among Muslims themselves (Imhoff and Recker 2012; Kunst, Sam, and Ulleberg 2013; Helbling and Traunmüller 2018; Lajevardi 2020).

Expressions of Islamophobia reveal individual attitudes, but they also constitute an intense form of "boundary-making." Since the 1960s, researchers have examined how societal distinctions are created, reinforced, or effaced through a variety of interactions (Barth 1969; Brubaker 2009; Wimmer 2013). The boundary metaphor evokes a line that separates two groups, or, as Lamont and Molnár (2002, 169) describe it, "segmentation between 'us' and 'them.'" In theory, boundaries can distinguish groups seen as equals, but in practice they often lead to social hierarchies, with some groups viewed as more favored, trusted, or welcomed as "ingroups" and others as disfavored "outgroups" (Hagendoorn 1995; Sidanius and Pratto 1999; Dovidio and Gaertner, 2010; Axt, Ebersole, and Nosek 2014; Bleich, Nisar, and Vazquez 2018). The stigmatization associated with Muslims in American society may partly be a function of expressions of Islamophobia, but it need not be so. The "othering" that creates social hierarchies of insiders and outsiders can be communicated through a variety of signals that fall short of unambiguous forms of outright prejudice.

Attitudes and beliefs about Muslims and Islam that constitute these important boundaries are shaped by a wide range of factors, each of which may affect individuals to a different degree. When asked in a 2007 survey about the biggest influence on their views on Muslims, for example, just over 10% of respondents cited religious beliefs, while just under 20% named education

or personal experience. The single most important factor listed by those sur-
veyed, however, was the media. Almost a third of all respondents said that
the media had the largest impact on their views of Muslims, a proportion
that rose to 48% among those who held negative views of Muslims (Pew
Research Center 2007). Since most people in the United States have limited
contact with Muslims in their everyday lives, it makes sense that the media
play a key role in forming attitudes. They do so when they report statements
by politicians or publish opinion pieces by writers sympathetic or hostile to
Muslims (Ali et al. 2011). They also do it when they identify either a terrorist
group or a sports star as Muslim, and when they choose to write stories about
Islamic museum exhibits or Muslim charities instead of a foreign war zone.
What the media communicate both reflects and reinforces perceptions of
Muslims that shape social boundaries in our societies.

The significance of the media: Negativity, representations, and effects

If we want to understand the stigmatization of Muslims, we have to know
more about media coverage and how it matters. We focus in particular on
negative coverage, which research shows is relatively widespread and meaningful for attitudes and actions. Studies of media gatekeeping—the process by which journalists select which events from the real world are worth
reporting—have frequently emphasized the particularly strong perceived
newsworthiness of negative coverage (Shoemaker 1996; Soroka 2012). The
prevalence of negativity also has a disproportionate influence on cognition
and attitudes, given that "negative information receives more processing and
contributes more strongly to the final impression than does positive information" (Baumeister et al. 2001, 323–24; Soroka and McAdams 2015; Soroka,
Fournier, and Nir 2019).

Studies of political attitudes suggest that negative information about
groups can be gleaned through skimming newspaper articles or even
headlines (Weinberger and Westen 2008), but the impact is greater if exposure is repeated. As Fairclough (2013, 45) argues, "the effects of media
power are cumulative, working through the repetition of particular ways
of handling causality and agency." Once an opinion about another group—
including a prejudice—takes root, it is difficult to change. Social psychological theories suggest that even "repeated exposure to counter-stereotypical

information" is unlikely to undo negative evaluations of groups (Lupia et al. 2015, 1).[3] Stereotypical information thus leaves a long-term residue of subconscious (implicit) negative attitudes that can trigger conscious (explicit) responses toward marginalized groups as well as toward policies that affect them (Erisen, Lodge, and Taber 2014; Arendt and Northup 2015; Pérez 2016; Kroon, van der Meer, and Mastro 2021).

Scholars have shown how this dynamic operates with respect to marginalized groups in a wide variety of settings (Eberl et al. 2018). In the US context, for example, Gilliam and Iyengar (2000) demonstrate through experimental methods that even brief exposure to a television news report identifying a Black perpetrator of crime amplifies White respondents' beliefs that African Americans are not part of the cultural mainstream, and intensifies their preferences for punitive policies. Similarly, Arendt and Northup (2015) find that long-term exposure to local television news (known for stereotypically depicting African Americans as criminals) correlates with negative implicit attitudes toward African Americans. They also find that heavy readers of Austrian tabloid crime stories express relatively more negative implicit attitudes toward foreigners. In other European countries, scholars have identified a relationship between negative media tone and perceptions that immigration is a significant societal problem (Boomgaarden and Vliegenthart 2009), stereotypes about immigrants (Schemer 2012), and views that immigrants endanger the host society (Schlueter and Davidov 2013).[4]

Studies over the past two decades confirm that coverage of Muslims has been markedly negative (Ahmed and Matthes 2017), regardless of whether the method of analysis involves close readings of relatively few articles (Abrahamian 2003; Jackson 2010; Powell 2011) or larger overviews of hundreds or even hundreds of thousands of articles (Moore, Mason, and Lewis 2008; Trevino, Kanso, and Nelson 2010; Baker, Gabrielatos, and McEnery 2013; Terman 2017; Yazdiha 2020). Even when research reveals a more complex portrayal of Muslims, it tends to find that positive depictions exist alongside negative ones, not that the former outweigh the latter (Nacos and Torres-Reyna 2007; Bleich et al. 2015; Bowe, Fahmy, and Matthes 2015). The epigrammatic joke by the comedian Maz Jobrani that opened this chapter

---

[3] Other research suggests, however, that positive media portrayals can help offset negative stereotypes under certain circumstances (Mastro and Tukachinsky 2011; Schemer 2012).
[4] These relationships were nuanced by other factors such as intensity of coverage (Boomgaarden and Vliegenthart 2009), political knowledge (Schemer 2012), or the size of the immigrant population (Schlueter and Davidov 2013).

Table 1.1 Feeling thermometer results for three religious groups

Year	Poll name	Catholics	Jews	Muslims
2007	American Faith Matters Survey	62	57	42
2011	American Faith Matters Survey	61	58	44
2014	American Trends Panel Survey	62	63	40

aptly captures the widespread assumption that even a rare light story might quickly be tempered by a dark turn.

What is the effect of such negative coverage on public attitudes? There is substantial indirect evidence that it generates aversion, skepticism, and hostility to Muslims. Table 1.1 displays the results of three comparative "feeling thermometer" polls, in which American respondents give groups a score between 0 and 100 based on the warmth of their feelings, where 50 represents a neutral sentiment.[5] The average score for Muslims is below 50, and substantially lower than that for other major religious groups.[6] These measures of explicit attitudes are consistent with studies of implicit attitudes, which demonstrate that Muslims are a disfavored category compared to White individuals (J. Park, Felix, and Lee 2007) as well as with respect to Christians, Jews, Buddhists, and Hindus (Axt, Ebersole, and Nosek 2014).

A growing number of scholars also provide more direct evidence of the impact of the media on attitudes toward Muslims. Survey research of over 16,500 New Zealanders identified a correlation between news consumption and elevated levels of anger and lower levels of warmth toward Muslims (Shaver et al. 2017).[7] Experimental work among American respondents demonstrates that exposure to negative stories increases not only general resentment toward Muslims, but also preferences for discriminatory restrictions on Muslim Americans and for military action in Muslim countries (Saleem, Yang, and Ramasubramanian 2016; Saleem et al. 2017; Lajevardi 2020, 108–31). Moreover, negative media coverage has been shown

[5] The data are from Putnam et al. (2007); Putnam et al. (2011), and Pew Research Center (2014a), respectively.

[6] Similar findings in British surveys indicate that a moderately larger Muslim population does not automatically lead to greater warmth (A. Park et al. 2010; National Centre for Social Research 2010; ICM Unlimited 2015).

[7] Research by Ogan et al. (2014) showed that survey respondents who paid greater attention to news stories about the 2010 Park51 Islamic community center controversy in New York City had stronger anti-Muslim attitudes.

to affect Muslims themselves. When Muslims feel that the media are biased against them, they are more likely to feel lower trust in government (Saleem et al. 2019), to feel lower identification with their national communities (Kunst et al. 2012; Saleem et al. 2019), and to feel a greater affiliation to an imagined global Muslim community (Güney 2010). In short, negative media coverage matters for public attitudes toward Muslims and for Muslims' own attitudes and identities.[8] All this underscores the importance of developing a better understanding of how the media represent Muslims.

What more can we learn? Tone-checking, explaining negativity, and four comparisons

Existing research largely concurs that coverage of Muslims is negative. Yet this masks how much we still do not know. In particular, there has been no clear or consistent way to gauge precisely how much negativity is present in stories about Muslims. Given that media producers and consumers are drawn to negative coverage in general (Soroka 2014; Trussler and Soroka 2014), it is possible that the bulk of reporting on Muslims is no more negative than the average story. Even if journalism about Muslims is negative overall, this finding may simply parallel coverage of other religious or ethnic groups, particularly those seen as cultural outsiders. What we need is a common baseline for measuring tone across sets of stories. This would allow us to accurately describe media coverage of Muslims and to understand how it compares to coverage of other groups, how it has shifted over time, and how it varies by country. It would enable us to "tone-check" articles for their positivity or negativity, much in the way that organizations "fact-check" reporting for its accuracy.

What makes some Muslim articles more negative than others? Perhaps pervasive negativity is linked to *geography*, given that stories about foreign locations are often associated with more negative coverage (Peterson 1981; Nossek 2004) and that the press extensively covers Muslim-majority countries with which the United States has tense relations. It is also plausible that negative coverage is primarily related to specific violent *events*, such as terrorism or political conflict more broadly, which have been found to create

---

[8] As Schlueter, Masso, and Davidov (2020) show, however, media tone is not always the most important factor in all contexts.

"media storms" that amplify negativity (Hamilton 2000; Boydstun, Hardy, and Walgrave 2014; Harcup and O'Neill 2017). Perceived or actual *cultural differences* are another possible source of negativity in reporting. Stories revolving around extremism, religiosity, and women's rights or other "value clashes" have frequently been associated with societal tensions (Sniderman and Hagendoorn 2007; Helbling and Traunmüller 2018; Sides and Mogahed 2018). Finally, some research finds that *market* characteristics of newspapers can affect coverage of Muslims, given that journalists and readers of conservative or tabloid newspapers may be more inclined toward skeptical or sensationalist coverage (Conboy 2005; Mullainathan and Shleifer 2005; Moore, Mason, and Lewis 2008; Gentzkow and Shapiro 2010). To pinpoint more clearly the main drivers of negative coverage, we must examine all of these elements, both separately and together.

Articles mentioning Muslims and Islam have been widely argued to be negative, but are they more negative than those touching on comparable groups? Most research on media portrayals of Muslims focuses uniquely on Muslims. It may be the case, however, that journalists write about religious or ethnic groups primarily when they are involved in significant controversies. If this were true, articles about other world religious groups, such as Catholics, Jews, or Hindus, might focus largely on topics such as pedophilia scandals, harsh treatment of Palestinians in Israeli-occupied territories, or extreme nationalism and riots in India. Stories about US groups such as African Americans, Latinos, Mormons, or atheists—often perceived or treated as outgroups—may also disproportionately focus on controversial events likely to spark strong reader reactions. In short, the negativity inherent in articles about Islam and Muslims may contribute to stigmatization, but it might stand out as less noteworthy if it were consistent with coverage of other world religions or marginalized groups in the United States. We need to compare coverage of a wide variety of religious, racial, ethnic, and social groups to see if reporting on Muslims is distinctly negative.

Some scholars have argued that 9/11 generated a significant shift in media portrayals of Muslims (Martin and Phelan 2002; Abrahamian 2003; Bail 2012). Others have noted a longer-standing propensity of the media to cover Muslims and Islam using simplistic or negative frames (Mortimer 1981; Said 1997; Silva 2017). Still others have argued that 9/11 actually engendered somewhat more nuanced or even positive coverage (Nacos and Torres-Reyna 2007; Alsultany 2012; Bleich, Nisar, and Abdelhamid 2016). Did the tone of articles about Muslims become substantially more negative following

9/11, did it become more positive, or has negativity simply been a pervasive and enduring feature of the American media landscape? It is essential to grasp these long-term patterns, but it is equally important to understand the short-term effects of particular events. Terrorist incidents like 9/11 generate a spike in coverage. But how do dramatic events affect not just the amount of coverage but also its tone, as well as the specific words likely to appear? How long do these effects endure? Fine-grained, day-by-day information about the tone of stories can help us to discern patterns over time more clearly than ever before.

Most studies of media portrayals of Muslims are situated within a single country. While this facilitates an understanding of a particular setting, it has been nearly impossible to compare cross-national coverage of Muslims. Scholars have shown that stories about Muslims are negative in almost every individual location (Ahmed and Matthes 2017). Yet we do not know whether the tone of coverage is similarly negative everywhere, or if it varies dramatically depending on the country. This uncertainty holds with respect to the tone of coverage as well as with regard to the specific terms that journalists are most likely to use. Does international coverage of Muslims resemble American coverage, or is US journalism unique in certain ways? Are the principal words used to describe Muslims and Islam substantially the same or quite different across countries? Answering these questions allows us to understand whether there are important national distinctions in media coverage or whether, instead, there is something approaching a Western or perhaps global media discourse about Muslims.

Finally, while existing research provides insights into the topics most associated with Muslims in the media, we know less about variation within and across topics. Stories about Muslims frequently contain references to conflict and violence, for example; but what proportion of those stories cast Muslims as victims of violence rather than as instigators of conflict? And do the media use different words when covering Muslims in these different ways? Because existing scholarship has focused attention on the most negative aspects of coverage, it has been difficult to identify how often stories touch on topics that may not be as resolutely negative. What noteworthy themes are present in a significant number of US newspaper articles related to Muslims and Islam that have not been analyzed by researchers, and to what extent do they function as sources of relative positivity?

In short, there are a series of important questions about media coverage of Muslims that have not been adequately addressed until now:

1. How negative are stories about Muslims compared to the average media story?
2. Is the bulk of the negativity in stories about Muslims accounted for by coverage of foreign locations, by violent events, by cultural differences, or by newspaper type?
3. Is coverage of Muslims more negative than that of comparable world religious groups? Is coverage of Muslim Americans more negative than that of other marginalized domestic racial, ethnic, or religious groups?
4. Is negativity an enduring feature of the US media landscape, or has the tone of Muslim articles fluctuated over time? Was 9/11 a major turning point? How do article frequency, tone, and prominent words shift in response to events?
5. Is negativity unique to the US or is it more widespread? Do newspapers outside of the United States tend to cover Muslims in a similar way with respect to tone and prominent words found in coverage?
6. What meaningful nuances exist within coverage of Muslims that have not yet been identified by researchers? Are there any topics associated with Muslims that are not resoundingly negative?

Answering these questions will provide a much richer understanding not only of the factors that shape media representations of Muslims, but also of how such representations compare across groups, time, countries, and topics. Tone-checking coverage can help us see whether the media may be wittingly or unwittingly contributing to the stigmatization of Muslims by constructing, reinforcing, or reconfiguring the symbolic and social boundaries that define marginalized groups within our societies.

Our approach

To address the six sets of questions, we introduce a systematic way to gauge the tone of articles. We focus our analysis on newspaper coverage, as newspapers offer several key advantages for the long-term study of representations of social groups. They have circulated for decades (some for more than a century), which allows us to explore periods prior to key historical turning points, such as September 11, 2001, in our case. Newspapers typically offer a wider range of daily stories than their counterparts in television or radio, providing a richer array of information. They commonly serve as agenda-setters for other media outlets (Golan 2006; Zhang 2018), including, to some degree, for social media platforms in the contemporary era (Harder, Sevenans, and Van Aelst 2017; Vargo and Guo 2017; Stern, Livan, and Smith 2020). In addition, compared to other forms of media, newspapers are generally more factual and less emotional (Nisbet, Ostman, and Shanahan 2009, 174–76), and thus less prone on average to sensationalism or hyperbole. If we discern negativity in newspapers, in other words, it is likely to exist at least as strongly on other media platforms.

We start by examining a representative sample of 48,283 newspaper articles drawn from over a dozen American sources across a 20-year period. Assessing the tone of this essentially random set of stories provides a baseline against which other articles can be compared. We then use computer-assisted methods and corpus linguistics techniques to analyze all 256,963 articles that mention Muslims or Islam in 17 national and regional US newspapers over a 21-year period. By calibrating this set (or *corpus*) of articles against the representative sample, we can say with confidence that articles about Muslims are negative. More importantly, we can demonstrate precisely how negative they are compared to the average newspaper article. We also explore the degree to which people are able to discern differences in the tone of texts and show that most can identify which is more negative even when the tone varies by a relatively small amount. This suggests that readers are capable of tone-checking articles in real time.

We then carry out four types of comparison: across groups, across time, across countries, and across topics. First, we gather all 641,982 articles that mention Catholics, Jews, and Hindus from the same US newspapers and time period. This allows us to understand whether coverage of Muslims is negative compared to other religious groups. We also collect 175,447 articles mentioning African Americans, Latinos, Mormons, and atheists. We compare those to the 30,445 articles focusing more specifically on Muslims in the United States to see whether this subset of Muslim articles differs from coverage of other domestic outgroups. Because our articles about Muslims extend from January 1996 to December 2016, we can track the evolution of coverage across more than two decades of daily newspaper production. We can thus identify long-term patterns and compare articles pre- and post-9/11. It also means we can assess the short-term effects of multiple events on article frequency, tone, and word selection. Looking beyond the United States, we assemble a corpus of 528,444 Muslim articles from Britain, Canada, and Australia. These articles allow us to see how American media coverage of

Muslims compares to coverage in other Anglophone countries, situated both nearby and on two different continents. We also conduct a probe on 79,397 articles from six newspapers drawn from different countries in South Asia, Southeast Asia, and Africa to understand whether the patterns we discern in the Anglophone North hold elsewhere in the world. In total, we analyze the tone of more than 1.6 million articles in the process of assessing how US Muslim coverage compares along these multiple dimensions.

To get the most complete picture of how the media cover Muslims, we use a combination of deductive and inductive methods. Our deductive approach aims to advance scholarly theories about what drives negative coverage of Muslims and Islam. We identify specific, concrete expectations about particular factors that are presumed to be associated with negative coverage. As noted above, researchers have argued that the geographic location of a story, a focus on events or on cultural differences, or market incentives of right-leaning or tabloid newspapers may account for negativity in stories about Muslims or Islam. We test these propositions by tagging all articles containing specific words or phrases that are associated with different topics, as well as marking different types of newspapers. This allows us to estimate which factors are most strongly associated with negativity in articles about Muslims.

Our inductive approach lets the articles speak for themselves. We use computer-assisted topic modeling algorithms to wend through the 256,963 articles in our US Muslim corpus. This method identifies clusters of words found together within articles. These words suggest the main themes of coverage in our articles. They confirm the presence of some topics previously identified by scholars, but also uncover some that have not been heavily emphasized in the deductive literature, and that are comparatively more positive. Our inductive approach thus reveals more about what journalists cover than we can see through a deductive lens alone. It also adds greater nuance to our deductive findings.

When working with more than a million articles, it is impossible for a researcher to read even a small fraction of them. Our computer-assisted methods are designed to capture systematic elements in large bodies of articles. They are also replicable in ways that human coding is not, given the variability that individuals bring to interpreting the same text. Yet computer coding is not well-equipped to handle irony, word-play, metaphors, or emotional stories that simultaneously evoke sympathy while conveying the brutality of an event. We therefore regularly draw samples of articles from our corpora and read the words on the page. This helps ensure that our data analysis does not lead us to unwarranted conclusions. Reading these articles—and conveying portions of them in this book—also provides a more direct connection to what articles about Muslims and Islam are actually saying.

What we find

Are articles that mention Muslims or Islam more negative than the average news story? Simply put: yes, and overwhelmingly so. While it is not surprising that there are more negative articles than positive ones, the extent of the disparity is striking. As we show in chapter 2, there are more than four times as many negative articles in our Muslim corpus as positive ones. And they are not just slightly more negative. The *average* Muslim article is more negative than over 84% of our *entire* representative sample of American newspaper articles.

To convey a sense of the disparity, consider this sentence that has a neutral tone: "A Muslim cleric from the US Navy will arrive today to discuss religious issues." As anodyne as those words may sound, they are unusual. The tone of Muslim articles is better reflected in sentences like the following, each of which has a tone equivalent to the average article in our Muslim corpus:

- "The Russian was made to believe by undercover agents that the radioactive material was to be delivered to a Muslim organization."
- "Sami Al-Arian, 49, a former professor of computer science at the University of South Florida, began the hunger strike on January 22 to protest efforts to force him to testify before a grand jury investigating Muslim charities in northern Virginia."
- "One person was killed and at least 10 wounded yesterday when suspected Muslim militants threw grenades at people celebrating a Hindu festival in northeastern India, police said."
- "Moderski also has had business relationships with Shamsud-din Ali, the Muslim cleric and friend of Mayor Street who was convicted last year on racketeering and related charges, and given a seven-year jail sentence."[9]

---

[9] *New York Times*, April 15, 2009; *Washington Post*, February 16, 2007; *Philadelphia Daily News*, October 14, 2002; *Philadelphia Daily News*, January 20, 2006.

The typical Muslim article simply contains much more negativity than positivity. Reading strongly negative articles that touch on Muslims or Islam is the norm, not an exception. Muslim stories that are neutral or positive when compared to the average newspaper article are, by contrast, unusual. We conduct an experiment in chapter 2 to test how well readers can accurately identify which texts are more positive or negative at a variety of levels of tone difference. Our results suggest that approximately three-quarters of readers would recognize the average Muslim story as more negative than the average story in our representative sample of US newspaper articles.

What accounts for the negativity of Muslim articles? In chapter 3, we review scholarship on geography, events, cultural differences, and market characteristics of newspapers as likely drivers of negativity. We use statistical techniques to estimate the associations between these types of factors and the tone of coverage. We find that stories set in foreign locations, those that touch on conflict or extremism, and those published in tabloids are most strongly associated with negative coverage in American newspapers. By contrast, articles that touch on religiosity or presumed value clashes and those published in right-leaning newspapers are not substantially more negative. Importantly, however, even setting aside articles associated with the most negative factors, coverage of Muslims remains negative. In other words, articles about Muslims that are not set exclusively abroad, that make no mention of violence or extremism, and that are published in broadsheets rather than tabloids are *still* negative.

Chapter 3 also delves into cross-group comparisons. Muslim articles are strongly negative compared not only to randomly selected newspaper articles, but also to stories touching on other world religions and domestic outgroups. At various points in US history, Catholics and Jews were considered cultural minorities and viewed with substantial suspicion. The boundaries between these groups and the "mainstream" have faded over the past few decades—a transition that may well be reflected in the fact that the average article about each of these groups is close in tone to the average of our representative corpus. By contrast, Hindus share many similarities with Muslims: they are primarily associated with foreign locations, make up under 1% of the US population, do not belong to what some argue is the "Judeo-Christian" cultural tradition of the country, and are predominantly non-White. We expected, therefore, that articles touching on Hindus would more closely resemble those about Muslims than those about Catholics or Jews. Yet articles in our Hindu corpus are only modestly negative in tone compared to those in our representative corpus. Hindu articles resemble those about the other major religious groups much more closely than they resemble Muslim articles.

We find the same distinctive quality when we compare coverage of Muslim Americans to that of other domestic outgroups. Articles about Muslims in the United States are less negative than articles about Muslims taken as a whole, yet they are still strongly negative. Moreover, they are substantially more negative than articles that mention historically stigmatized racial or ethnic groups such as African Americans or Latinos.[10] In addition, they are more negative than articles that touch on other, relatively smaller groups that surveys consistently show are viewed skeptically by American respondents, such as Mormons or atheists. There is something distinctly negative about coverage of Muslims that cannot be explained simply by demographic, geographic, cultural, or ethno-racial differences.

This is not because of 9/11. Our analysis in chapter 4 definitively demonstrates that long-term coverage of Muslims was just as negative prior to September 11, 2001 as after. The tone of articles immediately following prominent terrorist attacks almost always drops measurably, but the effect is typically short-lived. The overall tone most commonly reverts to pre-attack levels within a month or two. The 9/11 and other terrorist attacks do generate spikes in the amount of articles mentioning Muslims or Islam, as well as shifts in the prevalence of different topics. The raw number of Muslim articles jumped dramatically in the wake of 9/11 and had not receded to pre-9/11 levels by 2016. There has also been much greater coverage of terrorism and extremism since 9/11. Corresponding positive events, such as a major speech by President Obama or the celebration associated with the annual Islamic holy month of Ramadan, do not have as much of an influence on either the amount or the tone of coverage. Major terrorist events like 9/11 thus drive surges in articles, but only temporary increases in negativity. Over the 21 years of our study, there has been no overall long-term rise or fall in the tone of Muslim articles.

In chapter 5, we confirm that our findings for the United States hold in the three other Anglophone countries we examine. Muslim articles in Britain, Canada, and Australia are similar to those in American newspapers in most

---

[10] In other work, we have shown that Muslim articles are also much more negative than articles touching on Asian Americans or Native Americans (Media Portrayals of Minorities Project 2019, 2020, 2021).

key ways. Patterns in both the amount and the tone of coverage closely parallel our US findings, as do the factors associated with the greatest negativity,
as well as the words most commonly used to describe Muslims or Islam. The
evidence from these four countries is consistent with a view that there may
be a common Western journalistic approach to stories touching on Muslims
or Islam, or at least one that holds in predominantly Anglophone countries
in the Global North.

Our probe into six newspapers from South Asia, Southeast Asia, and
Africa, however, demonstrates that coverage of Muslims is not simply dictated by world events. In most of these newspapers, coverage of Muslims remains negative on average, but this negativity is simply far less intense than
in the United States, Britain, Canada, or Australia. In fact, in the Malaysian
newspaper we analyze, the tone of the average Muslim article is modestly
positive. In addition, the specific words most commonly associated with
Muslims and Islam in these six newspapers are much more varied than those
in our Anglophone North newspapers. Media around the world have more
latitude to select stories and to frame discussions than an analysis of US
newspapers alone would imply.

Nor is there a uniform media discourse within the United States, as we
show in chapter 6. Our topic modeling analysis demonstrates, for example,
that newspapers cover Muslims differently depending on the geographic
context in which the stories are set. Reporting on Muslim-majority countries varies from that on Muslim-minority countries, where stories are more
likely to highlight separatism, militancy, and extremism. By further contrast,
in contexts where Muslims have been victimized by non-Muslim groups
(such as in Bosnia or Kosovo in the 1990s, or with respect to the Rohingya or
Uighurs in the 2010s), we see an emphasis on Muslims as a vulnerable group
or simply as civilians. Our inductive approach also reveals that approximately
a third of all stories are not primarily associated with the major themes identified by previous research. While almost no topic related to Muslim coverage is positive, several of these themes are linked with far less negativity
than others, suggesting pathways for journalists to pursue if they are seeking
more balanced coverage of Muslims and Islam over the longer term.

Our concluding chapter summarizes the main findings of our research,
the most important of which bears emphasizing here: coverage of Muslims
in the United States is strikingly negative by any comparative measure.
This negativity is not simply explained by radical Islamist violence, by coverage of foreign conflict zones, or by any other factor we explore, alone or in

combination with others. Articles mentioning Muslims or Islam are negative compared to those touching on all groups we investigate. They are consistently and enduringly negative across time. If US newspaper articles tend to be more negative than stories in many Global South locations, their negativity is mirrored in countries from the Anglophone North. This negativity is somewhat nuanced when we take a closer look at different topics covered by newspapers, but the vast majority of themes associated with Muslims remain highly negative.

We draw on these core findings to reflect on whether American newspapers—and the media more broadly—may be fostering Islamophobia, and how they serve to reinforce boundaries between social groups that contribute to ongoing stigmatization of Muslims. We also suggest that journalists and citizens develop the instinct to tone-check the media in an effort to limit the harmful effects of the deep and abiding negativity so commonly associated with Muslims and Islam.

2

The tone of Muslim coverage

Twice as many people use negative words as positive words to describe their impressions of the Muslim religion (30% vs. 15%).
— Pew Research Center (2007)

When the Pew Research Center asked Americans for one-word impressions of Islam, many of the responses could be classified readily as positive or negative: the top three positive words were "devout," "peaceful," and "dedicated"; the top three negative words were "fanatic," "radical," and "terror." Not all words had an immediate positive or negative association, however: "different" and "strict" were among top words Pew identified as neutral (Pew Research Center 2007). Yet, as the epigram indicates, negative words sprang much more easily to mind than positive words for most people. Given that the same survey showed the preponderant influence of the media on respondents' views, we need to learn more about how the media cover Muslims and Islam.

There is little disagreement among experts that reporting on Muslims is negative (Ahmed and Matthes 2017). The challenge, until now, has been to pin down exactly what this means: Negative compared to what? And just how negative? Neither of these questions can be answered without reference to a measure of tone—the positivity or negativity of a text—that is reproducible, reliable, and comparable across groups, time, countries, and topics. Our focus in this chapter is to explain how we tackle this challenge. As we shall show, print media coverage of Muslims is systematically very negative, compared to a representative sample of all articles published by the newspapers we study. Moreover, this negativity is not subtle: it is at a level most readers can readily recognize.

We begin the chapter by discussing our method for measuring tone, articulating the strengths and weaknesses of our approach to sentiment analysis. The method builds on the intuitive appeal of homing in on positive and

Covering Muslims. Erik Bleich and A. Maurits van der Veen, Oxford University Press. © Oxford University Press 2022.
DOI: 10.1093/oso/9780197611715.003.0002

negative words, as was done in the Pew survey cited earlier. In addition, we explain how we calibrate, or benchmark, our measure of tone so as to be able to identify not just *whether* an article is positive or negative, but also *how* positive or negative it is. As the proof of the method is in its performance, we discuss how we have validated our approach against texts whose positivity or negativity is known and, most importantly, against human evaluations of segments of newspaper articles coded using our method. Significantly, we show that people can identify even comparatively small differences in tone between two texts.

Next, we introduce our corpus of more than 250,000 articles mentioning Muslims or Islam, drawn from 17 US newspapers over a period of more than 20 years, from 1996 to 2016. Applying our sentiment analysis method to this corpus allows us in effect to quantify our central puzzle about the negativity of Muslim coverage. We show that this coverage is very negative, and that the negativity is not limited to specific newspapers or time periods. Moreover, while there are some differences between the tone of articles mentioning only Islam, only Muslims, or both, strong negativity holds across the board.

A crucial question is whether this negativity is higher or lower than we would expect, given what we know about the factors that tend to shape media coverage. Setting up our analyses in the next four chapters, the last part of this chapter discusses how we identify aspects of media coverage that are likely to shape the tone of an article. In particular, we specify which particular words we expect to be associated with important features of an article, such as whether it is set in a foreign location and whether it covers violence or religiosity. In doing so, we also note some challenges in interpreting whether negative coverage is negative *about* Muslims and Islam.

Measuring the tone of coverage

One of the most intuitive ways to measure whether a text is positive or negative is to look for words that are obviously positive or negative, and tally them to arrive at an overall assessment. Consider the following three-sentence snippet taken from an article in our corpus:

> To be sure, there are no easy solutions to Algeria's crisis, which dates back to the military government's 1992 decision to cancel elections in which Islamic factions held a commanding advantage. Muslim insurgents are said

to have killed more than 80,000 civilians in an effort to topple the unelected junta that still holds power. The government has consistently rejected outside offers for help in ending the conflict.[1]

This is clearly a negative text. It is easy to identify some of the words that make it so: "crisis," "killed," and "conflict," for example. On the other hand, despite the overall negative tone, there are some positive words as well: "sure," "easy," and "advantage" (although "easy" is preceded by the word "no"). Significantly, "factions" and "insurgents" are arguably negative words, and are closely associated here with "Islamic" and "Muslim," respectively. Since 99% of Algeria's population is Muslim, the second reference could equally have been "Insurgents are said to have killed more than 80,000 Muslim civilians." As such, this article illustrates that explicitly referencing a religion or its adherents in a particular context is often a choice; a choice, moreover, that may affect public perceptions.

For us to say anything systematic about the negativity of Muslim coverage and the contexts in which it appears, we need to be able to gauge negativity in a replicable and reliable way. Scholars across the social sciences have long been interested in how best to solve this challenge (Holsti 1964; Singer 1965), and recent years have seen an explosion of interest, as automated methods have become increasingly accessible and accurate (e.g., Meyer-Gutbrod and Woolley 2020; Shapiro, Sudhof, and Wilson 2020). Many existing approaches, however, share two important weaknesses for our purposes. First, recall that, in discussing the text about Algeria, we simply noted its general negativity. Most sentiment analysis methods do the same, classifying texts as positive or negative without defining and identifying the reference point: positive or negative *compared to what*? Second, most approaches are unable to identify sentiment strength—is a text very positive or negative, or just modestly so?

Until recently, the modal sentiment analysis approach has been to select a set of texts and code them manually, usually into just two categories: positive and negative.[2] Manual coding of texts has been a preferred approach because people are better at interpreting language than are computers, requiring no special training to understand grammar, metaphor, or sarcasm, among

---

[1] *Tampa Bay Times*, January 10, 1998.
[2] Thus, the watershed 1997 Runnymede Trust report *Islamophobia: A Challenge for Us All* asserted that the British media contained broadly unfavorable views about Islam, basing this conclusion on a hand-coded selection of such negative articles. However, it made no attempt to ascertain how representative this selection was, nor whether coverage of Muslims was more negative than coverage of other groups (Runnymede Trust 1997, 20–30).

others (Conway 2006; Sjøvaag and Stavelin 2012). On the other hand, people *do* require training in particular coding procedures and rules. Moreover, coding standards may change over the course of a coding project; coders may become tired and introduce inadvertent errors; and different coders will often apply coding standards in ways that vary, limiting inter-coder reliability (Riffe and Freitag 1997; Lovejoy et al. 2016).

Fortunately, a growing body of evidence indicates that automated approaches frequently perform just as well as, or even better than, human coders. They make up for weaknesses in language understanding by being systematic, adjustable, and completely replicable (Rosenberg, Schnurr, and Oxman 1990; King and Lowe 2003; Aust 2004). Many approaches use supervised learning, in which a computer is trained on a set of texts pre-classified by human coders, after which it is tasked with classifying similar texts that have not yet been classified. In contrast, unsupervised methods use lexica (lists of words, phrases, etc.) to classify texts. Supervised approaches work best on texts similar to those they learned from, with performance degrading rapidly when they are applied to other topics or text types (Blitzer, Dredze, and Pereira 2007; Loughran and McDonald 2011). Unsupervised methods, meanwhile, do not require pre-classified sample texts and tend to be less domain-dependent, performing equally well across a wide range of topics and issues (Blitzer, Dredze, and Pereira 2007; González-Bailón and Paltoglou 2015).

However, different sentiment lexica capture different sets of words. Returning to our opening example about Algeria, not all lexica identify "sure" as a positive word or "topple" as a negative one. As a result, applying different lexica to the same text produces different results (Young and Soroka 2012; González-Bailón and Paltoglou 2015). Rather than attempting to improve the performance of a particular lexicon on a single, predetermined corpus, our approach produces a high-quality measure that maximizes the cross-domain validity, replicability, and interpretability of valence.

There is, of course, no such thing as an objectively neutral text. Words that may strike one reader as purely factual and descriptive might impress someone else as highly value-laden. There is also no such thing as a completely balanced sentiment lexicon. A lexicon may contain more positive than negative words (or vice versa), its positive words may appear more frequently in "normal" texts than its negative words, its positive words may be more positive than its negative words are negative, and so on. In addition, human beings may well be primed—perhaps even hardwired—to pay more attention to negative words (Shoemaker 1996), causing even texts with more positive than negative words to be interpreted as having a negative tone overall.

Our goal, then, is not to identify a specific valence level that every human reader would recognize as neutral, but rather one that readers, on average, would consider neutral. To do so, we collect a large corpus of newspaper articles whose tone we expect to be representative of the average tone of US newspaper articles in general, and calibrate our valence calculations so that texts in this benchmark corpus are neutral, on average. More specifically, we standardize the valence results so that the mean is 0 (neutral) and the standard deviation is 1. This makes the degree of positivity and negativity of a text easier to interpret, and produces an easily applicable pair of calibration parameters for the lexicon used (simply subtract the pre-standardization mean and then divide by the pre-standardization standard deviation).

Since different lexica capture different sets of positive and negative words, we repeat the same process using eight different, widely used, general-purpose sentiment lexica. We average those results (the mean will remain 0), and divide by the resulting standard deviation to once again produce a standard deviation of 1 (and, in the process, generate our final calibration parameter).[3] While the mean article tone is 0, the median article from our representative corpus has a tone of .05; 52% of all representative corpus articles are positive and 48% are negative. Together, this indicates that negative articles are somewhat more intensely negative and positive articles are somewhat more mildly positive. Still, as expected from an approximately normal distribution, more than two-thirds (71%, in our case) of the articles have valence scores between −1 and +1; 95% between −2 and +2, and 99% between −3 and +3.

Based on this distribution, and on our experience working with a wide range of corpora, we have developed a scale that indicates the substantive significance of tone scores. Articles with a valence between −.1 and +.1 we consider essentially neutral. Those between −.1 and −.3 are modestly negative. An article between −.3 and −.5 is clearly negative. Finally, a text with a score of −.5 or lower is strongly negative: at that level, an article is more negative than 71% of the representative corpus. The cut points for positive articles occur at the corresponding positive thresholds. Figure 2.1 illustrates these

---

[3] The overall distribution of valences in the representative corpus approximates a normal distribution, as the Central Limit Theorem predicts.

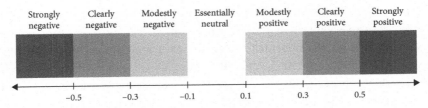

Figure 2.1 Simplified interpretation of article tone

segments. While actual tone scores are continuous, this helps to quickly communicate the substantive significance of scores in our analyses.

As we do for the texts in the representative corpus, we can calculate the valence of any other text by summing the values of the positive and negative words from a lexicon. Since a positive (or negative) word by itself has a greater impact than a single positive (or negative) word embedded in a long text of nonvalenced words, we scale by the total number of words in the text. The positive or negative value of a word is adjusted if it is immediately preceded by one or more modifiers: words that can intensify, attenuate, or negate the meaning of what follows, such as "very," "not," and "hardly." Thus, "very good" is more positive than "good," and "not good" is negative rather than positive.[4] The resulting length-scaled sum of positive and negative values in the text is adjusted by the calibration parameters calculated for the lexicon based on the representative corpus. Finally, the eight values that result for the eight different lexica are averaged and divided one last time by the final calibration parameter. The value that results is a valence that is easily interpretable relative to our representative, benchmark corpus, either directly—by seeing what proportion of the benchmark corpus lies on either side of that value—or indirectly, by assuming a normal distribution and simply calculating the cumulative density function for that value.

The following extract shows how this works for the sample text we introduced earlier. If a word serves as an intensifier or negater, it is followed by an asterisk. If it appears in one or more of our sentiment lexica, a number in parentheses shows how many such lexica and whether it is positive or negative.[5] The overall valence for this piece of text by itself is −2.87—a score that

---

[4] More details are provided in the appendix.
[5] Several of our lexica rank words by sentiment intensity. As a result, we cannot simply calculate the sum of positive and negative occurrences, as shown here, to get an overall valence.

puts it nearly 3 standard deviations away from the mean of our representative corpus: very negative indeed.[6] As we can see, in addition to the words
we easily identified as positive or negative earlier, a number of less obvious
words also contribute to the overall valence, albeit with much less impact,
since they appear in only one or two lexica. This example also shows where
"no" modifies the meaning of "easy" ("no easy" is a negative phrase overall)
while "consistently" intensifies "rejected" (making it more negative).

To be sure (4), there are no (*) easy (7) solutions (2) to Algeria's crisis (−7)
which dates (1) back (2) to the military government (−1) 's 1992 decision
to cancel (−3) elections in which Islamic factions (−1) held a commanding
advantage (8). Muslim insurgents (−2) are said to have killed (−4) more
than 80,000 civilians (2) in an (−1) effort (2) to topple (−5) the unelected
junta (−1) that still holds (−1) power (2). The government (−1) has (1) consistently (*) rejected (−7) outside (−1) offers (2) for help (5) in ending the
conflict (−7).

Validation

In looking at the words flagged in the sample text snippet, it may come as a
surprise that "dates" is considered a positive word by one lexicon, while "government" is considered negative. We might wonder how that came about,
and whether we might not be better off finding lexica that do not have such
puzzling entries. Unfortunately, there is no way to decide *ex ante* which potentially valenced words to include and which to leave out. Different lexica
deal with this challenge differently, and none is systematically better than the
others. Rather than try to second-guess the decisions that went into the construction of each lexicon, we instead average across them, thus drawing on
all their strengths while minimizing the impact of any particular lexicon that
might be ill-suited to a particular text or topic.

A number of different validation tests support this choice. As we report
in the appendix, our method—including the calibration against a representative sample of US newspaper articles—successfully identifies the tone
of more than 75% of a large dataset of movie reviews, a success rate that

---

[6] Our valence calculation is scaled by the length of a text; the overall article from which this snippet
was drawn has a valence of −2.45, indicating that the remainder of the text was slightly more positive
than this snippet, on balance.

compares favorably with some widely used machine-learning algorithms. It also outperforms most or even all leading alternatives on three smaller sets of more social science–focused texts, including op-eds in the *New York Times*. Moreover, while it is important to perform well at classifying individual articles, we are actually much more interested in correctly identifying patterns and trends across sets of texts (Hopkins and King 2010). Here, too, our method performs very well. As we report in the appendix, for sets of texts as small as 12 articles, our ability to correctly identify them as positive or negative climbs to 99%. This further increases confidence in the sentiment values we present throughout the book, which are generally based on hundreds if not thousands of articles, even when we home in on smaller subsets of our overall corpus.

The most important test, for our purposes, is whether average newspaper readers are able to identify the finer-grained distinctions in tone that our method provides. When reading two texts that have scores of 0 and −1, respectively, can most people correctly say which is more negative? What about when reading texts with scores of +.5 and 1? We conducted an experiment that provided short texts with different tone scores to readers and asked them to identify which was more positive and which was more negative. The experiment was conducted through Crowdflower during the fall of 2018.[7]

We selected three-sentence vignettes from our Muslim corpus at various valence levels. The text snippet about Algeria's civil war discussed earlier in this chapter was one of the more extreme vignettes we used. Vignettes were paired at random, while constraining the difference in valence between the two texts to fall between .05 and 2.80—any higher than that, and the differences are obvious to all. In the experiment, readers moved through a random sequence of pairings and, for each pair, selected which vignette they thought was the more positive (or less negative) of the two. Respondents had to be residents of the United States, were limited to answering at most 10% of the different pairings available, and were eliminated from the task if they failed a test comparison that was inserted roughly every 10th pairing with a large valence gap (5 or more), to make sure they took the task seriously.

To provide a sense of our respondents' task, compare the following two vignettes, which differ in tone by about 1.5 points:

---

[7] Crowdflower, which no longer exists, operated similarly to Amazon's more familiar Mechanical Turk.

"Some of us say the Welfare Party is going to change Turkey into an Iranian Islamic regime," he said recently over a Diet Coke. Turkey would face a civil war if that happens. Horrible things could happen in Turkey. So far however, even Turkey's elite seems to be coming to terms with Islam's heightened influence. (valence −.62)

It is your time now; your time to make a difference. The Atlanta event and Saturday's Million Youth March in New York grew out of 1995's Million Man March, organized by Nation of Islam leader Louis Farrakhan to build responsibility among black men. Jackson, using a chanting refrain of self-esteem, urged listeners to retain the civil rights movement's legacy of non-violence. "Young people you have got to keep marching," Jackson said. (valence +.85)

Now compare these two vignettes, which have a tone difference of about .5 points:

Although their relationship regularly has its ups and downs, and they have strong cultural links, India and Pakistan have fought two previous wars over Kashmir, which is strategically located where India, Pakistan, and China intersect. It is the only majority Muslim state in predominantly Hindu India. India and Pakistan both claim the state as their own. (−.35)

Serbian legislators in the Kosovo Parliament, meanwhile, would be able to stop at least some legislation if they believe it discriminates against the Serbian minority, diplomats said. Serbian religious institutions would also be guaranteed special protection. Kosovo, nearly the size of Connecticut, has about two million people, 90 percent of whom are ethnic Albanian Muslims, a legacy of Ottoman rule. (+.13)

In both cases, the second vignette has a more positive valence score than the first. On balance, people found it easier to discern this difference in the first pairing than the second. Indeed, the greater the difference in valence between two vignettes, the more likely respondents were to correctly identify the higher-valence vignette as more positive. Overall, respondents faced pairings with 395 different values of the valence gap (all between .05 and 2.80). For each gap, we obtained between 6 and 11 different responses. In total, the survey produced 3,720 responses. By aggregating the results across all of the responses, we are able to estimate the valence distance at which

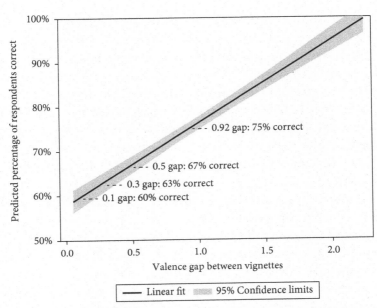

Figure 2.2 How well can survey respondents identify valence differences?

readers can reliably identify the more positive vignette as coded by our method.

Figure 2.2 shows the result of calculating a best linear fit (i.e., a linear regression) for these responses, along with a 95% confidence interval. Since actual responses can take only two values—1 for correctly identifying the higher-valence vignette, and 0 otherwise—we can think of this line as the expected probability that a reader will correctly identify the more positive vignette, as coded by our method. It turns out the best fit line crosses the maximum possible value of 1.0 well before our maximum gap level of 2.8; we eliminated any observations for which the estimated value exceeded the maximum, to prevent these from biasing the regression line. Accordingly, the figure shows the best linear fit for responses with valence gaps up to 2.3 (a total of 385 different gap values, and 3,614 different responses).[8]

The figure identifies the percentage of respondents predicted to correctly identify which of two text snippets is more positive at valence gaps of .1, .3, and .5, respectively. These values correspond to the distances from 0 marked

---

[8] Including gap values up to 2.8 results in a slightly flatter line, which artificially boosts (by a small amount) how well people are predicted to do at identifying very small valence gaps.

in figure 2.1 as demarcating moderately, clearly, or strongly negative/positive texts. The most important takeaway from this figure is that even at a valence difference of just .1, we can expect people to identify the vignette assigned a higher valence as being more positive more than half the time. Indeed, the bottom edge of the confidence interval at .1 (the first vertical line) remains well above 50% (the bottom of the figure), which represents a random guess. In addition, the match between our method and people's responses improves quite rapidly: even before the valence gap reaches 1 (at about .92), we can expect three out of four readers to correctly identify the more positive of two text vignettes.[9]

These results demonstrate that readers are capable, more often than not, of consciously recognizing relative positivity and negativity when comparing texts, even for quite small differences in valence. It is much easier for readers to do so when the texts differ in valence score by more than 1, but we expect 67% of respondents to succeed already when the tone score differs by .5. In other words, about two-thirds of people can reliably distinguish between a text our method codes as having a valence of −.5 (defined as strongly negative, in figure 2.1) and one that we code as neutral. In fact, as we just saw, a majority will do so even when the valence is just −.1 (modestly negative).

The tone of Muslim coverage in US newspapers

Our sentiment analysis method can be applied to any set of texts. Indeed, the corpus whose sentiment we are interested in measuring—in our case, a large corpus of newspaper articles mentioning Muslims and Islam—need not be drawn from the same sources as our representative, or benchmark, corpus. When it is, as is the case here, the benchmarking is of course more direct. Our primary goal, however, is to select texts from a set of media sources that, together, can be seen as indicative of overall US print media coverage, which in turn is a key segment of US media. Why choose newspapers for this purpose? And why choose the specific set of 17 different newspapers we draw from here?

Newspapers, as compared to other types of media such as radio, television, or social media, have two important advantages for our purposes, one

---

[9] There is no meaningful difference in our results between difference comparisons straddling (or including) the neutral point and those where both vignettes were either positive or negative.

pragmatic and one substantive. Pragmatically, if we wish to study trends across a number of years, from the 1990s to the present, newspapers offer the widest range of candidate sources available for the full period. Studying a longer period of time allows us to identify whether there are key turning points in coverage, analyze long-term patterns, and distinguish short-term movements from such longer patterns; none of that would be possible if we looked at just a few more recent years.

In particular, social media did not become widely used until about a decade ago. While some digitized transcripts of radio and television go back as far as digitized newspaper archives, the number of different sources for which that is the case is far smaller. More substantively, radio and television programs also offer a narrower range of stories: a nightly television news program might feature a few dozen news stories at most; a daily newspaper can easily feature 5–10 times as many, offering a far more detailed and fine-grained spectrum of stories.

In addition, many studies show the importance of inter-media agenda setting: media outlets tend to take cues from one another on what to cover (McCombs 2005, 549) and at times even how to cover it (Vargo and Guo 2017). Indeed, until about a decade ago, the three main national-circulation newspapers—the *New York Times*, *Wall Street Journal*, and *Washington Post*—had a powerful agenda-setting influence on all other media outlets, including local print media or local/national broadcast media (Golan 2006; Zhang 2018). Even with the current visibility of online media, newspapers still find themselves prominently positioned in the inter-media agenda setting network, including social media, in part because social media are often used to share newspaper stories (Vargo and Guo 2017, 1042; Vu, Guo, and McCombs 2014, 682).

In selecting the newspapers from which to draw our corpus, we began by including the four main national-audience papers: the three already mentioned plus *USA Today*. We added a range of newspapers with various political leanings and from major cities spread across the United States. A paper's political leaning is relevant both because it is known to affect readers' views of political issues (Kahn and Kenney 2002) and because evidence suggests that consumers of right-leaning media (newspapers as well as television) hold beliefs that are more critical of perceived outgroups, including Muslims (Jones et al. 2011, 10–11; Ogan et al. 2014). We operationalize political leaning by looking at the presidential candidates that each paper endorsed over the two decades covered by our corpus.[10] We characterize

---

[10] Presidential endorsement data was taken from Noah Veltman's aggregation of this information (noahveltman.com/endorsements/; accessed November 15, 2019). We also estimated ideological

as right-leaning those papers that endorsed Republican candidates four or five times during the five election cycles included in our corpus: the *Arizona Republic, Las Vegas Review-Journal, Richmond Times-Dispatch* and *New York Post*.[11] We also included several tabloid titles, as studies in other countries have found that tabloids are likely to report on outgroups differently than do broadsheet titles (Conboy 2005).

In selecting sources, we were constrained by their availability through standard university subscriptions to one of the major online news databases (LexisNexis, ProQuest, and Factiva).[12] Our final list of 17 titles appears in table 2.1. In addition to the four national-level newspapers, the *Boston Globe*, the Minneapolis *Star-Tribune*, New York's *Daily News*, and the *New York Post* are often ranked among the top 10 US papers by circulation.[13] The latter two are also the two largest tabloid papers in the country. New York and Philadelphia—represented by more than one paper each—are also cities with comparatively large Muslim populations; in contrast, Phoenix (*Arizona Republic*), Las Vegas, and Denver are home to comparatively few Muslims.[14]

Our corpus includes articles for the 21-year period from January 1, 1996 to December 31, 2016. This includes five years prior to the 9/11/2001 attacks, often seen as a watershed moment in the coverage of Muslims and Islam (e.g., Morey and Yaqin 2011). Going back any further would rapidly restrict the number of newspaper titles available in digitized form. As it is, only three of our sources are not available to us for the full 21-year range: the *New York Post* starts in December 1997; the *Arizona Republic* begins at the start of 1999; and the *Las Vegas Review-Journal* ends at the end of 2012. Our corpus stops at the end of 2016, so as to coincide with the United States presidential cycle.

---

effects using text-based slant scores (Gentzkow and Shapiro 2010). Though not all our papers have such scores, the substantive findings were similar.

[11] Analogously, left-leaning papers are those that endorsed Democratic candidates four or five times. The *Wall Street Journal*, whose editorial page—but not necessarily its news coverage—is often considered right-leaning, generally does not endorse particular candidates, and hence is coded as centrist.
[12] In particular, we were unable to include the *Los Angeles Times* as well as the *Chicago Tribune*, two papers generally among the top 10 highest-circulation US titles, and representing cities with considerable Muslim populations.
[13] Exact circulation data varies by year and by how circulation is measured (subscription, paid individual copies, etc.). Data from https://www.cision.com/us/2019/01/top-ten-us-daily-newspapers/ and https://www.infoplease.com/arts-entertainment/newspapers-and-magazines/top-100-newspapers-united-states (both accessed June 2020).
[14] Muslim population data from https://www.pewforum.org/religious-landscape-study/religious-tradition/muslim/ and https://www.thearda.com/rcms2010/ (both accessed July 2021).

This gives us, for the post-9/11 period, nearly two full terms of a Republican presidency and two full terms of a Democratic presidency.

We construct our corpus by including all articles published in one of our 17 titles from 1996 through 2016 that include one or more of the word roots Muslim*, Moslem*, and Islam*. The asterisk after these words indicates that we accept any word beginning with the letters that precede it (i.e., a word whose "root" is those letters). In other words: Muslim, but also Muslims; and Islam, but also Islamic, Islamist, Islamophobia, etc. Moslem, once a common transliteration of the original Arabic term, has virtually disappeared from general usage, but occurs intermittently throughout our corpus, primarily prior to 9/11 (cf. Baker, Gabrielatos, and McEnery 2013, 76–78).[15] For the word root Islam*, we exclude four proper names that begin with those letters: two locations—Islamabad (the capital of Pakistan) and Islamorada (part of the Florida Keys)—and two that can serve as last names: al-Islam and Islami. Articles that mention Muslims or Islam as well as any of these four excluded words are included, but an article that only mentions Islamabad, for example, is not.

Table 2.1 displays the total number of articles mentioning Muslims or Islam between 1996 and 2016 in each newspaper.[16] This includes articles from all sections of the newspaper: front page news as well as entertainment, sports, letters to the editor, etc.—anything that is not paid (advertising) content is included. As the table shows, the New York Times and Washington Post each account for roughly one-fifth of the total corpus. Given that these are the two leading general-interest newspapers with a national readership, and that they have the largest general reporting newsrooms among US newspapers, this comes as no surprise (Edkins 2016). These two titles are of particular importance for our purposes, too, since other newspapers often follow their reporting through their respective news services (Peake 2007, fn. 6). As such, any coverage of Muslims and Islam that appears in these papers is often reflected across many smaller American newspapers not in our corpus.

[15] Only 649 (0.25%) of the articles in our corpus include the word root Moslem*.
[16] In addition to the core US Muslim corpus, in chapter 3 we use analogous corpora, from the same sources and time period, for a number of other comparison groups. In chapter 5, we use comparable corpora of Muslim coverage, using the same search terms and for the same time period, for three other countries: Britain, Canada, and Australia. Details about titles and article counts appear in the appendix.

Table 2.1 Newspaper sources for our main corpus, with article count

Title	Type	Leaning	Article count
New York Times	National	Left	59,693
USA Today	National	Center	8,749
Wall Street Journal	National	Center	23,581
Washington Post	National	Left	49,431
Arizona Republic (1999–2016 only)	Regional	Right	4,923
Atlanta Journal-Constitution	Regional	Center	10,737
Boston Globe	Regional	Left	17,096
Denver Post	Regional	Left	6,104
Las Vegas Review-Journal (1996–2012 only)	Regional	Right	2,324
Philadelphia Inquirer	Regional	Left	15,317
Richmond Times-Dispatch	Regional	Right	6,412
San Jose Mercury News	Regional	Left	13,752
Star-Tribune (Minneapolis)	Regional	Left	4,978
Tampa Bay Times	Regional	Left	11,094
Daily News (New York)	Tabloid	Center	9,477
New York Post (1997–2016 only)	Tabloid	Right	9,315
Philadelphia Daily News	Tabloid	Left	3,980
Corpus total			256,963

Applying our sentiment analysis to this corpus of more than a quarter of a million articles produces a set of valences whose average is a strikingly negative −.94. What does that mean in practice for a human reader? Perhaps the simplest way to convey the tone of Muslim articles is to note that over 80% of them are negative. In other words, if we choose five individual Muslim stories at random, we expect four to be negative. By way of a small but illustrative test, we selected a random sample of sentences from the last year (2016) of our data that contain one of our word roots and that have 20 or fewer words:

1. General Flynn is an outspoken critic of political Islam and has advocated a global campaign led by the United States against radical Islam.
2. A Pakistani Taliban offshoot claimed the attack as did the Islamic State, though analysts say the latter claim is dubious.
3. "Look," says Donald Trump, "we are having problems with the Muslims."

4. Mumbra, one of the largest, is over 90 percent Muslim.

5. For the Americans the cease-fire could create an opportunity to cooperate with Russia against the Islamic State.[17]

The first three sentences are clearly negative, while the fourth is a simple and neutral description of a city in India. However, since an average text in our representative corpus contains at least one positive word, our method marks this sentence (with no such words) as very slightly negative. The last sentence contains the words "create," "opportunity," and "cooperate" and is the most positive of the five, even though it alludes to a war zone.

While this glimpse into our corpus is revealing, we want to know more than just whether we are likely to come across negative sentences or articles. Figure 2.3 reproduces figure 2.1, indicating for each tone segment the proportion of our corpus that falls in that range. Note that the left-most and right-most "boxes" cover a much larger valence range than the others do, as they go from +/−.5 to whatever the valence of the most positive/negative article in our corpus is. As the figure shows, nearly two-thirds of all articles in our Muslim corpus qualify as strongly negative.

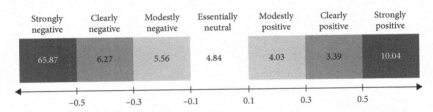

Figure 2.3 Proportion of corpus at different degrees of positivity and negativity

Because we calculate the tone of every article in our representative sample, we can illustrate the distribution of positivity and negativity within our Muslim corpus even more finely and compare it to the distribution of articles in our representative corpus. As a reminder, for purposes of benchmarking or calibration, we set the mean of our representative corpus to 0 and its standard deviation to 1. Figure 2.4 overlays kernel density plots—essentially smoothed histograms—of the Muslim corpus and the representative corpus.

---

[17] The sentences appeared in articles in the *New York Times*, December 1, 2016; the *Washington Post*, August 10, 2016; the *Washington Post*, March 2, 2016; the *New York Times*, March 16, 2016; and the *New York Times*, December 31, 2016.

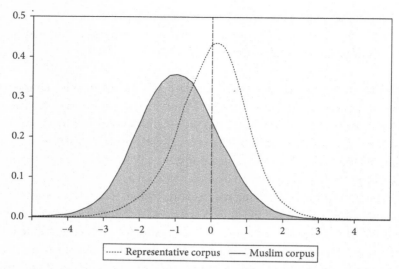

Figure 2.4 Valence distribution estimates (kernel density) of the Muslim corpus, compared to the representative corpus

It shows that Muslim articles are not concentrated just a little to the left of the zero mark (the vertical line on the plot). Rather, the peak value is far closer to −1. The average Muslim article is, in fact, more negative than 84% of all articles in our representative corpus.

What does it mean that the average score of a Muslim article is −.94? An easier way to understand this is to imagine reading that average Muslim article. Would a reader notice that it is more negative than a generic article about healthcare, car maintenance, or the economy? Our survey experiment suggested that three-quarters of readers would do just that. To provide a more grounded sense of what an actual article with an average valence feels like, here are two relatively short texts whose valence is within .001 of the corpus average:

"Bin Laden Mocks Grab at His Assets." Washington. Terror master Osama bin Laden taunted the Bush administration from his mountain hideout yesterday, saying efforts to freeze his financial assets will not stop his global mission of mayhem. Bin Laden's latest declaration was delivered to an Urdu-language Pakistani newspaper that has been a frequent conduit for his propaganda. "Freezing of the assets or accounts of al Qaeda will not make any difference," the newspaper quoted bin Laden as saying. "By the grace of God, al Qaeda has got three alternate financial systems which are separate and independent. This system is run by people who love jihad, and if the whole world tries to remove them, they will not succeed. These people are not a few hundred. They are in the thousands and hundreds of thousands," bin Laden said. Bin Laden is believed to have gone into hiding in Afghanistan with his four wives, ten children and hundreds of bodyguards hours after the September 11 terrorist attacks on the World Trade Center and the Pentagon. US analysts believe he is directing his words at ordinary people in the Arab world who he hopes will rise up against the United States in the name of Islam. Bin Laden's latest statement appeared to be in response to President Bush's order on Monday to freeze the assets of 27 people and organizations. Bin Laden also repeated his earlier denials that he masterminded the terror attacks on New York and Washington. "I want to clarify that my job is to inspire Muslims and to tell them what is in their interests and what is bad," he said, according to the newspaper.[18]

Letters to the Editor. "Christians in Iraq since the Beginning." Vincent Carroll and the people quoted in his Houses of Worship column, "Help Unwanted," Weekend Journal, May 16, concerning evangelical Christian outreach in Iraq, seem blithely unaware that Christian churches are already well-established there, and have been since the first century AD. About 3 percent of Iraqis are Christian, about the same percentage as the rest of the Middle East. They largely belong to one or another of the Orthodox or Coptic churches, though there are also some "Eastern rite" Roman Catholics. This Western blindness toward indigenous Arab Christians is unfortunately common. Charles M. Sennott's book, *The Body and the Blood*, cites many examples of Western tourists innocently asking Arab Christians, "When did you convert," not realizing these Arabs' families have been Christian since their churches were started by Christ's apostles. They have been dealing with the difficulty of existing in a Muslim society for more than a thousand years, and are increasingly embattled. As a former evangelical Christian and convert to the ancient Orthodox Christian faith, I hope Samaritan Purse and the other organizations cited are working with, not against, the existing Arab Christian churches, and not naively trying to "bring Christianity" into a land that has had Christianity since its beginnings 2,000 years ago. Michael Baum, Madison, Wis.[19]

---

[18] *New York Post*, September 29, 2001.
[19] *Wall Street Journal*, May 22, 2003.

While neither is unrelentingly negative, most readers are likely to come away from both articles with a negative impression. In the first, the impact of negative words such as "terror," "mayhem," and "attacks" outweighs the more positive words ("grace," "family"). In the second, "unwanted," "unaware," and "embattled," among others, outweigh positive words such as "innocently," "hope," and "faith." It is worth noting that the author of the second article is critical primarily of evangelical Christian outreach and Western tourists. As such, the article reminds us that a text can be negative and refer to Muslims or Islam without being negative *about* Muslims or Islam. This underscores the importance of going beyond just looking at an article's valence to examining the context in which our key terms of interest (Muslim, Islam) are used, as well as the general topics discussed in an article. We turn to this challenge in the next section of the chapter.

Before we do so, however, it is worth briefly examining broad patterns in valence across newspapers, over time, and within articles. The two texts just shown are drawn from two different sources and cover two very different issues, even though they have the same overall valence. If newspapers differ systematically in terms of valence even when they discuss the same events or topics, pooling all our articles in a single corpus might obscure more than it illuminates. This would be particularly true if either of the two main contributors to our corpus, the *New York Times* and *Washington Post*, were outliers. In fact, however, average article valence for these two papers is −.94 and −.93, respectively: right at our corpus mean. The most negative paper is the *New York Post* (average valence −1.41), and the least negative is the Minneapolis *Star Tribune* (−.35); neither contributes enough articles to the corpus to meaningfully sway overall patterns.[20]

There is no clear trend over time in the valence of articles about Muslims and Islam. Both in 1996 and 2016, average valence in our corpus was −.90. During the years in between, annual averages ranged from −1.05 (2002) to −.74 (2008), again without any clear trend. In chapter 4, we look at over-time patterns in more detail, with a particular emphasis on the impact of the 9/11 attacks. For now, suffice it to say that no single year is enough of an outlier to have a large impact on any overall patterns we identify in the next chapter.

---

[20] In the next chapter, we examine whether newspaper characteristics such as tabloid format and political leaning have a systematic impact on article valence. Table II.2.1 in the appendix breaks down average valence by paper.

Finally, we check whether the tone of coverage might be affected by the contexts in which Muslims and Islam are discussed. Might it be the case that the specific parts of an article that mention them are more positive than the rest of the article? We assess this possibility in two ways. First, a substantial majority (67%) of the 256,963 articles in our Muslim corpus contain just one or two mentions of Muslims or Islam. Sometimes these articles are focused on Muslims, but often—as in our second sample article—they mention them only in passing. If we whittle down our dataset to include only the 83,782 texts with three or more mentions of our keywords, to be more certain that the articles are truly "about" Muslims, we are left with articles whose average valence is even more negative, at −1.04. An article with that valence would be more negative than 86% of articles in our representative sample of American newspaper articles.

Another way to home in more closely on parts of texts that are specifically about Muslims or Islam is to isolate those sentences that contain one of our word roots Muslim*, Moslem*, or Islam*. After all, what if our keywords frequently appear in relatively negative articles, but sentences specifically about Muslims or Islam cast the group in a more positive light? To test this possibility, we stripped away all sentences in each of our 256,963 articles that did not contain those word roots. We then assessed the tone of each resulting compressed "article." The average tone of these texts is −1.20. A full text article with that valence would be more negative than 89% of articles in our representative corpus. In short, the more frequently Muslims are mentioned in a text, the more negative it tends to be, and sentences about Muslims tend to be more negative still. Overall, it is safe to say that no matter how we parse the data, there is a substantial amount of negativity in the US media's coverage of Muslims and Islam.

The contents of Muslim coverage

As we noted earlier, the tone of an article does not tell us everything we might want to know about how the article portrays Muslims. It matters, for example, whether Muslims are the subject or the object of a negative article: If it discusses violence, are Muslims the perpetrators or the victims of such violence? While articles discussing Muslims as the victims of violence may nonetheless leave readers with a negative image associated with Muslims, such an association is likely to be weaker than would be the case for articles discussing them as perpetrators. Similarly, an article using negative terms to describe Muslims' religious practices is less likely to worsen a reader's mental picture of Muslims than one using the same negative terms to describe terrorists claiming to act in the name of Islam. In other words, context matters.

One obvious aspect of context is what term caused an article to be included in our corpus. As noted earlier, we pool together all articles containing one or more occurrences of the word roots Muslim*, Moslem*, or Islam*.[21] Yet it might be the case that articles touching on Muslims as people are distinct from those mentioning Islam as a religion. To make sure there are no dramatic differences in tone that would argue against pooling all the articles together for our analysis, we constructed three separate subsets of articles, as shown in table 2.2. Each of these subsets has a strongly negative average article valence. Articles including the word root Islam* are somewhat more negative than the corpus average, while articles including only references to Muslims are a bit less negative. Overall, however, the average values are sufficiently close—and so many articles include references to both Muslims and Islam—that treating this as a single corpus makes sense.

Table 2.2 Proportion of corpus and average valence for articles referencing Muslims and/or Islam

Corpus	Number of articles	Average valence
All	256,963	−.94
Islam* but not Muslim*	105,646 (41%)	−.99
Muslim* but not Islam*	81,798 (32%)	−.81
Both Islam* and Muslim*	69,120 (27%)	−1.01

In the following chapters, we look in more detail at the contents of the articles in our corpus, testing existing theories about the factors that drive negative coverage as well as identifying new patterns.[22] In order to do so, we need a systematic way to identify and characterize the content of a text. We do so using three different methods: (1) searching for and examining the occurrences and prevalence of specific words; (2) analyzing collocations: the

---

[21] Cf. Vultee (2009, 623), who notes that for certain media outlets, "Islam is inseparable from what Muslims do, and Muslims are inseparable from each other."

[22] In appendix II.2, we also provide an overview of the most common positive and negative words in the overall corpus. The positive words are fairly generic, but the negative words strongly point to a specific type of discussion regarding Muslims, involving conflict, violence, and terrorism.

words that are co-located with our corpus keywords Muslim and Islam; and (3) allowing an algorithm to identify words that frequently co-occur, a technique known as topic modeling. We turn to topic modeling in chapter 6, and explain it there. Here, we focus on the keywords we tag as indicative of a text touching on issues highlighted in the theoretical literature as shaping negative coverage. Following that, we briefly explain how we use collocation analysis.

Words to look for

Among the four umbrella elements identified in chapter 1 as potentially associated with negative coverage—geography, events, cultural differences, and the market for news—we noted earlier that right-leaning and tabloid papers represent two dimensions of the last element. Here, we look at five additional factors that guide the discussion in the empirical chapters: (1) foreign story locations; (2) references to (political) violence, and references related to three types of cultural differences: (3) extremism; (4) aspects of religiosity; and (5) social values at times alleged to be incompatible with some interpretations of Islam, often summarized in the literature as a "value clash" (Norris and Inglehart 2002).

We test for the impact of foreign story locations by identifying country names as well as names of major foreign cities in the newspaper articles we analyze, along with major domestic cities and smaller cities and towns in the immediate coverage area of a newspaper (e.g., suburbs of Boston for the *Boston Globe*). This allows us to distinguish between stories that feature only domestic locations, those that reference domestic as well as foreign locations, and those that only mention foreign locations.[23] We are particularly interested in stories involving an *exclusive foreign setting*, as these are most likely to involve a high degree of negativity.

For violent events in the news, scholars have focused largely on broad patterns of stories about political violence. As such, we flag articles that contain key political conflict-related terms related to wars and insurgencies, such as "warring," "separatist," and so on. In addition, we include references to political violence and conflict directly associated with Muslims, including

---

[23] The practice of adding a reporter's location to a story ("Dateline Washington . . . ," for example) means that a few articles referring only to people and events outside the United States will nevertheless be coded as also featuring a US location.

Taliban, 9/11, and ISIS, among others. Finally, we mark references to terrorism. We combine all of these different references into a single *violence* variable, allowing us to systematically assess the impact of violence and conflict on the tone of newspaper coverage involving Muslims.[24]

To analyze the tone of Muslim articles associated with *extremism*, we identify those that mention extremist and fundamentalist beliefs in general, based on words such as radical, militant, fanatic, extremist, and fundamentalist. To those, we add references to extreme and politicized versions of Islam—Islamist, the caliphate, islamofascism—as well as extremist political ideas not explicitly linked to Islam: theocracy and fascism. We combine this with a variable tallying explicit references to sharia; in theory, sharia need not have any fundamentalist or extremist connotations, but in common media usage it often does.

In order to test whether markers of religiosity and devotion are associated with particularly negative or positive coverage of Muslims, we identify explicit references to devotion (keywords such as devotion, devout, observant, pious, etc.), as well as references to religious practices in general (prayer, pilgrimage, fasting, worship) and to Muslim practices in particular (Ramadan, Eid). In addition, we capture "physical" attributes of religiosity, including references to clothing, beards, and religion-related dietary practices (halal, ritual slaughter, etc.). We combine these components to form a *religiosity* variable.

Finally, to flag topics where some scholars have argued a clash of values is likely, we identify all references in our corpus to sexual orientation and gender identity (gay, lesbian, homosexual, transgender, queer, etc.), along with references to women and children.[25] To this category we further add references to particular issues associated with women's rights, specifically female genital mutilation and polygamy. As noted earlier, we name the resulting variable "value clash."[26]

---

[24] Note that we do not include references to physical violence, such as fights, brawls, murder, etc. Such references are also likely to be associated with negative article tone (indeed, in other work we have found this to be the case (Media Portrayals of Minorities Project 2019, 2020, 2021). However, the theoretical predictions associating Muslims with violence are primarily associated with political violence, as we shall see in chapter 3.

[25] Different approaches to childrearing often feature in discussions of clashing values (Sniderman and Hagendoorn 2007).

[26] To guard against the possibility that stories mentioning women and/or children were not referencing themes of clashing values, we replicated our main analyses using a value-clash variable that excluded each of these terms separately and together. The results were substantively similar.

Table 2.3 summarizes each of the variables (other than geographic location) and the word roots we include. We capitalize the words and word roots here as appropriate, but the actual text searches were executed without regard to capitalization. In addition, for "al Qaeda" and "bin Laden," listed under "Violent Islamism" in Table 2.3, we look for several different spellings (with and without spacing, Laden as well as Ladin, etc.).

Unavoidably, our search specifications are not perfect. For instance, not every reference to revolution is associated with violence: among others, people often talk about scientific advances representing a revolution. Similarly, not every reference to sharia is associated with extremism in beliefs, though in practice most are. In addition, some terms could arguably

Table 2.3 Search criteria for content-based variables

Variable	Conceptual components	Words and word roots
Violence	Terrorism	terror*
	War	war, wars, warring, warlike, warred, warfare
	Insurgency	revolution*, separatis*, insurgen*, militia*, armed
	Violent Islamism	Taliban, 9/11, September 11*, jihad, alqaeda, binladen, ISIS, ISIL, Islamic State, Daesh
Extremism	Extremism	extreme, extremis*, fundamentalis*, ultraconservativ*, radical*, militan*, fanatic*
	Theocracy	theocra*
	Fascism	fascis*
	Sharia	sharia
	Political Islamism	islamis*, caliph*, islamofascis*
Religiosity	Religion	religio*, convert*, interfaith, god, faith, worship*, Allah, mosque*, minaret*, imam*, koran*, quran*, prophet M*
	Devotion	devout*, devotion, observan*, pious, piety
	Observance	Ramadan, Eid, pray*, pilgrimage*, fasting
	Clothing	garb, attire, dress, veil*, headscar*, scarf, scarves, hijab*, jilbab*, burqa, burka*, burkini*, niqab*, chador*
	Diet	halal, diet*, ritual slaughter
	Other	holy, calendar*, lunar, beard*
Value clash	Women	woman, women, girl*, female*, feminin*
	Children	child*, kid, kids, young, youth*
	LGBT	gay*, lgbt*, homosex*, lesbi*, transgender*, bisex*

fit into a different variable: maybe the Taliban is better characterized as political Islamism than as violent Islamism? It is also not difficult to think of words that seem worthy of inclusion into our search criteria: for example, perhaps "boy" should be added to the "children" category.

We adopted the specific set of search criteria shown here—as opposed to the nearly infinite number of alternative possible criteria—in an iterative process. First, we randomly selected a small number of texts containing each term we adopt—and a number we did not adopt—and examined their immediate context to see whether the term was used in ways that correspond to our categorization; this is often referred to as a "keyword in context" (KWIC) search. For example, while "revolution" can be used in many different ways, in our corpus it is primarily mentioned in the context of violent insurgencies. Next, to assess possible omissions, we ran a collocation analysis—explained in more detail in the following section—on the immediate context of each term, to identify other words often used in conjunction with the term. Words with related meanings frequently occur together in the same context, an insight often summarized as "You shall know a word by the company it keeps" (Firth 1957, 11). Any plausible additions were then subjected to a KWIC analysis to make sure their modal occurrence in our corpus represented the category for which they were a candidate. As noted, the result is not perfect; however, we are confident that our variables do a good job of capturing the concept(s) of interest. Moreover, since they reflect the aggregation of a number of related search terms, adding or dropping any single search term would make little difference in terms of which articles get flagged for a variable.

Collocations

Collocation analysis is not only helpful in homing in on specific words associated with our key concepts of violence, religiosity, etc.; it can also shed light on how the word roots Muslim* and Islam* are used throughout our corpus. Collocation analysis is one of the fundamental tools of text analysis, with a pedigree going back centuries.[27] KWIC searches show where and how

---

[27] For example, early theological scholars compiled long tables of the different contexts within which particular words occurred in the Bible.

a particular term is used in a corpus; statistical collocation analysis examines word usages and contexts systematically, to see whether a word's appearance in a particular context is statistically and substantively significant. For example, if we look at the immediate neighbors of the word "Muslim," do we encounter the word "baker" more or less often than we would expect to, given the latter word's overall frequency in newspaper articles? If it occurs a lot more than we would expect it to by chance, that indicates that the word is associated, textually, with "Muslim" and—as a result—may well become associated with Muslims in readers' minds. In chapters 4 and 5 we look at the collocates of Muslims and Islam to get a sense of what kinds of associations newspaper readers are likely to form.

Collocations are also important tools to illuminate where Muslims and Islam figure into positive and negative texts. After all, it makes a real difference whether, in a discussion of political violence, Muslims are depicted as the aggressors and perpetrators or as the victims. As we noted at the start of the chapter, in some stories they are both, and the journalist can choose to identify either or both sides as Muslim. Collocation information will shed some light on the balance between perpetrator and victim contexts in our corpus, among others; in addition, our topic modeling analysis in chapter 6 will identify topics where Muslims are victims—a possibility not widely discussed in the literature. If political violence stories mentioning Muslims are evenly balanced between those where Muslims are the perpetrators and those where they are the victims, readers may form a very different impression than if there is a strong imbalance in either direction.

However, it is important to note that reading about Muslims as victims may also strengthen rather than counterbalance preexisting negative impressions people have: well-established cognitive patterns such as illusory correlation (Hilton and von Hippel 1996) and victim blaming (Chagnon 2017) may predispose some media consumers to such a result. For example, reading a negative article that merely mentions a group (even when the group is not described negatively) may lead readers who have a preexisting negative impression to remember the article as being negative about the group (cf. Mastro and Tukachinsky 2014). In addition, recent research in one context finds that when a group is portrayed as being the victim in a text, readers may actually emerge with *more* negative impressions of that group (Bos et al. 2016).

Conclusions

In September 2016, the *New York Times* published an article noting that hate crimes against Muslims in America had risen to levels not seen since 2001 (Lichtblau 2016). In presenting one possible explanation of this trend, the article quoted a Muslim businessman as saying: "There is a lot of negative rhetoric; the negative rhetoric is causing the hate, and in turn the hate is causing the violent acts." This view echoes that of scholars who have identified the causal links between discourse and rhetoric, ideas and attitudes, and actions and policies (Simon and Jerit 2007; Islam 2008; Perloff 2010). How Muslims and Islam are discussed in the media and elsewhere matters—not just in and of itself, but also because it shapes beliefs about Muslims that in turn can shape policy preferences and policy outcomes, and even spur some to engage in violence (Ivandic, Kirchmaier, and Machin 2019; Saleem et al. 2017).

In this chapter we presented a way of quantifying the notion that there is "a lot of negative rhetoric," and applied it to our corpus of more than a quarter of a million articles mentioning Muslims and/or Islam in the US print media. Our calibrated method of measuring the tone of coverage in a fine-grained way, coupled with recent advancements in the digital availability of media coverage and developments in computational text analysis, make it possible for the first time to offer systematic and precise answers to the question of how negative a particular set of newspaper articles is compared to any other set, across groups, time, countries, and topics.

We showed that coverage is systematically strongly negative: the average article mentioning Muslims or Islam is more negative than four out of five newspaper articles that do not mention them. Moreover, coverage is negative across all newspapers included in our corpus, and it is negative regardless of whether we focus on the word roots Muslim* or Islam*. We also presented experimental evidence indicating that the level of negativity in these articles is more than enough for most people to readily and consciously identify it. Finally, we outlined the words that mark articles as referencing foreign locations, (political) violence, extremism, religiosity, and social values: five variables that will be central to the analysis in the next chapter and beyond.

3

United States newspaper coverage
of Muslims

Main patterns and group comparisons

Articles about Muslims in American newspapers run the gamut from extremely positive stories about Muslim patriotism and generosity to extremely negative coverage of Islamist militant attacks. Yet identifying examples on either end of the spectrum does not help us grasp patterns across the media as a whole. As we have seen, the tone of the average article in our Muslim corpus is a strikingly negative −.94. One main goal of this chapter is to understand why. We begin by reviewing some common reasons scholars believe articles about Muslims are likely to be negative, and then assess the degree of negativity associated with these factors. We show that coverage set exclusively in a foreign location, articles related to violence or that mention extremism, and stories published in tabloids are associated with the greatest degree of negativity. Other prominent elements we examine are not linked with as much negativity as some suggest. Most telling, however, is that even once we filter out articles that touch on the most negative factors, the remaining articles about Muslims are still negative. The average article that is not set exclusively abroad, makes no mention of violence or extremism, and is not published in a tabloid is still more negative than the average article in our representative sample of newspaper stories.

What if newspapers only cover religious groups when crises, conflicts, or cultural tensions erupt? To understand whether our findings about Muslims are noteworthy in this respect, we compare coverage to that of three global religious groups that are also minorities within the majority-Protestant United States, though with different degrees of perceived outsiderness (Kalkan, Layman, and Uslaner 2009). Catholics are Christians and mostly White, though a high percentage of ethnic Latinos—who may or may not be White—are Catholic; Jews are part of the so-called Judeo-Christian tradition, but also remain targets of anti-Semitism even if most self-identify

Covering Muslims. Erik Bleich and A. Maurits van der Veen, Oxford University Press. © Oxford University Press 2022.
DOI: 10.1093/oso/9780197611715.003.0003

as White; Hindus are closest to Muslims in many key respects: they are adherents of a demographically large world religion who constitute a similar percentage of the US population and are typically not viewed as White by the majority of Americans. We leverage these similarities and differences to explore whether Muslims are covered in a distinctly negative fashion, or whether Muslim articles only differ by degree from those touching on these other religious groups.

Muslims are not only associated with a major world religion, they are also viewed as a minority group within American society. As a subset of all Muslims, Muslim Americans can be more directly compared to ethno-racial groups within the United States that are frequent targets of discrimination and even violence, such as African Americans and Latinos. As a domestic religious group, Muslim Americans share consistently low ratings on feeling thermometer surveys with groups often viewed as outside of the American religious mainstream, such as Mormons and atheists. To deepen our understanding of how the press covers Muslims, we narrow our comprehensive corpus to just those articles that mention US-based Muslims. By excluding highly negative articles about violence or extremism set abroad, we can tone-check coverage of Muslim Americans compared to that of other American racial, ethnic, or (non)religious groups.

The core finding of this chapter is that Muslim articles are remarkably negative by any measure, and not only relative to our representative corpus: they are negative when we exclude articles touching on the most negative topics; they are negative compared to articles mentioning other world religious groups; and Muslim American articles are negative compared to stories linked to African Americans, Latinos, Mormons, or atheists. Of course, as already noted, individual articles in our corpus may be positive, and some are strongly so. Yet articles mentioning Muslims or Islam in US newspapers are undeniably and conspicuously negative overall, no matter what point of comparison we use.

Potential reasons for negative coverage

Why might coverage of Muslims in American newspapers be so negative? Scholars from political science, sociology, communication science, and economics have advanced arguments about what makes news coverage negative. We summarize these arguments here under four main rubrics: *geography* (foreign news), *events* (violence and conflict), *differences* (cultural factors), and *market* incentives (newspaper agendas). These areas capture not only scholarly research on negative media coverage, but also common intuitions about why articles about Muslims and Islam may be more negative than those about other groups. This approach allows us to assess the extent to which specific elements associated with each perspective are linked with negative coverage. It also means we can gauge the tone of Muslim articles after taking all of these factors into account. Is it the case that negativity associated with Muslims is simply a function of coverage of events or topics that are prone to elicit negative coverage?

Geography: The negativity of foreign news

Muslims constitute nearly a quarter of the total world population, but just around 1% of the US population (Pew Research Center 2015, 8, 16).[1] This inevitably means that if an article mentions Muslims or Islam it is often related to foreign news (Sheikh, Price, and Oshagan 1996). Scholars have long argued that the negativity bias of news operates more strongly for foreign than domestic news (Peterson 1981; Nossek 2004). Among others, this general pattern has recently been shown to apply to headlines about Muslims and Islam in the *New York Times* and the *Guardian* (Nisar and Bleich 2020), and to a cross-section of European newspapers (Mertens 2016).

In fact, the seminal early work on newsworthiness, Galtung and Ruge's "The Structure of Foreign News," suggests that negative foreign news is likely to be more surprising and more immediate than positive foreign news, which is often associated with processes that unfold over longer periods of time (Galtung and Ruge 1965, 69; Yu and Luter 1964, 8). Other scholars posit a funnel "through which news about foreign countries flows," turning "a relatively rich mixture of news . . . to a sparse, violent, and conflict-laden portrait of the world" (Wilhoit and Weaver 1983, 132; Nossek 2004, 344). The prevalence of negative news at the end of this funnel has been shown to increase with geographic and cultural distance (Balmas 2017). Since there are no Muslim-majority countries geographically close to the United States, news reported from such countries may well be even more negative than the

---

[1] Lajevardi (2020, 8) notes that there is uncertainty about the precise population of Muslims in the United States, with some estimates ranging as high as 4%.

average foreign news story. We test the hypothesis that articles set exclusively abroad are prone to be more negative than their counterparts that mention domestic locations or that contain no geographic references at all.

Events linked to violence: Both newsworthy and negative

If Muslims find themselves disproportionately involved in violence- and security-related events, this will drive down the average tone of news coverage of Muslims and Islam. Research going back at least two decades suggests there is something to this expectation (Sheikh et al. 1996). More recent scholarship shows that Muslim-majority countries are indeed disproportionately conflict-prone, not because they are Muslim, but because of the age composition of their populations (Urdal 2006), as well as lower levels of income and higher levels of state repression (Karakaya 2015). The importance of conflict in increasing a story's newsworthiness also contributes to this pattern (Harcup and O'Neill 2017; see also Phillips 2014). Violence is a major factor in making stories more attractive to publishers. This is true for domestic as well as for foreign news (Hamilton 2000). Indeed, foreign news covering the Global South—where most Muslim-majority countries are located—has long been dominated by "violence and disasters" (Hackett 1989, 824).

Most of the violence and conflict involving Muslims takes place outside the borders of the United States and hence also qualifies as foreign news. However, it is important to keep the two categories separate: not all news about violence and conflict is foreign, and not all foreign news is violent. Moreover, some types of violence are not limited to a single location. The 9/11 attacks, for example, had important domestic as well as foreign aspects. For violent events in the news, scholars have been particularly interested in broad patterns of stories about *political* violence. As such, we flag articles that contain the key political conflict-related terms we outlined in detail in chapter 2 into a single *violence* variable, allowing us to systematically assess the hypothesis that violence and conflict are associated with a great deal of negativity. Our approach also allows us to explore the extent to which violence and foreign news play distinct roles in newspaper coverage involving Muslims.[2]

---

[2] In fact, the correlation between articles mentioning an identifiable foreign location and those containing a reference to violence is just .26, meaning that the two factors are indeed distinct.

Cultural differences: Grappling with the "Other"

Most newspaper coverage of Muslims and Islam is not exclusively set in foreign locations, and much of it is not tied to specific conflicts or violence. What might drive such coverage to be more negative than comparable coverage involving other (religious) groups? Scholars across a number of different disciplines have identified cultural differences between Christianity (or "the West") and Islam as a likely key factor explaining negative coverage of Muslims (Ahmed and Matthes 2017; Semati 2010; Whitaker 2002). We discuss such differences under three rubrics: extremism, religiosity, and value clash.

Extremism and fundamentalism

Most people regard religious fundamentalism negatively (Bolce and De Maio 2008; Yancey 2010), and unease with Muslim immigrants may largely be a function of such negative attitudes (Helbling and Traunmüller 2018). Here, it is not the religion of Islam as such that causes a negative tone, but rather a particular (extreme) set of values associated with it. As Said argued well before the 9/11 attacks, Islam has long been "almost automatically" associated with fundamentalism; this association evokes "every negative fact associated with Islam—its violence, primitiveness, atavism, threatening qualities" (Said 1997, xvi). Said also notes that the terms "fundamentalism," "radicalism," and "extremism" are often used interchangeably, without precise definitions, and that prominent mainstream commentators see all as profoundly threatening: "fundamentalism equals Islam equals everything-we-must-now-fight-against" (Said 1997, xix).[3] To analyze the tone of Muslim articles associated with extremism, we isolate those that mention extremist and fundamentalist beliefs to understand whether such references are indeed associated with an increase in negativity.

Religiosity and devotion

Many people believe that Muslims are, on average, more conservative and traditionalist in their religious and societal attitudes (Sides and Mogahed 2018).[4] As most Western societies have undergone a rapid process of

---

[3] Research in Europe has identified more widespread fundamentalist attitudes among certain types of Muslims when compared to Christians (Koopmans 2015).

[4] In an extensive, cross-national study, Fish (2011, 255–56). finds little evidence of differences in religiosity, but support for the idea that Muslims tend to be more socially conservative.

secularization in recent decades (Casanova 2006; Lewis and Kashyap 2013; Brubaker 2017), clear or intense expressions of religiosity may increasingly make people, including journalists, uncomfortable. Indeed, numerous scholars argue that secularization has brought along with it an increased skepticism and disparagement of all religious practices—not just the most fundamentalist manifestations—directed predominantly toward non-Christian religions (Casanova 2006; Cesari 2007; Roy 2016; Brubaker 2017).

Many scholars making such claims focus on Islam in Europe. Cesari, for example, argues that "European perceptions of certain manifestations of Islam as troublesome or even unacceptable are thus a consequence of a more general invalidation of religion (Cesari 2007, 37). Brubaker, similarly, is interested in Western European secularist rhetoric, which he views as "directed against Muslim immigrants and their descendants, whose religiosity is seen as threatening despite the fact that Islam has little institutional power, political influence, or cultural authority in the wider society" (Brubaker 2017, 1201). Whether these findings translate to the US context is an open question. According to at least one author, "The American news media presuppose that religion is a good thing. . . . As hostile, ham-handed, or ignorant as their approach may sometimes appear, the media will never be caught attacking religion as such" (Silk 1998, 57). Research examining the coverage of Muslim devotional practices appears to bear this out (Bleich, Souffrant, et al. 2018).

Aside from potential skepticism about devotion and religiosity in general, certain Muslim religious practices may be particularly likely to generate tensions or to tangibly affect how Muslims and non-Muslims interact in society. The best known examples here are religious clothing (which may violate social norms as well as official rules about religious displays) and the observance of fasting during Ramadan (Adida, Laitin, and Valfort 2016, 80–81; see also Cesari 2007; Roy 2016). Our *religiosity* variable enables us to explore whether articles touching on devotion and religious practices are associated with greater negativity than those not mentioning religiosity words.

Clash of values
Beyond associating Islam with extreme beliefs and highly visible displays of religiosity, many people feel that most Muslims—not just those who are fundamentalist—hold attitudes at odds with contemporary Western values (Sides and Mogahed 2018). The values frequently highlighted in this context are those concerning attitudes toward women and toward members of

the LGBTQ+ community (e.g. Whitaker 2002; Adida, Laitin, and Valfort 2016, 85–86). Data from successive rounds of the World Values Survey indicate that such attitudes differ considerably between Christians and Muslims (Inglehart and Norris 2003; Fish 2011). Attitudes toward childrearing constitute an additional potential vector of value differences, with over 75% of respondents in one Dutch survey, for example, agreeing that "Muslims in the Netherlands raise their children in an authoritarian way" (Sniderman and Hagendoorn 2007, 24).

It is empirically the case that women and LGBTQ+ people have fewer rights and face more discrimination in most Muslim-majority countries than they do in most Western countries (Ross 2008; Cherif 2010). As such, reporting on rights and discrimination is more likely to be negative when set in such countries. Moreover, since Muslim attitudes regarding gender roles, sexual orientation, and gender identity are often perceived to violate widely shared norms in Western countries, reporting on those attitudes is also more likely to be critical. A study of the *Washington Post* and the *New York Times*, for example, shows that stories about Muslim women are more likely to emphasize rights violations and gender inequality, whereas stories about non-Muslim women are more likely to emphasize rights being respected (Terman 2017).

We identify all references in our corpus to sexual orientation and gender identity, along with references to women and children. To this category we further add references to particular issues associated with women's rights, specifically female genital mutilation and polygamy. Since these are issues where there is a presumptive clash in values, we call this variable *value clash*, without intending to prejudge whether such a clash will be evident in our corpus. This allows us to assess whether such articles are associated with more negativity than other articles within our Muslim corpus.

The market for news: Giving consumers what they like

Market forces shape media content, especially in profit-driven media markets such as the United States (McManus 1994; Hamilton 2004). When readers hold particular ideological preferences, news outlets have an economic incentive to cater to these preferences in their reporting (Mullainathan and Shleifer 2005; see also Gentzkow and Shapiro 2010). Given that a newspaper's ideological slant is affected by market incentives, it is no surprise that the coverage of specific political issues is similarly influenced. For example, Dunaway (2013) shows that election campaign coverage is affected by market incentives as well as by an outlet's ownership.

We identify two different dimensions along which newspaper consumers are likely to vary: political leaning and socioeconomic status. On the former, most evidence suggests that consumers of right-leaning media (newspapers as well as television) will hold beliefs that are more critical of Muslims and Islam (Jones et al. 2011, 10–11; Ogan et al. 2014). We therefore examine whether right-leaning outlets are more likely to convey negativity in our Muslim corpus than centrist or left-leaning newspapers. Newspaper audiences also vary in socioeconomic status, with broadsheet papers generally seen as more up-market, while tabloids are more popularly oriented (Conboy 2005). This tabloid orientation is expected to generate more negative coverage of Muslims, both because tabloid consumers are drawn to sensationalist stories, which are more likely to feature violence and extremism (Moore, Mason, and Lewis 2008), and because these readers hold more negative opinions of Muslims overall (Conboy 2005). Identifying right-leaning and tabloid newspapers thus permits us to test the hypothesis that market forces are associated with negativity in our Muslim corpus.

Assessing negative coverage

The tone of the average Muslim article in US newspapers is an extremely negative –.94. The scholarship that we just reviewed about media coverage—and about Muslims in particular—draws our attention to seven types of stories that might help account for this negativity: those (1) set exclusively in a foreign location; those containing words related to (2) violence, (3) extremism, (4) religiosity, or (5) value clash; and those found in (6) right-leaning or (7) tabloid newspapers. To understand the relative significance of each factor and the combined effect of all of them, we explore the prevalence and assess the tone associated with these elements in the 256,963 articles in our Muslim corpus. We also test the proposition that articles that are not associated with any of the most negative factors are essentially the same, in terms of valence, as articles from our representative corpus. If this were the case, the intense negativity linked to newspaper reporting on Muslims may be viewed as a function of the newsworthiness of particular stories or of media bias due to market incentives.

Table 3.1 Articles containing at least one
word associated with each element

	Count	Percentage
Violence	188,842	73
Extremism	116,519	45
Religiosity	137,426	53
Value clash	127,530	50

How common is it for articles that mention Muslims or Islam to contain words linked to any of these seven factors? Thirteen percent of all articles in our Muslim corpus were set uniquely in a foreign location. These explicitly mention one or more foreign countries or cities, and contain no references to the United States or to any domestic geographic markers.[5] A much greater percentage of articles include at least one word associated with violence, extremism, religiosity, or value clash, as summarized in table 3.1. Given that individual articles often contain more than one type of reference, the counts add up to more than 256,963 and the percentages to more than 100%.

Articles with words linked to violence immediately stand out. Almost three out of four articles that include the words Muslim or Islam also contain words like terrorism, war, militia, armed, or al Qaeda. In addition, 45% of articles include extremism words like fundamentalist, militant, radical, or extremist. As might be expected, there is substantial overlap between these categories: taken together, violence and/or extremism words are present in just under 80% of articles in our Muslim corpus. Words related to religiosity (such as devout, faith, God, imam, Ramadan, or veil) and value clash (such as women, homosexuality, transgender, or polygamy) are also present in half or more of our articles. Rounding out the overview, 9% of articles were published in right-leaning papers, and 9% in tabloids, with 4% appearing in the sole right-leaning tabloid in our pool of newspapers (the *New York Post*).

How many articles are not set exclusively abroad; contain no references to violence, extremism, religiosity, or value clash; and are not published in right-leaning or tabloid papers? Strikingly, only just under 3% of our articles

---

[5] Nine percent of our articles are set uniquely in a domestic location, while 77% contain references to both foreign and domestic locations; 1% do not contain explicit references to either a foreign or domestic location.

are not linked to any of the factors generally associated with negative coverage of Muslims. Even in newspapers that are not right-leaning or tabloids, only just over 3% of all articles contain no references to violence, extremism, religiosity, value clash, and are not set exclusively in foreign locations. This suggests that when newspapers write about Muslims or Islam, they tend to link them to specific subjects, most of which the current literature presumes to be negative.

We take a first cut at assessing each of these seven elements by calculating the percentages of positive and negative articles associated with each factor. Figure 3.1 shows that between 76% and 89% of articles linked with each element are negative. Even two-thirds of the small number of articles that contain none of the factors in our investigation are negative. Thus, while 50,827 articles—20% of the total—have a positive tone, almost all of these articles nonetheless contain words linked to one or more factors that scholars argue are likely to be negative.

The evidence presented in figure 3.1 is revealing, but it cannot show just how much more positive or negative the presence of each element makes an

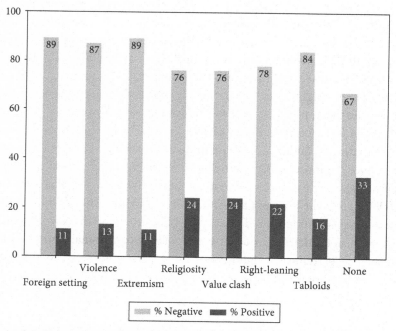

Figure 3.1 Proportions of negative and positive articles associated with each factor (rounded to the nearest whole number)

article. Moreover, because articles may contain more than one element, we want to know the effect of each individual factor while also controlling for the potential influence of other factors that happen to be in an article. For example, if articles in a right-leaning paper mention violence and religiosity, which of those three elements is driving the negativity? Is it primarily one factor, two of the three, or are all three equally linked to the negative tone? A multivariate regression allows us to estimate the association between tone and each of our main factors, while controlling for the others. Figure 3.2 displays coefficient plots from such an analysis; all seven factors are coded simply for their presence or absence, facilitating direct comparisons.

The location on the x-axis of the dot associated with each variable provides information about whether articles containing that factor are likely to be more positive (to the right of the vertical line at 0) or negative (to the left) than articles that do not mention that element, holding all else equal. Each dot represents the regression's estimate of just how much more positive or negative; the very short horizontal line through each dot represents the 95% confidence interval (indicating how certain we are about this estimate). The magnitude of each plotted coefficient shows which factors are associated with the greatest shift in the predicted tone of the articles. For example, articles containing violence words are strongly more negative than those not containing violence words. Articles set exclusively in a foreign location have

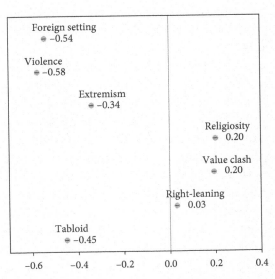

Figure 3.2 Factors associated with the tone of Muslim articles

a roughly similar negative association with article tone. These two factors are thus associated with more negativity than are any other elements. Articles that mention extremism and those published in tabloids are also clearly more negative than articles containing no mentions of extremism or those not found in tabloids.

On the other side of the spectrum, articles in right-leaning papers are very slightly more positive than those in non-right-leaning papers, although this difference is so small that it is not meaningful in substantive terms. Articles that mention religiosity words or value-clash words are modestly more positive than those with no such words. This is surprising in light of the assumption, derived from the theoretical literature on secularism and clashing values, that such discussions tend to be highly negative. It is important to stress, however, that, as we saw from figure 3.1, these coefficients do not mean that articles touching on religion or values are likely to be positive. Instead, they are simply likely to be less intensely negative compared to articles that do not mention those topics.

To communicate what this means, it is helpful to understand the average tone of articles with different combinations of our seven variables, compared to the Muslim corpus average of −.94. For instance, stories that mention both violence and extremism words and are not tagged for any of the other five variables we analyze make up 9% of articles in our Muslim corpus and have an average valence of −1.24. Meanwhile, only 6% of Muslim corpus articles mention both religiosity and value-clash words and contain none of the other five elements; these 14,178 articles tend to be essentially neutral, with a mean tone of +.04.

Our analyses thus reveal which factors are associated with the greatest degree of negativity, as well as those associated with less negativity than expected. In particular, articles that mention violence and those set exclusively in foreign locations are most likely to be markedly negative. Articles that mention extremism and articles published in tabloids are also associated with clear negativity. By contrast, articles that touch on religiosity or mention words associated with value clashes are actually modestly more positive than those that do neither of those things. Stories published in right-leaning papers, finally, are not more negative than those appearing in centrist or left-leaning outlets, but neither are they substantially more positive.

While some of these findings are highly intuitive—it is difficult to imagine articles containing violence or extremism words being positive—others are less obvious. That tabloid articles are far more negative than those in right-leaning papers (which themselves are no more negative than articles in centrist or left-leaning papers) is only apparent through our comparative analysis. That stories mentioning religiosity or "value clash" words related to women, sexual orientation, or gender identity are less negative than articles without such words is also surprising, given the scholarly expectations outlined above.

Comparing Muslims to other religious groups

So far we have looked just at articles that mention Muslims or Islam. But what if the negativity associated with those articles simply reflects a general negativity whenever religious groups draw media attention? To address this question, we gathered every article from the same 17 newspapers across all 21 years that mentioned Catholics or Catholicism, Jews or Judaism, and Hindus or Hinduism.[6] Some of these groups garner more coverage than others. Figure 3.3 shows the monthly article count for our four religious group corpora between January 1996 and December 2016. The spike in Muslim coverage occasioned by the 9/11 attacks is clearly visible. Overall, Catholics are mentioned most often, while Jews and Muslims traded second and third place for most of the 21 years we cover.

Hindus are by far the least-covered group among the four. There are only 20,466 articles that mention them across our 21 years, compared to 365,062 Catholic articles, 256,963 Muslim articles, and 256,454 Jewish articles. This may not be surprising, but it is noteworthy, given that Hindus make up approximately the same percentage of the US population as Muslims (0.7% compared to 0.9%). Moreover, with an estimated 1.1 billion adherents, Hinduism is the third-largest world religion, behind only Christianity and Islam, which have approximately 2.3 and 1.8 billion followers, respectively. To round out the demographic context for our comparison, Judaism has 14 million adherents worldwide and Jews make up a little less than 2% of the American population, while there are approximately 1.1 billion Catholics in the world and Catholics constitute around 21% of the US population.[7]

---

[6] Lists of search terms associated with each religion and its adherents are available in the appendix.

[7] Estimates of American religious demographics are for 2018 (CIA 2020). Estimates of global populations of Christians, Muslims, Hindus, and Jews are for 2015 (Pew Research Center, Cooperman, and Schiller 2017, 8–10). Estimates of the global Catholic population are for 2010 (Pew Research Center 2011, 21).

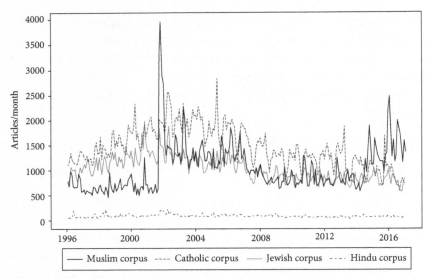

Figure 3.3 Monthly article count, by religious group corpus

The percentages of positive and negative articles referencing these three groups decidedly do not mirror those mentioning Muslims. Eighty percent of all articles in our Muslim corpus were negative and only 20% were positive. Figure 3.4 shows the four groups ordered from least to most positive. As the figure indicates, coverage has tended to be neutral or even positive, rather than negative, for the three groups other than Muslims.

What about the average article tone for each group? As table 3.2 shows, the average Hindu, Jewish, and Catholic full-text articles have tones of −.16, −.05, and +.08, respectively, compared to −.94 for Muslim articles. As we saw for Muslims in chapter 2, if we focus on articles that mention each group at least three times—ones more likely "about" each group rather than perhaps containing passing references—the tone for Muslim article drops to −1.04. It declines to −.32 for Hindus, but dips only marginally for Catholics and Jews. Finally, looking at articles stripped down to retain only the sentences that mention each group, the average tone for Muslim stories drops even more, to −1.20. The corresponding average tone for Hindu, Jewish, and Catholic articles is −.13, −.04, and +.24, respectively. In short, the more an article mentions Muslims and the more we focus on Muslim sentences, the more negative the tone. The same is not uniformly true for any other group.

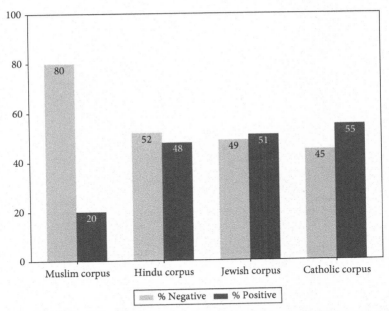

Figure 3.4 Percentage of negative and positive articles in each religious group corpus (rounded to the nearest whole number)

Table 3.2 Mean valence for articles associated with groups under three conditions

	Muslim	Hindu	Jewish	Catholic
Full-text articles	−.94	−.16	−.05	.08
Three or more mentions	−1.04	−.32	−.12	.04
Sentence-level articles	−1.20	−.13	−.04	.24

To ensure that our observation of the conspicuous negativity associated with Muslims applied across the entire spectrum of articles, we illustrate the distribution of articles among the four groups in comparison to the representative corpus of randomly selected articles. We include a vertical line at 0 to aid interpretation of the overlapping distributions. Figure 3.5 shows that articles touching on the other three groups resemble the representative corpus much more closely than the Muslim corpus. The valence distribution of Muslim articles is notably distinct from those of Catholic, Jewish, or Hindu articles across the entire range of valences.

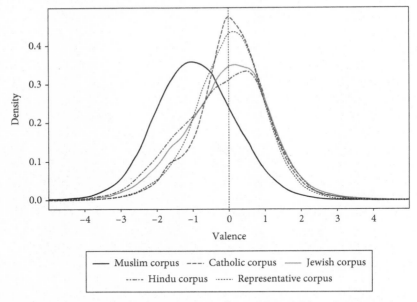

Figure 3.5 Valence distribution estimates (kernel density) by religious group corpus, compared to the representative corpus

What if all of the data presented so far concealed a significant uneven-ness in tone over time? Figure 3.3 reveals a sharp spike in coverage in the months following 9/11. Is it the case that those months account for the bulk of the intensely negative articles? Perhaps if we exclude them, the remaining Muslim articles are similar in tone to those touching on other religious groups. To check, we examine whether coverage became more positive, more negative, or held relatively steady over the span of our 21-year time period. Figure 3.6 shows trend lines for the average monthly tone for each group, superimposed on monthly fluctuation patterns. The figure reinforces the point that articles about Muslims have been systematically and dramatically more negative than articles about any other group in virtually every month. Only articles about Hindus approach the level of negativity associated with Muslims for brief periods. Yet there were only two months (out of 252, across our 21 years) where Hindu articles were more negative than Muslim arti-cles on average: in June 1998, following UN condemnation of India's nuclear weapons tests, and in March 2002, in the midst of riots in India that resulted in dozens of deaths. In addition, while articles touching on Catholics, Jews,

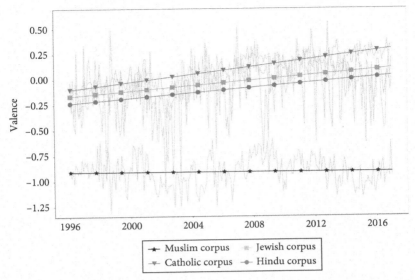

Figure 3.6 Average monthly article valence over time, by religious group corpus

and Hindus became more positive over time on average, the same is not true of articles about Muslims.

As a final step to ensure full understanding of the comparison across the four groups, figure 3.7 displays a linear regression coefficient plot similar to the one in figure 3.2. We use the same variables we tested on the Muslims-only corpus, applied to the 898,945 articles for all groups. In addition, we include a variable, "Muslim article," which has a value of 1 only for articles in the Muslim subcorpus.[8]

There are a number of immediately visible similarities between figure 3.7 and figure 3.2. Articles set exclusively in foreign locations, those that mention violence or extremism, and ones published in tabloids are more negative compared to those that are not. Articles mentioning religion, values, or published in right-leaning papers are more positive, with articles in right-leaning papers now modestly more positive. However, the Muslim article variable is independently very negative (with a regression coefficient of −.53). This means that the factors associated with positivity and negativity are relatively similar

---

[8] To test whether pooling the three groups obscures across-group differences, we re-ran the analysis with additional group dummies for Jews and Catholics; the distinctiveness of Muslims remains. The results are reported in table II.3.2 in the appendix.

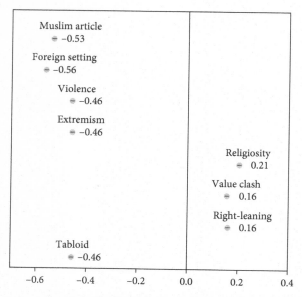

Figure 3.7 Factors associated with the tone of all articles, across religions

for all groups, but that articles mentioning Muslims are simply associated with more negativity than those touching on the other three religious groups, all else being equal. In short, even setting aside articles that exclusively reference foreign locations, that contain violence or extremism words, and those published in tabloids, articles touching on Muslims are *still* likely to be much more negative than articles about the other groups.[9]

To illustrate this point, we isolate full-text articles that contain no links to these four most negative factors. This describes 64%, 44%, and 41%, respectively, of Catholic, Jewish, and Hindu articles, but only 15% of Muslim articles. The average article tone for Catholic, Jewish, and Hindu articles under these conditions is +.20, +.38, and +.44, respectively, as befits sets of stories devoid of highly negative factors. By striking contrast, the tone of the average Muslim article not set exclusively abroad, not mentioning violence

---

[9] No two variables are highly correlated with one another, so there is no reason to be concerned about multicollinearity. Table II.3.1 in the appendix presents a correlation matrix for these variables. In addition, table II.3.2 reports the results of an OLS regression with interaction effects between Muslims and our principal variables, in order to isolate the differential effect of variables on the Muslim subcorpus. The results show that violence is associated with additional negativity in the case of Muslims, and that right-leaning papers are comparably less positive about Muslims than they are about other religious groups.

or extremism, and not published in a tabloid is still negative, at −.15. In other words, when newspapers write about other religious groups, they are both much less likely to associate them with the most negative elements and much more likely to produce positive stories when those negative elements are missing. This is true even for Hindus, which comprise a similar percentage of the American population as Muslims, are predominantly associated with foreign settings, and are frequently constructed as racial and cultural outsiders in American society.

There is thus a clear "Muslim penalty" in newspaper coverage—similar types of articles are more negative when they touch on Muslims than when they cover Catholics, Jews, or Hindus. To convey a more intuitive sense of why this might be, we randomly drew sentences about Muslims and Hindus from our corpus, and selected texts not associated with any of the most negative elements. These four sentences about each group are representative of the types of stories we found:

- "When he creates a piece, he lives with the craftsmen and says his work emphasizes craftsmanship to express the spirituality of Islam."
- " 'Even in New York,' said Ferida Osman, 21, a Hunter College senior and a Muslim, who recalled being spat on by a stranger as she waited for a train at Pennsylvania Station last week."
- "Yet the Hillsborough Area Regional Transit Authority has denied an advertisement sponsored by the Florida Council on American-Islamic Relations in support of diversity."
- "But their differences have implications for all the big issues the West grapples with in considering the Muslim world."[10]

- "Hinduism isn't one religion but many religions, with deities beyond counting."
- "Area Hindus wound up the weeklong holiday with a festival of lights religious program last night at the Hindu center of Virginia in Glen Allen."
- "Throughout the performance she was accompanied by live classical Indian music and danced against a backdrop depicting a Hindu temple."
- " 'Last year the Hindu American Foundation launched a campaign to highlight the Hindu roots of yoga exercises which are meant to prepare

[10] Articles are from the *San Jose Mercury News*, January 25, 2013; *New York Times*, November 25, 2015; *Tampa Bay Times*, August 12, 2013; and *New York Times*, April 27, 2008.

the body for higher forms of meditation,' says the group managing director Suhag Shukla."[11]

The sentences about Muslims are quite varied. They include one that is clearly positive, but also some that imply or openly address stresses between Muslims and American citizens, local governments, or the entire West. The Hindu sentences are almost uniform in their positive emphasis on religion, festivals, or cultural contributions. Newspapers may not intend to depict Muslims and Hindus differently, but this comparison reveals how daily decisions about reporting add up to disparate representations of two groups that are similar in many ways.

Comparing Muslim Americans to US racial, ethnic, and religious outgroups

Muslims are members of a global religion, but in the American context they are also a distinct minority that can be compared to other domestic racial, ethnic, and religious groups (Jamal 2009; Lajevardi 2020; Oskooii, Dana, and Barreto 2019). To do this, we narrow our lens to focus on Muslim Americans as a category within our broader set of Muslim articles. We identify this subset of our Muslim corpus by selecting two types of articles. We include any article that specifically mentions "Muslim Americans," "Muslims in the United States," and variations that clearly indicate the article is related to Muslims located in the United States.[12] We also include all articles that explicitly mention a domestic location and no foreign location.[13] Such articles set stories about Muslims in the United States only, as in the sentence just above that refers to New York without explicitly identifying Ferida Osman as a Muslim American. Altogether, our Muslim American corpus contains 30,375 articles, or just under 12% of the full Muslim corpus.

Kalkan, Layman, and Uslaner (2009) have examined Muslims as part of what they call "bands of others," noting that they are both a religious minority

---

[11] Articles are from the *New York Times*, July 22, 2005; *Richmond Times Dispatch*, November 16, 2001; *Arizona Republic*, August 14, 2016; and *USA Today*, February 1, 2011.

[12] Our search terms were "Muslim American*," "American Muslim*," "Muslim* in the United States [or US]," "United States [or US] Muslim*," "Black Muslim*," and "Nation of Islam." There are 10,338 articles that match these search criteria.

[13] In our Muslim corpus, 22,783 articles explicitly and uniquely mention a domestic location. Of these, just 2,746 also explicitly reference Muslim Americans.

and a cultural outgroup. For these authors, prejudices against groups associated with ethnic, racial, and religious characteristics tend to fade over time, particularly with interpersonal contact. However, negative attitudes toward those associated with "behaviors or values that many find unusual or offensive" may persist (Kalkan, Layman, and Uslaner 2009, 2). Oskooii, Dana, and Barreto (2019) have also demonstrated that tapping Islam-specific prejudices in surveys induces negative evaluations of Muslim Americans and opposition to mosque building. We therefore analyze Muslim American articles in comparison to those touching on two important racial or ethnic groups in the United States, as well as two religiously related groups that American survey respondents consistently rate disfavorably.

African Americans and Latinos are prominent examples of racial or ethnic minorities that suffer from systemic disadvantages in the United States, including discrimination, hate crimes, and police violence (FBI 2019; Edwards, Lee, and Esposito 2019). At the same time, opinion polls have demonstrated that most respondents hold generally warm feelings toward these groups (American National Election Studies 2020). Mormons and atheists, by contrast, receive relatively low ratings on feeling thermometer surveys and are more often seen to fall outside of the American religious mainstream (American National Election Studies 2020; Pew Research Center 2007, 2014a). Attitudes toward these groups are comparatively negative, but it is unlikely that they experience the same degree of systemic disadvantages suffered by African Americans or Latinos.

Scholars have long explored public opinion and forms of disadvantage that shape the social boundaries around American racial, ethnic, and religious groups. Yet there have been few studies that use a consistent baseline to compare how the media represent such domestic outgroups.[14] Here, we tone-check American newspapers' reporting on African Americans, Latinos, Mormons, and atheists, comparing it to coverage of Muslim Americans. If newspapers tend to write primarily about the systemic disadvantages commonly associated with African Americans or Latinos, or if they convey views about the "unusual or offensive" values of Mormons or atheists, the tone associated with these groups will be negative. If, on the other hand, newspaper reporting of these four groups resembles that of Catholics, Jews, or Hindus

---

[14] The Media Portrayals of Minority Project (2019, 2020, 2021) annual reports provide information on the tone of articles about a number of US groups.

by counterbalancing negative elements with positive coverage, the overall average article tone for each group will be closer to neutral.

What about coverage of Muslim Americans? It is likely the case that US newspapers write about Muslim Americans less negatively than about Muslims in general or Muslims abroad. The Muslim American corpus by definition excludes the vast majority of articles about foreign conflict zones that are among the most negative articles in our broader corpus. Consequently, we expect the tone of our Muslim American corpus to be more positive than the tone for all other Muslim articles. But Muslim Americans are distinctive among our ethno-racial-religious groups. Not only are they similarly situated in public opinion polls to Mormons and atheists (Pew Research Center 2007), they also suffer many of the same systemic disadvantages as African Americans and Latinos.[15] They are, in this sense, double outsiders. If American newspapers reflect this status, coverage of Muslim Americans may remain markedly negative even compared to other domestic outgroups.

Before we look at the tone of articles touching on our five American groups, we should note that important distinctions exist across these categories. African Americans and Latinos constitute approximately 13% and 18% of the US population (CIA 2020), respectively, while Mormons and atheists make up an estimated 2% and 3%, respectively (Pew Research Center 2014b). As noted earlier, Muslims account for approximately 1% of American residents. Correspondingly, there are many more articles that mention the larger groups than the smaller ones in the newspapers we sampled. There were just 20,524 Mormon articles and 11,382 that mentioned atheists in the 16 outlets to which we had access across our 21-year period from January 1, 1996 to December 31, 2016. However, for the same time period, there were 77,614 African American articles and 65,927 Latino ones just in the four "national" newspapers in our dataset.[16] Although all of these groups are present both in the United States and abroad, domestic newspaper articles that mention them are extremely likely to situate them in an American context.

---

[15] It is important to note that 20% of Muslim Americans identify as Black, and 8% as Latino (some of which may also identify as Black), which highlights the potential for intersectional forms of stigmatization (Pew Research Center 2017, 35).

[16] Our data for Mormons and atheists do not include articles from the *Denver Post*, which was unavailable at the time we downloaded articles on these groups. Our data for African Americans and Latinos are drawn uniquely from the *New York Times*, *USA Today*, *Wall Street Journal*, and *Washington Post*.

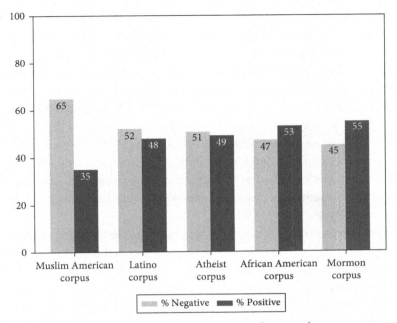

Figure 3.8 Percentage of negative and positive articles in each group corpus (rounded to the nearest whole number)

Figure 3.8 shows the percentage of positive and negative articles about each group, ordered from least to most positive. That only 35% of Muslim American articles are positive—compared to between 48% and 55% for the other groups—is a first indicator that they are covered in a distinctive way among the racial, ethnic, and religious groups in the United States. To account for this disparity, we need to understand what might explain the relative positivity in stories touching on these other groups. In previous research regarding American racial and ethnic groups, we found that highly negative stories about law and order prevalent within coverage of African Americans and Latinos were largely offset by positive coverage of culture or achievements, such as stories about the National Museum of African American History and Culture, or celebrations of Latinos winning prestigious awards (Bleich, Callison, et al. 2018; Media Portrayals of Minorities Project 2019, 2020). The lower frequency of positive articles related to Muslim Americans suggests that there are simply fewer of these types of stories counterbalancing negative themes.

Before turning to the five-group comparison, it is important to note that coverage of American Muslims is indeed significantly more positive than that of all other stories in our Muslim corpus. While the average article tone is −.94 for the full corpus, the American Muslim subset has a decidedly less negative average tone of −.50; meanwhile, all other Muslim articles have an average tone of −1. At the same time, this finding is tempered to some extent by the fact that articles mentioning Muslim Americans three or more times still have an average tone of −.62, and those stripped down to include just sentences that mention Muslim Americans have a tone of −.73. On the whole, then, stories related to Muslim Americans remain strongly negative, and articles or sentences that focus intensely on Muslim Americans are even more strongly so.

How does this compare to the average tone of articles touching on the other four groups? Table 3.3 juxtaposes the tone associated with the five groups across the three ways of analyzing our articles: full-text articles, articles that mention the group three or more times, and all articles stripped down to include just the (one or more) sentences mentioning the group. In all respects, Muslim Americans are associated with coverage that is far more negative than that of any other group. The average tone for non–Muslim American articles under most circumstances ranges from approximately −.12 to +.11, roughly the same range we found for articles mentioning Catholics, Jews, or Hindus. The most positive articles are those about Mormons. That is partly a function of the 2,377 articles that mention the musical *The Book of Mormon*: those together have an average valence of +.48. However, full-text Mormon articles that do not mention the musical still have an average valence of +.02 and sentence-level articles have a tone of +.10. The most negative score among all non–Muslim American groups, in contrast, is for sentences mentioning

Table 3.3 Mean valence for articles associated with group corpora under three conditions

	Muslim American	Latino	Atheist	African American	Mormon
Full-text articles	−.50	−.12	−.05	.01	.07
Three or more mentions	−.62	−.11	−.05	.02	.11
Sentence-level articles	−.73	−.11	−.29	.11	.17

atheists, with an average valence of −.29. While this is noteworthy, the tone is less than half as negative as the corresponding score for Muslim American sentences.

To visualize the comparison across these groups, figure 3.9 displays the valence distribution estimates of all full-text articles. Those touching on African Americans, Latinos, Mormons, and atheists are quite similar. Those containing references to Muslim Americans stand out as markedly more negative. This reinforces the conclusion that Muslim Americans are associated with a greater degree of negativity in US newspapers than other outgroups in American society. To be clear: African Americans, Latinos, Mormons, and atheists indisputably face significant stigmatization in many quarters in the United States. Yet newspaper coverage does not overwhelmingly associate these groups with negativity. Muslim Americans also contend with negative attitudes and concrete acts of bias. In addition, their representation in American newspapers is strikingly negative, especially when it is juxtaposed to that of other racial, ethnic, and religious outgroups.

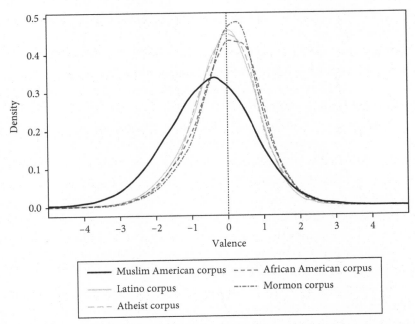

Figure 3.9 Valence distribution estimates (kernel density) by group corpus

Conclusions

Coverage of Muslims is distinctive in American newspapers, and distinctly negative. Virtually no matter the types of articles we set aside from our analyses, and no matter the comparison group, coverage of Muslims has a negative tone. Our conclusion that articles about Muslims are negative is not new. Dozens of studies have produced similar findings (Ahmed and Matthes 2017). Our contribution is in demonstrating with precision how negative this coverage is—not only for a few dozen or a few hundred articles, or in a single year or from a single newspaper, but for hundreds of thousands of articles collected over a 21-year span from 17 national and local newspapers. There are positive articles about Muslims in American newspapers, but the vast majority are negative, and strongly negative at that.

Why is coverage of Muslims so negative? Some of the answer revolves around articles set in foreign locations and those linked with violence or extremism. Stories about the Islamic Republic of Iran or the Muslim Brotherhood in Egypt, or about groups like the Islamic State or Islamic Jihad are typically highly negative. In addition, when militants or terrorists claim to be motivated by Islamism, negative coverage follows. Even articles depicting Muslims as victims of violence—such as Muslim Bosniaks during the Bosnian war, the Rohingya of Myanmar, or the Uighurs in China—are likely to be negative because they often contain words linked to death or oppression. Journalists naturally write extensively about consequential political turmoil and conflict zones where lives are lost.

At the same time, setting aside all of these types of articles, coverage of Muslims remains negative. Only 15% of the 256,963 Muslim articles are not exclusively linked to foreign settings, do not touch on violence or extremism, or are not published in tabloids. These 39,754 articles still tend to be modestly negative on average when compared to the representative corpus, which *does* include such negative topics. When we compare this restricted set of Muslim articles to Catholic, Jewish, or Hindu articles that also eliminate references to the main negative elements, we see even more clearly the distinctive negativity embedded in articles that touch on Muslims.

Even when we pare down our corpus to focus on Muslim Americans, coverage remains notably more negative than that for other US racial, ethnic, or religious groups as varied as African Americans, Latinos, Mormons, and atheists. Elsewhere, we have explored whether additional ethno-racial groups may be the subject of coverage as negative as that of Muslims, examining newspaper articles about Asian Americans and Native Americans (Media Portrayals of Minorities Project 2019, 2020, 2021). Our findings show that Muslims remain the group associated with the most negativity by a substantial margin. There is simply no group we have identified for which the tone of coverage is anywhere near as negative as it is for Muslims.

4

Time and tone

Major events and their impact on coverage

In this chapter we ask how major events—often, but not exclusively, terrorist events—shape the volume, tone, and content of American media coverage of Muslims and Islam. Our primary interest is the effect of 9/11 on US news-paper coverage. In chapter 3, we examined several key factors that are associated with article tone to varying degrees. We found that stories about violence and extremism tended to be among the most negative. Here we are interested in whether events such as 9/11 help to create a turning point in coverage, rendering not only the tone much more negative, but also affecting the number of stories and the types of language used in articles about Muslims.

The notion that major events have the ability to dramatically shape news coverage over the long term is widespread, and not limited to the United States. In the specific case of Muslim coverage, for instance, a recent *Guardian* story on the British media read: "After the Rushdie affair, and then particularly after 9/11 and 7/7 [the London bombings] . . . [t]he story of Muslims became the story of terrorism and of clashing civilizational values" (Subramanian 2018). Nor is this idea new: similar claims about the negative effect of events have been made at least since the Iranian revolution (Mortimer 1981; Said [1981] 1997).

But what precisely are the effects of events like 9/11, and how long do they last? Can one seminal event have an enduring impact on the media's coverage of a religion associated with that event? In chapter 3, we highlighted not only violence, but also geography, cultural differences, and the beliefs of newspaper readers as key factors identified by scholars as potentially driving negative coverage. Major terrorist events have the ability to affect all of these: in addition to producing a "media storm" of reporting about the event itself (Boydstun, Hardy, and Walgrave 2014), they can reshape a public's mental geography—how close or how far different places feel—as well as highlight

Covering Muslims. Erik Bleich and A. Maurits van der Veen, Oxford University Press. © Oxford University Press 2022.
DOI: 10.1093/oso/9780197611715.003.0004

cultural differences and change the public's appetite for more stories about an issue going forward.

In this chapter, we home in on the impact of such events on three different aspects of coverage: the total volume of articles about Muslims and Islam; the tone of articles both about the event and about other issues during the same time period; and the content of those articles, as reflected in the prominence of key words or themes. We begin with a focus on 9/11, which stands out for its unparalleled impact, but in the second half of the chapter we broaden our focus to examine a number of additional events associated with Muslims and Islam over the past two decades. This allows us to assess whether the impact of the 9/11 attacks was unique. In addition, we examine whether nonconflictual, positive events have a comparable, but opposite, impact on overall media coverage. This allows us to gauge whether positive events help counterbalance the impact of the better-known negative events.

As we shall see, 9/11 does stand out, albeit not exactly as one might expect. It is particularly noteworthy for its impact on the *volume* of coverage. However, as already indicated in figure 3.6 in the previous chapter, the shock to the *valence* of articles about Muslims and Islam is both more limited and less exceptional. We find that terrorist events like 9/11 create a predictable, but temporary, downturn in the tone of articles. This impact affects not only articles about terrorist incidents, but also those not directly related to these events. Even though not all additional coverage is explicitly negative (cf. Alsultany 2012), terrorist events have an indirect negative effect on valence that goes beyond the direct effect of generating additional negative articles about the event itself. Positive events have corresponding, but not offsetting, effects. Our analysis shows that positive shocks, while comparable in some respects, are shorter and weaker than the negative shocks we examine. For example, Ramadan, a recurring positive event, produces some additional coverage, but the tone of articles during Ramadan barely differs from that of articles produced during the rest of the year.

We also take a closer look at what negative articles in our corpus are *about*. We show that 9/11 produced an enduring jump in the proportion of coverage dedicated to terrorism and extremism. In addition, there has been a shift from a focus on distant groups acting in their local settings to one on global radicalism and threats to the United States. While these findings do not speak directly to the negativity of the articles in our corpus, they have clear implications for the likely impact of those articles on the average news consumer: not all negativity is equal, and changes since 9/11 appear likely to strengthen the perceived connection between Muslims and terrorism or extremism, even if the average tone of articles in our corpus remains steady.

We begin the chapter by reviewing what the literature would lead us to expect about the impact of 9/11 on the media coverage of Muslims and Islam. Next, we analyze that effect on both the volume and the tone of coverage, followed by a closer look at trends in key themes of that coverage. The final part of the chapter broadens the analysis to consider other negative as well as positive events, comparing their relative impact to one another as well as to 9/11.

Major events and media coverage: Expectations

When and why are articles mentioning Muslims and Islam published? Media coverage of policy issues tends to be irregular: periods of low coverage are interrupted by short spikes in attention. During such spikes, often referred to as "media storms" or "media hypes," the media produce many articles for a sustained period of multiple days, weeks, or even months (Boydstun, Hardy, and Walgrave 2014, 509–10; see also Kepplinger and Habermeier 1995; Vasterman 2018). They do so because major precipitating events produce two mutually reinforcing effects: the newsworthiness threshold for including a story is lowered (Galtung and Ruge 1965, 82), and competing media outlets face pressures to cover the issue no less extensively than their peers, leading to increased coverage across multiple sources (Hardy 2018).

In this chapter, we are interested in better understanding how patterns of Muslim coverage change over time, especially in the wake of major events. Spikes in coverage are particularly meaningful to track, as the likelihood that a newspaper consumer sees and reads an article about Muslims increases when many more such articles are published. We focus not just on major spikes in coverage, but also on smaller or recurring spikes that may affect overall patterns. We begin by examining in some detail the impact of 9/11, the single biggest event involving Muslims and the United States during our coverage period. What should we expect to see in terms of the volume of coverage, the effect on the average valence of article tone, and the contents of articles?

Scholars and observers vary surprisingly widely in their assessments of what exactly 9/11 changed, in part because many findings are based on small samples of media coverage before and/or after 9/11 (cf. Yazdiha 2020, 5). In terms of article tone, some find that the coverage of Muslims became more negative (Lajevardi 2019, 10; Trevino, Kanso, and Nelson 2010). In apparent contrast, Nacos and Torres-Reyna (2003) find more positive stories on newspaper front pages after 9/11. Turning to the content of these stories, some find that the shock of 9/11 resulted in less stereotypical, less unidimensional reporting on Muslims than had been the case before (Strawson 2003), and in an "increase in sympathetic representations of Arab and Muslim Americans in the US media after 9/11" (Alsultany 2012, 4). In direct contrast, Morey and Yaqin argue that 9/11 "has thrust a certain type of Orientalist stereotype firmly back . . . into our news media, and into the mouths of politicians," focusing in particular on portrayals that highlight "behavior, the body, and dress" (Morey and Yaqin 2011, 3; see also Kumar 2010). Finally, a survey of a number of different studies found that after 9/11, Muslims were often described as " 'terrorists,' 'extremists,' 'fundamentalists,' 'radicals,' and 'fanatics' " (Ahmed and Matthes 2017, 231).

We can also derive some general expectations from the broader literature on media coverage. First, 9/11 is certainly significant enough to produce a media storm, and other scholars have argued that it did (Boydstun, Hardy, and Walgrave 2014). Therefore, we expect a large spike in newspaper articles mentioning Muslims and Islam; moreover, given the significance of the event, we would expect the jump in coverage to be larger and last longer than any other spikes occurring between 1996 and 2016. Media storms are, by definition, events of limited duration. But seminal events have a secondary effect on media coverage of a related broader issue—in our case, Muslims and Islam—that may last indefinitely. In 2003, Vice President Cheney famously argued, "In a sense, 9/11 changed everything for us" (Cheney 2003). Where the media is concerned, one potential effect is to permanently change the threshold of what counts as "news" when Muslims and Islam are involved. Such a change is likely to happen only when an event changes the way media consumers view the world around them, the way Cheney suggested 9/11 had. As Vliegenthart and Roggeband (2007, 299) note, this requires that the event "dominate the news for a longer period" and "be incongruent with the way the issue has been framed before the event"—conditions that appear likely to hold for 9/11 but not for any other events.

While some have suggested that a larger number of stories on terrorism and extremism may be balanced out by additional positive and more nuanced stories (Strawson 2003; Alsultany 2012, 4), this still means the average reader will encounter additional negative stories. Does it also mean that the average story a reader sees becomes more negative? We certainly expect 9/11 to produce a negative shock in tone in the short run, as lots of articles discuss the event and its impact. But how large and enduring is that shock likely to be? The literature on media storms suggests that most such storms last from one to several weeks (Boydstun, Hardy, and Walgrave 2014). Toward the end of an event-driven media storm, additional coverage will increasingly be not about the shock of the event itself but about other issues; therefore, we expect that the spike in coverage will outlast the shift in average article tone, even for an event such as 9/11.

This brings us to the impact of events on coverage content. Again, we expect an immediate shift in content driven by reporting on the event itself, be it 9/11 or other salient events. Moreover, 9/11 likely stands out both for the duration of the media storm and for the contrast between how people thought about Muslims before and after the attacks. As such, we expect that the type of negative stories will shift in the direction of more stories about terrorism and extremism going forward. This expectation is reinforced by other findings in the literature. For example, the media tend to overreport terrorist events that are associated with Muslims, compared to those that are not (Kearns, Betus, and Lemieux 2019); the media often jump to conclusions and generalizations about Islamist responsibility for terror attacks (van der Veen 2014; Ahmed and Matthes 2017), and even articles about completely different issues may mention terrorism. This last point in part reflects the temptation for political actors and media producers since 9/11 to "securitize" nearly any issue related to Muslims, arguing that it has implications for the terrorist threat facing the United States.[1] Several scholars have pointed to the significance of this process with respect to Muslims and Islam (Brown 2010; Cesari 2012; Hussain and Bagguley 2012). Analogous arguments apply to references to extremism. For this reason, too, we expect the association of extremism with an event as seminal as 9/11 to produce a sustained increase in the share of articles mentioning Muslims or Islam that include one or more of our extremism keywords (cf. Hoewe and Bowe 2021).

Over the course of this chapter we also look more systematically at patterns in coverage—especially shifts in volume and tone—not associated with the 9/11 attacks. This brings us to the question of what types of other events might produce a shift in coverage. What counts as major news where Muslims and

---

[1] Most strongly associated with the "Copenhagen school" of international relations, securitization theory highlights the degree to which security threats are socially constructed (Buzan, Wæver, and De Wilde 1998; Stritzel 2007; Balzacq, Léonard, and Ruzicka 2016; Balzacq 2019).

Islam are concerned? In other words, what types of events might generate media storms, and what should we expect to be the corresponding impact on the tone of media coverage? While the literature on media storms has not yet addressed this question, the general media bias toward negative news suggests that negative events are seen as more newsworthy (Galtung and Ruge 1965; J. Young and Cohen 1973; Harcup and O'Neill 2017; Soroka and McAdams 2015), and thus should be more likely to produce such storms. Given the negative baseline tone of Muslim coverage, this appears all the more likely in our case. We thus expect the largest spikes in coverage to be associated with negative events. As a result, we also expect the tone of coverage to drop as the volume of media coverage rises. In other words, there should be a negative correlation between the number of articles published on a given day and the average valence of those articles.

As for spikes in the average valence of stories, these will depend in part on the volume of coverage: during periods of low volume, a few positive stories on a few consecutive days might suffice to produce a positive valence spike. Thus, if we look only at valence spikes, ignoring volume, we *do* expect to find some positive events represented, even though they are still likely to be fewer in number than the negative valence spikes. Since a focus on spikes is likely to produce less information about the nature and impact of positive events, we end the chapter by specifically looking at one major positive event—President Obama's speech addressing the Muslim world in Cairo in 2009—as well as at a recurring positive "event" associated with the religious calendar: Ramadan. Given the American media's general tendency to see religion as "a good thing" (Silk 1998, 57), we expect religious celebrations and holidays to be associated with a measurable rise in article tone. Since we know both the precise timing of these events and their expected effect on article tone, studying them allows us to develop a better understanding of the impact of positive events in general. Our expectation is that we will see shocks of the same nature as we see for major negative events, only noticeably smaller and shorter.

Media storms and long-term shifts: Patterns in the volume and valence of coverage

Figure 4.1 shows the average daily article count across the entire 21-year period we cover, from 1996 to 2016. Rather than charting the precise daily

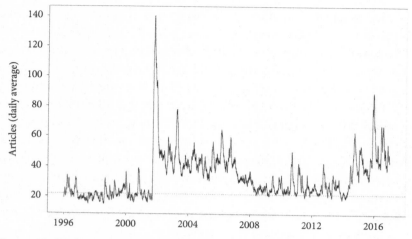

Figure 4.1 Daily count of articles mentioning Muslims and/or Islam (30-day exponential moving average)

article count, which has too many fluctuations to be easily readable, this figure shows a 30-day exponential moving average (EMA), in which each day's count is averaged along with a weighted combination of the values from previous days. The weighting is exponential, so that the most recent days are weighted most heavily.[2] Another way of thinking about this is that the impact of a shock is greatest on the day it happens, but the overall effect is spread over the next 30 days. The horizontal dotted line in the figure shows the average daily article count (22) for the period prior to September 11, 2001. The 9/11 attacks are easily identified, as they are associated with the largest spike during the entire period by far, as expected. No other single event even comes close. This immediate spike lasts about five months.

The figure also shows that 9/11 caused a long-term shift in the average daily count of articles mentioning Muslims. The event dominated the news for long enough to have an enduring impact on coverage volume, as newspaper readers' interest in and perceptions of Muslims and Islam changed during this initial media storm. The number of articles remains elevated far above the pre-9/11 level for years, and even when it declines to approach that

[2] Specifically, the weighting factor for our 30-day average is $2/(30+1) \approx .065$. This means the previous day receives a weight of $1-.065 \approx .935$, the one before that $(1-.065)^2 \approx .874$, and so on. The 30th day has a weight of just .133).

level, what was once the average now seems to function as something closer to a lower bound.

Next, we turn to the impact of 9/11 on the valence of newspaper articles mentioning Muslims or Islam. As already noted, we expect the average valence to drop, but we do not expect that drop to outlast the spike in coverage. After all, one of the features of a media storm is to lower the threshold for newsworthiness of any story even indirectly associated with the event (or, in this case, with Muslims or Islam). As direct coverage of the event tapers off, such indirectly related stories, which are not necessarily negative, will come to constitute a greater fraction of the added coverage, mitigating the event's impact on average article tone. A return to "normal" reporting should also bring a return to a "normal" average tone. Figure 4.2 shows the fluctuation in valence over time. The horizontal dotted line again marks the pre-9/11 average: −.90. Since average daily article valence is greatly shaped by day-to-day fluctuations in stories and story content, these data are smoothed by a 90-day exponential moving average, rather than the 30-day average we used for figure 4.1.

The figure makes clear that the direct impact of 9/11 on the average tone of articles was minor at best. Indeed, its impact can be clearly identified only on the smaller inset chart: on the main figure, it looks like just another downward slide in a series of such slides that had brought the moving average down from a peak of around −.71 in late September 2000 to a value below

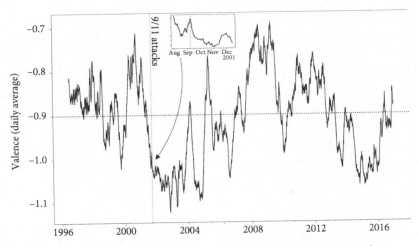

Figure 4.2 Daily average valence (90-day exponential moving average)

−1.0 by early September 2001. On the figure's inset, we can see that the 9/11 attacks reversed an upswing that had begun in August, initiating a renewed decline that lasted until November.

Looking at the main figure again, we can understand why other scholars have found that coverage of Muslims the year or so after 9/11 was more negative than that of the year before. However, the figure also shows that this difference is at most only partially due to 9/11 itself, lending support to those who have argued that 9/11 marked less of a sea change. Indeed, a number of larger valence shocks are evident in the figure; we'll discuss these in more detail in the second part of the chapter. Overall, there is no systematic over-time trend in the tone of Muslim coverage over this two-decade span.

We hypothesized earlier that days with larger numbers of articles should have lower valence, on balance. A visual comparison of figures 4.1 and 4.2 offers some support for this expectation, with some of the lowest areas of figure 4.2 coinciding with the higher areas of figure 4.1. Calculating the correlation between the figures provides concrete evidence to support this impression: the correlation coefficient is −.51, meaning that as the article count climbs, the tone drops.[3] This is particularly important, because periods of intense coverage are likely to make a stronger impression on readers. In other words, since peaks in coverage are associated with below-average article valence, the tone of articles readers will encounter in moments when they are most likely to be interested in and exposed to news about Muslims—such as in the months after 9/11—will be lower than the average tone of articles in our corpus.

Finally, we look at the subset of articles identified in chapter 3 as least likely to be negative: those not set exclusively in a foreign location, mentioning neither violence nor extremism, and not published in a tabloid paper. Even this subset experiences a negative shock after 9/11, with average tone dropping from −.43 during the four weeks beforehand to −1.24 for the first week after. In other words, even when neither violence nor extremism is explicitly mentioned, the average tone of articles mentioning Muslims or Islam still becomes more negative. That is not altogether surprising, since many of these articles will still be indirectly about the event, as some sample headlines from the days immediately following 9/11 show: "Muslims brace for angry

---

[3] This is the correlation between the exponential moving averages, which smooth out day-to-day shocks. Even without any smoothing, the correlation is −.16. This may seem less impressive, but given how many other, exogenous sources of variation there are in the two measures, it remains both substantively and statistically significant.

response"; "Anguish gives way to rage"; "Offices try to prevent harassment of Muslim staff"; and "An atmosphere charged with anger and fear."[4] Such articles are not negative *about* Muslims, but they do place Muslims in a negative context, and add to the prevailing negativity in reporting about Muslims and Islam after 9/11. However, average valence for this subset of articles bounced back to pre-9/11 levels after just three weeks.

In sum, the 9/11 attacks had a meaningful but comparatively short-term impact on the tone of articles about Muslims; if we look at average daily valence over the course of a week, it took about two months for valence levels to return to their value prior to 9/11—in figure 4.2 this is visible in the bump in November 2001 (visible in the inset) that reverses the post-9/11 slide. In contrast, by the analogous volume measure—daily article count, averaged over the course of a week—the coverage shock lasted more than 12 *years*.[5]

Not all negativity is the same: A look at content

The 9/11 attacks had a large impact on the number of stories published about Muslims and Islam, and a smaller effect on the tone of those stories. Did they also affect the *types* of stories published? In other words, did the attacks have an effect on the topics or themes mentioned in articles? Our expectation was that we would see more stories mentioning terrorism and extremism. To investigate this dimension of coverage, we first examine the presence of keywords linked to different topics. Figure 4.3 shows the proportion of articles containing keywords related to terrorism and extremism. Once again, it is obvious when the 9/11 attacks happened: they caused an immediate, very large jump in the share of articles about Muslims or Islam that mentioned terrorism, from a pre-9/11 level of around 25% to a short-lived peak over 65%.

While the jump for extremism was less pronounced, it too became much more prominent in discussions of Muslims and Islam after 9/11, rarely returning even close to pre-9/11 levels.

The figure also shows that for several years after 9/11, terrorism was mentioned more frequently than was extremism. This suggests that media consumers were exposed to a steady stream of articles that mentioned Muslims

---

[4] Sources, respectively: *Tampa Bay Times*, September 13, 2001; *Washington Post*, September 13, 2001; *USA Today*, September 14, 2001; *New York Times*, September 25, 2001.

[5] In appendix tables II.4.1 and II.4.2, we provide additional information about the time it takes volume and valence to return to their pre-event levels.

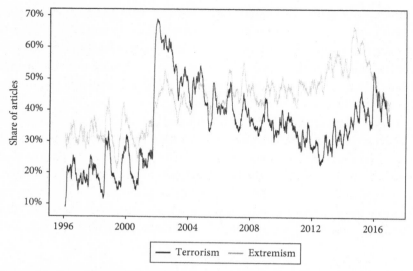

Figure 4.3 Prevalence of topic keywords over time (90-day exponential moving average)

or Islam in the context of terrorism without necessarily qualifying this by indicating that terrorist attacks were committed by extremists.[6] In fact, the *New York Times* journalist Clyde Haberman (2004) asked, "Is it possible to talk about Islam in the post-9/11 world without a single reference to the dread T-word?"[7]

We can see from the figure just how common discussions of both terrorism and extremism have become: prior to 9/11, 23% of stories mentioning Muslims also mentioned terrorism; since 9/11, this figure has risen to 44%. Breaking these figures down by newspaper source is also informative. Tabloids referred to terrorism in 27% of articles prior to 9/11, and 53% after that date. Right-leaning papers, meanwhile, refer to terrorism in 26% of articles prior to 9/11 and 48% after. These patterns are as we expected: both tabloids and right-leaning papers are more likely to feature terrorism references, and for both types of papers the shock caused by 9/11 is greater than for our overall corpus.

---

[6] Similarly, even by 2016, 15 years after the attacks, 8% of articles mentioning Muslims and/or Islam still mention 9/11.

[7] More than a decade later, this same tendency of the media to inject mentions of terrorism into stories about Muslims and Islam that otherwise have nothing to do with terrorism was once again noted by another *New York Times* journalist (Walsh 2016).

For extremism, the proportion of post-9/11 articles in our corpus including words that fall into our extremism category rises to 48%, from a pre-9/11 baseline of 33%. Interestingly, both right-leaning and tabloid papers are comparatively *less* likely to use extremism words than other papers, and the difference only grows after 9/11 (tabloids went from 26% pre-9/11 to 41% after; right-leaning papers from 28% pre-9/11 to 40%). This helps explain our earlier point that many articles post-9/11 referenced terrorism without mentioning extremism: right-leaning and tabloid papers, in particular, are comparatively more likely to feature articles that mention terrorism without mentioning extremism.[8]

In terms of content, then, 9/11 *does* appear to have permanently changed newspaper coverage of Muslims and Islam: a far greater proportion of stories now mention terrorism and extremism. Combine this with the increase in the total number of stories published (seen in figure 4.1), and since 9/11 the average newspaper consumer has been exposed to many more stories about Muslims associated with terrorism and extremism than was the case before, even during periods when no terrorist events are directly in the news. The sheer volume of such stories likely has an impact on perceptions and associations that readers have with Islam and Muslims.[9] In this context, it bears repeating that the top three single-word impressions of Islam offered by respondents to a Pew survey in 2007 were fanatic, radical, and terror: two words referencing extremism, and one referencing terrorism (Pew Research Center 2007). Contrary to what some have argued, however, the 9/11 attacks do not appear to have "thrust a certain type of Orientalist stereotype firmly back . . . into our news media" (Morey and Yaqin 2011, 3; see also Kumar 2010). In particular, references to Muslim dress—hijab, burqa, etc.—are less common post-9/11 than they were before (4.1% of all articles before; 3.8% after). This is not to say the media does not trade in such stereotypes; only that they have not become more common in the aftermath of 9/11.

That brings us to the more general question of what else may have shifted in the media's representations of Muslims and Islam. To see how 9/11 may have altered the way Muslims and Islam are described, we analyze changes in the frequency of the words that appear immediately to the left or the right of our word roots Muslim* and Islam*. These are commonly referred to as L1R1

[8] The newspaper most likely to feature extremism words in the post-9/11 era is the *Wall Street Journal*, which does so in no less than 61% of all articles mentioning Muslim and Islam.
[9] As Mastro and Tukachinsky (2014) note, "repeated exposure can make stereotypes chronically accessible, and therefore more likely to be applied in the future."

Table 4.1 Words most over-represented
directly adjacent to Muslim* or Islam*

Pre-9/11	Post-9/11
salvation	radical
fundamentalists	jihad
fundamentalist	extremists
fundamentalism	radicals
guerrillas	militant
militants	extremism
devout	devout
militant	non-
holy	fundamentalist
jihad	fundamentalism
predominantly	fundamentalists
strict	radicalism

(1 word to the left and 1 word to the right) collocates. Those that appear to the left are typically adjectives and adverbs; those to the right are more commonly nouns. Our expectation is that these should have changed along with the broader reframing of Muslims and Islam in the media.

Table 4.1 shows the words that stand out the most. To obtain these lists, we look at the frequency with which words appear immediately to the left or the right of Muslim* or Islam*, and compare that to the frequency with which they appear in the rest of our corpus.[10] We filter out any proper names, any words that appear fewer than 100 times, and any words whose frequency here is less than double that of their frequency in the overall corpus. The table displays the top dozen words, ranked in declining order of how closely a word's appearance is associated with the context of one word on either side of our search terms. We see that "radicals" and "extremists" first appear after 9/11 and immediately occupy top positions, while "fundamentalists" remains, but move down the list. A number of words disappear post-9/11, including "holy," "strict," and "salvation," along with "guerrillas." In other words, while

---

[10] We ignore any words for which differences in this frequency are not statistically significant (p >= .05) or are substantively close to zero (normalized pointwise mutual information (PMI) <= .005). For details about normalized PMI, see (Bouma 2009).

Table 4.2 Top descriptive words surrounding Muslim/Islam root words (L1R1 collocates)

1996–2000 (vs. 2012–2016)	5 months pre-9/11 (vs. 5 months post-9/11)	5 months post-9/11 (vs. 5 months pre-9/11)	2012–2016 (vs. 1996–2000)
militants	jihad	world	*radical*
group	militant	**radical**	*anti-*
militant	group	countries	*extremists*
leader	militants	**extremists**	*community*
holy	law	nations	*non-*
law		center	*all*
jihad		movement	*terrorism*
revolution		all	*extremist*
government		**extremist**	*terrorists*
fundamentalist		**terrorists**	*extremism*
rebels		press	*ban*
groups		faith	*communities*

extremism becomes more prominent, religiosity and locally focused conflicts become less so.

While the table indicates that coverage did change over time, these data alone cannot tell us whether it was 9/11 that precipitated that change. To examine that question more closely, we turn to comparing analogous pre-9/11 and post-9/11 periods directly against one another, rather than separately against our overall corpus. Table 4.2 shows two paired comparisons. Since we saw that the initial post-9/11 media storm lasted about five months, the two central columns compare all articles published in the five months preceding 9/11 (2,983 in total) to those published in the five months immediately after 9/11 (14,579 articles). The columns on the left and the right compare all articles published in the first five years of our corpus (1996–2000; 40,193 articles) to those published in the last five years (2012–2016; 67,301 articles). Each column lists words that are strongly associated with our word roots Islam* and Muslim* in that particular period, in declining order of frequency; the focus is thus on words readers are most likely to encounter.[11]

[11] As with table 4.1, we include only those whose frequency difference across the two subcorpora is both statistically significant and not too small. Also as before, we filter out proper names, as well as a few prepositions and "filler" words ("the," "of," "all," "many," "other," "against," "and," "by").

The comparison in the central columns allows us to identify immediate changes; that in the outer columns gives a better indication of how the media's coverage of Muslims has changed over the full period covered by our corpus. Be that as it may, it is striking how similar the last two columns are, even though they are more than ten years apart: the most notable changes that emerged immediately after 9/11—the introduction of radicalism, extremism, and terrorism words (bolded in both periods to facilitate identification)—have persisted through the ensuing decade and a half, indicating that 9/11 really did serve as a key turning point.

The contrast between the two pairs of time periods is similar: in the earlier period, there are more references to militants and particular groups; in the latter, in addition to the obvious emphasis on radicalism, extremism, and terrorism, there is a focus on Muslims considered as a single group: "world," as in "Muslim world" and also "all." The fact that the patterns are comparable whether we look immediately before and after 9/11, or at the beginning and end of the timeframe covered by our corpus, shows that 9/11 had an enduring impact on the words readers are most likely to encounter right next to Muslim* or Islam*.[12]

Since our interest is not only in the words that stand out, but also in the words readers are simply likely to encounter most often, we end this section by broadening our focus from words disproportionately likely to occur immediately before or after the word roots Muslim* or Islam* to include all the words that appear in those positions during the entire post-9/11 period.

Figure 4.4. shows a word cloud displaying these words, with their size reflecting their frequency in those positions; as before, we filter out our corpus word roots as well as the words "Republic," "State," and "Brotherhood," which form part of proper names when following "Islamic" and "Muslim," respectively, as well as standard stopwords such as definite or indefinite articles, prepositions, etc. In the figure, words that fall within our terrorism and extremism categories are displayed in black; all others are in grey.

The figure underscores just how common it is for newspapers to identify Muslims as radical, militant, or extremist. As we saw in table 4.2, the association of Muslims with militancy predates 9/11; this last visualization makes

---

[12] The increase in the share of articles mentioning terrorism and extremism terms we encountered earlier already suggested as much. Also informative is the particular way the word "Islam" is modified in our corpus. By the same criteria of substantive and statistical difference, the words "Islamism/t(s)" and "Islamophobe(s)/ia/ic" appear only in the most recent five-year period. This suggests that coverage has in some ways become more nuanced over time, including by recognizing the existence of anti-Islam prejudice.

Figure 4.4 Top words in US print media coverage of Muslims/Islam since 9/11

clear that even if it does not stand out as much in the post-9/11 period as it did before, it remains very prominent in articles about them. Moreover, while it is perhaps encouraging that terrorism-related words are not quite as common overall (and thus smaller in the word cloud), the image nonetheless provides a discouraging snapshot of the terms an average American news consumer has been most likely to encounter in association with Muslims and Islam since 9/11.

Looking beyond 9/11: Identifying the impact of major events

The events of 9/11 precipitated an enduring shift in the volume of coverage of Muslims and Islam, as well as in the contents of that coverage, shifting the focus from articles about religious practices and local militants or guerrilla groups to global extremism and terrorism. On the other hand, the drop in article valence after 9/11 was neither particularly large nor enduring. In this section, we identify other event-driven shifts in the volume and tone of coverage to see how they compare. Specifically, we want to see if 9/11 was a unique event not only in its size, but also in its effects, and we want to understand more broadly how major events affect coverage of Muslims. We begin

Table 4.3 Largest spikes in coverage of Muslims and Islam, 1996–2016 (other than 9/11)

Start of spike	Associated event(s)	Rank
October 15, 2000	Attack on the USS *Cole* (Oct. 12)	9
September 11, 2002	Anniversary of 9/11 attacks	7
March 20, 2003	US invasion of Iraq	2
February 10, 2006	Danish cartoon controversy	6
August 22, 2010	Park51 ("Ground Zero Mosque") controversy	5
February 4, 2011	Arab Spring	8
September 22, 2012	Benghazi attacks (Sept. 11–12)	10
September 11, 2014	Obama speech about Islamic State (Sept. 10)	4
November 17, 2015	Paris attacks (Nov. 13–14) & San Bernardino attacks (Dec. 2)	1
June 14, 2016	Pulse nightclub (Orlando, FL) shooting (Jun. 12)	3

by looking at the events that had the greatest impact on the volume of coverage, and we follow that by looking more specifically at the largest spikes—both positive and negative—in the tone of coverage.

Table 4.3 lists the events (apart from 9/11) that caused the 10 largest spikes in coverage during the 21 years we study.[13] What types of events were these? As we can see, three of the spikes are associated with terrorist attacks, four with developments in the Middle East and North Africa, two directly or indirectly with the memorialization of 9/11, and one with global responses to the publication of cartoons about Islam in Denmark. As expected, each of these events is negative. The table also shows their relative ranking, as measured by the height of the peak at its highest point, compared to coverage volume prior to the peak. The greatest jump in coverage after 9/11 came after two terrorist attacks in quick succession in late 2015, in Paris and San Bernardino. However, the second and fourth ranked peaks are not associated with terrorist attacks, illustrating that terrorism is not the only driver of media storms associated with Muslims and Islam.

Since we are studying the US press, it is not a surprise that most of the events listed in the table have a direct connection to the United States. In this

---

[13] To identify the spikes, we first calculate the standard deviation of the entire time series of article counts from figure 4.1. Next, we look for periods during which the article count exceeds the average of the preceding three months by at least that standard deviation. Such periods are relatively rare: in addition to 9/11, there are just 10 such moments in our corpus.

context, it is interesting to note that the last two entries in the table involved terrorist attacks in quick succession in France and the United States. In 2015, the Paris attack preceded the San Bernardino attack, whereas in 2016, an attack in Nice, France, on July 14 occurred just a month after the Pulse nightclub attack. In each case, the US attack resulted in fewer casualties than the French attack. Nonetheless, when the US attack took place first, the subsequent attack in France produced a spike too small to register by itself on our table; when the French attack happened first, the subsequent US attack raised the spike higher still.

In each of these cases, the media storm associated with the coverage spikes is of limited duration. For 9/11, the immediate spike lasted 4–5 months; for most other events, it is over much faster. We can look at this more systematically by seeing how long it takes article counts to drop back down to their pre-event levels. While other events can intervene to drive coverage up subsequently, only in exceptional cases does the boost in coverage last longer than a couple of months.[14]

Next, we turn to spikes in valence. Adapting the same basic approach we used to identify volume spikes,[15] we find eight negative and five positive spikes, apart from 9/11. As shown in table 4.4, not only are the positive spikes fewer in number, as expected; they are also slightly smaller, overall: six of the eight largest spikes are negative. In addition, positive spikes are less clearly associated with individual events. Of the five that met our criteria, only two are associated with events directly linked to Muslim populations; one is associated with religion more generally, and two have no clear theme. In contrast, the negative spikes are more closely linked to a single event (or two events).

As with the volume spikes, not all of the negative valence spikes are associated with terrorist events, and some are not directly linked to the United States at all. As we discussed earlier, this is because during periods when average article volume is low, a few articles about a negative event (even a distant one) may suffice to produce a spike. That appears to be what happened in August 1999, for example: few articles overall, and two events that produced negative news, neither of which loomed large on the media's radar screen at the time. This underscores the degree to which the tone of articles about

---

[14] Table II.4.1 in the appendix shows the data for several of these major events; the length of the boost in publication volume is longest by far for 9/11, at more than 12 years.

[15] Since valence spikes are less extreme than volume spikes, we look for periods during which the valence deviates from the average of the preceding three months by at least three-fourths (.75) of the series' standard deviation.

Table 4.4   Spikes in valence, 1996–2016 (other than 9/11)

Start of spike	Associated event(s)	Rank
Positive valence spikes		
March 17, 2000	President Clinton visit to Bangladesh, India, and Pakistan	4
December 19, 2004	European Union agrees to begin accession negotiations with Turkey	1
April 2, 2005	Pope John Paul II dies (articles about faith, positive impact of religious leaders, etc.)	9
September 17, 2007	No single theme (articles about peaceful roots of Ramadan, success of democracy in Islamic Turkey)	11
November 13, 2013	No single theme (articles about art, music, education)	12
Negative valence spikes		
August 25, 1998	Response to US embassy bombings (including indictment of bin Laden)	5
August 22, 1999	Earthquake in Turkey; Russia's conflict in Dagestan	7
November 10, 2000	Aftermath of USS Cole attack; start of 2nd intifada	8
April 21, 2004	Bombings in Basra, Iraq	2
July 14, 2005	London bombings (July 7)	3
August 4, 2009	Ahmadinejad re-elected in Iran, in the midst of protests about election irregularities	6
January 12, 2010	Aftermath of Fort Hood attack; conflict in the Middle East	13
October 3, 2012	Attacks in Aleppo, Syria; aftermath of Benghazi attacks	10

Muslims and Islam is event-driven: stories about negative events are negative, of course, and if such events happen at a slow news time, they can easily drive the average valence to be more negative, even in the absence of a spike in overall coverage. On the other hand, this also means that positive events should have the potential to push valence levels in the opposite direction. We turn to that possibility in the last part of the chapter.

Positive events and positive coverage

Not all newsworthy events are negative; in the previous section, we identified a few positive events that were associated with a noteworthy spike in average article valence, even if not in volume. That there were only a few of these is not a surprise: the extensive literature on negativity bias suggests that positive events elicit weaker reactions than negative ones, at least for most individuals (Soroka, Fournier, and Nir 2019). In this last section of the chapter, we draw on our corpus of articles to see if there are systematic differences in both the volume and valence of coverage of positive events related to Muslims and Islam. Specifically, we look at one notable positive event that occurred on a single day—constituting a direct comparison to some of the single-day negative events appearing in tables 4.3 and 4.4—and one recurring annual event.

On June 4, 2009, President Obama addressed an audience at Cairo University, seeking, as he said, "a new beginning between the United States and Muslims around the world" (Obama 2009). As a story in USA Today noted, the speech was widely seen as an attempt to "repair the United States' relations with Muslims after a decade of violence and recrimination."[16] It received extensive media coverage, ranking as the top story that week across several media sectors (Pew Research Center 2009). The speech itself referred to Muslims and Islam in positive terms. We examine whether it also had a positive effect on the tone and content of the media's broader coverage of Muslims, and how that impact compares to the effects we have seen so far.

We also investigate the impact of Ramadan, a recurring event that is the ninth month on the Islamic calendar. It is observed as a month of prayer, reflection, and care for the community, with the festival of Eid al-Fitr marking the end of Ramadan. As the Islamic calendar is lunar, its 12 months last 354–355 days, making it 10–12 days shorter than a calendar year. As a result, Ramadan begins a few days earlier each year. This is helpful for our purposes, since we can distinguish any Ramadan-specific effects on media coverage from patterns based on the regular calendar year. Over the course of our study, the beginning of Ramadan ranged from January 22 in 1996 to June 6 in 2016. The final days of Ramadan, along with Eid, may attract more, and more positive, coverage than the rest of the month; accordingly, we look separately at coverage patterns for the entire month and for the last few days of the month.

[16] "Repairing Relations in the Muslim World: In Cairo, Obama to Face Hope and Skepticism Over USA's Intentions" (USA Today, June 3, 2009).

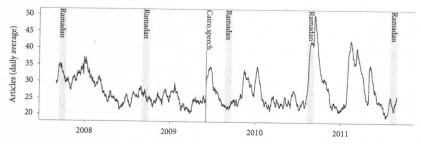

Figure 4.5 Average daily article count, 2007-2011 (30-day exponential moving average)

Figure 4.5 depicts a four-year section of our corpus, from September 2007 through August 2011, allowing us to examine the impact on coverage volume both of Obama's Cairo speech and of five consecutive Ramadan periods, shaded gray. Obama's speech is identified by a vertical gray line. It is worth noting that the major increases in the volume of coverage during this period are not associated either with Obama's speech or Ramadan; instead, they revolve around two coverage spikes we identified earlier: the fall 2010 controversy over the Park51 community center (better known as the Ground Zero mosque) and the Arab Spring, which began in late January 2011. The figure shows that Ramadan has at best a marginal influence on article count—much smaller than the two individual events just mentioned (one of which had its start during Ramadan). Over our entire 21-year period, in fact, our corpus contains an average of just 2.5 additional articles per day during Ramadan and the festival of Eid. During the final few days of Ramadan, plus Eid, this grows to five additional articles.

Figure 4.6 depicts developments in article valence over the same four-year period. The figure shows that the impact of Obama's Cairo speech on the tone of articles, while positive, is weaker than some of the negative spikes occurring during this same period, such as Mahmoud Ahmadinejad winning re-election as Iran's president in a disputed election not long after Obama's speech, and the Fort Hood shootings in early 2010.

Interestingly, even articles mentioning terrorism enjoyed a brief positive bump after Obama's address: in the week immediately following the speech, Muslim articles mentioning terrorism have an average tone of −.68, compared to a four-week average prior to the speech of −1.08.

Turning to Ramadan, if we consider the entire period, there is no significant difference in tone compared to the rest of the year, although our

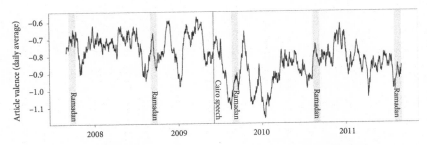

Figure 4.6 Article valence, 2007-2011 (30-day exponential moving average)

newspapers publish a few additional articles per day, as we have seen. For the final days of Ramadan plus Eid, average valence rises by .035: a statistically significant amount, but not one that is substantively meaningful.[17] It is safe to say that, compared to the impact on media coverage of major events such as those discussed earlier in this chapter, Ramadan and the festival of Eid pale in significance.

Overall, we can conclude that positive events do cause an increase in both volume and valence; however, this positive impact is smaller and has a shorter duration than the impact of negative events that are arguably comparable.

Conclusions

Scholars and media professionals alike argue that 9/11 changed a great deal with respect to the media (Greste 2018; Morgan 2009; Stohl 2012, 2018). The evidence presented in this chapter outlines both the truth and the limits of that claim: 9/11 *did* mark an enduring increase in the volume of coverage dedicated to Muslims and Islam, and in particular in references to terrorism and extremism within our Muslim corpus; on the other hand, it does not stand out from other significant negative events in terms of the size or the duration of the negative shock to the tone of coverage. Meanwhile, the content of negative coverage is perhaps where 9/11 had the most enduring impact: close to half of all articles mentioning Muslims or Islam published since 9/11 mention terrorism or terms related to extremism, a significant increase

---

[17] Table II.4.4 in the appendix provides additional information about the impact of Ramadan/Eid on article volume and tone.

from levels prior to the attacks. In addition, the words most likely to describe Muslims or Islam—or simply to appear in close proximity to those terms— also show a clear shift toward radicalism and extremism since 9/11. Indeed, "radical" and "extremist" are among the words a US newspaper reader has been most likely to see in the immediate context of the root words Muslim* or Islam* since 9/11.

The chapter also examined other events that produce spikes in the volume or tone of coverage. This allows us to put 9/11 in comparative perspective and helps improve our understanding of the dynamics of event-based patterns in coverage. We found that other negative events have also had a sizable impact on short- and medium-term patterns in coverage. In fact, the largest spikes in the volume of coverage are all associated with negative events, including, but not exclusively, other terrorist attacks. The fact that the largest spikes are all negative produces a significant negative correlation between volume and average daily valence. One important implication is that, on most days, the average valence of articles mentioning Muslims is less negative than the overall corpus average. However, readers are less likely to pay close attention to articles published in these quieter times unmarked by dramatic events.

Some positive events also stand out, especially when we focus on spikes in valence rather than coverage volume. Even there, however, negative spikes are more common and, on average, larger. Moreover, such spikes are sometimes driven simply by a few positive articles not specifically tied to a particular event. An expectation that the American media's general support of religiosity might make the annual observance of Ramadan a significant positive "event" was not confirmed: both volume and valence rise a little, especially toward the end of Ramadan and the festival of Eid, but the effect is marginal and in most years it is drowned out by individual events that simply happen to take place during the month.

Overall, these findings add depth to the investigation of our guiding question: "What makes coverage of Islam so negative?" We have shown not only how events drive negativity, but also how other factors—the volume of coverage and the prevalence of keywords related to terrorism and extremism— may add to or exacerbate that negativity as news consumers perceive it. They also raise an important question about whether the patterns we observe are specific to the United States. After all, while 9/11 had global reverberations, its impact was likely greatest in the country where the attacks took place. In addition, the word cloud in figure 4.4 shows that "American" (located just below "militant") is quite a prominent word in coverage about Muslims and Islam since 9/11. As such, it might be the case that our story so far is a uniquely American story. To assess that possibility, the next chapter expands our analysis to take in other countries: some whose coverage we might expect to be comparatively similar to the United States, and others where it is likely to be quite different, including several Muslim-majority countries.

5

Is the United States unique?

Examining newspapers from the Anglophone North and the Global South

So far, we have focused on coverage of Muslims in American newspapers and have explored comparisons across groups and over time. Our analysis shows that Muslim articles are more negative than those touching on other identity groups, and this negativity is intense and enduring. In this chapter, we ask whether American newspapers are unique in these respects. Given the centrality of the United States to the international system and the post-9/11 US declaration of a "war on terror," American newspapers may cover topics such as foreign locations, violence, and extremism to a much greater degree than other countries. Or they may simply infuse coverage of Muslims with a greater degree of negativity than do their counterparts elsewhere in the world. Are US outlets in fact more negative when writing about Muslims than newspapers in other countries?

We address this question primarily through an examination of Muslim articles drawn from a wide range of newspapers in Britain, Canada, and Australia. These countries have an extensive Anglophone press, making it possible to compare them to the United States using our methods. They differ, however, in a number of key ways. Geopolitically, they have varying levels of power: the United States and Britain are permanent members of the UN Security Council with nuclear capabilities; Canada and Australia have roughly a tenth or less of the US population and much smaller militaries. Geographically, Canada is a neighbor of the United States, Britain is heavily influenced by its interactions with other European countries, and Australia is more attuned to events in Asia. Each of the four countries has an immigrant-origin Muslim minority, but it ranges from approximately 1% in the United States to an electorally meaningful 5% in Britain. Tabloids are a smaller presence in the US and Canadian media markets, and a much larger force in the British and Australian ones. In short, these countries differ from the United

Covering Muslims. Erik Bleich and A. Maurits van der Veen, Oxford University Press. © Oxford University Press 2022.
DOI: 10.1093/oso/9780197611715.003.0005

States along multiple dimensions that may affect newspaper coverage of Muslims.

In spite of these differences, our exploration of 785,407 Muslim articles from the United States, Britain, Canada, and Australia reveals a striking degree of similarity. There was a sharp increase in articles following the 9/11 attacks, just as we documented for the United States in the previous chapter. More importantly, the tone of articles has consistently been extremely negative in all four countries. In addition, the same variables associated with intense negativity in US papers are linked with the greatest negativity in the other three countries: stories set abroad, those including violence or extremism words, and those published in tabloids are more likely to be negative in all four countries. Publication in right-leaning papers matters relatively little, and articles that touch on religiosity or value clash are associated with marginally less negativity in Britain, Canada, and Australia, just as they are in the United States.

These strong parallels raise the possibility that there may be a common global media discourse about Muslims. When newspapers in other countries write about Islam and Muslims, is it always as negative as it is in these four countries? For some, this is plausible, given the newsworthiness of international wars, terrorism, and forms of conflict that are staples of newspaper coverage in the United States and elsewhere (Galtung and Ruge 1965; Hackett 1989). For others, cross-national similarities may be a function of what sociologists call "institutional isomorphism" (DiMaggio and Powell 1983), or the tendency of institutions like the media to conform to an "industry standard" when journalists cover specific topics.

The United States, Britain, Canada, and Australia differ along important dimensions, but they are all advanced, industrialized, Global North countries, and they all have relatively small Muslim-minority populations. We therefore examine newspaper coverage of Muslims in pairs of countries drawn from South Asia, Southeast Asia, and Africa that have a majority and minority Muslim population, respectively. Because our methods make it most straightforward to compare English sources, we chose countries that publish an English-language newspaper available through a major international media database. Given that most of these newspapers are only available in recent years, we draw articles from the 2015–2019 time period.

Our probe of these newspapers is not directly comparable to the deeper and more systematic analysis we conduct on those from the US, Britain, Canada, and Australia. Yet it is revealing. It clearly demonstrates that not all newspapers are extremely negative when they publish stories touching on Muslims and Islam. The average article in five of these six countries is negative, but in four countries it is less than half as negative as in the Anglophone North newspapers. While one newspaper is equally negative when compared with the United States, the sixth has *positive* coverage of Muslims on average. In sum, there is a consistently strong negativity among newspapers in the US, Britain, Canada, and Australia, but this does not reflect a truly global discourse about Muslims.

Different countries, similar stories

Media coverage of Muslims is plentiful not just in the United States but also across the three other predominantly Anglophone countries we examine.[1] To understand its extent and nature, we assemble corpora of articles from prominent newspapers published in Great Britain, Canada, and Australia over the same 21-year period from January 1, 1996 through December 31, 2016. We mirror as closely as possible the broad sample of newspaper coverage that we obtained in the United States. Our sources thus range from left to right in political orientation, encompass different domestic geographic regions, and include broadsheets as well as tabloids. We ensure inclusion of high-circulation national newspapers that frequently influence regional and local newspapers and elite opinion in each country. Using newspaper database searches, we select all articles containing the root words Muslim*/ Moslem* or Islam* in the title or in the article text for each newspaper across the entire period. Including all four countries, our international Muslim corpus contains 785,407 articles: the 256,963 that make up our American corpus; 318,437 from fifteen daily and nine Sunday British newspapers; 121,588 drawn from six Canadian newspapers; and 88,419 from six daily and four Sunday Australian newspapers.[2]

Figure 5.1 displays patterns in the daily article count across the four corpora, illustrating the striking change in coverage in all four countries associated with the 9/11 attacks in the United States. As in chapter 4, we

[1] We use "Anglophone" and "Anglophone North" as a shorthand to describe these countries, while recognizing that multiple (at times officially recognized) language communities exist in each.
[2] Detailed information about the distribution of articles across newspapers is available in the appendix. Many British and Australian daily newspapers publish a separate Sunday edition that is related to the daily version.

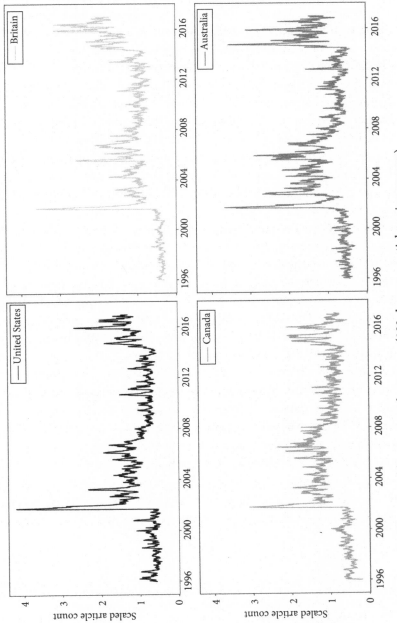

Figure 5.1 Scaled article publication rates by country (180-day exponential moving average)

use an exponential moving average (EMA) to smooth out the shorter-lived fluctuations and to ease interpretation.[3] Since our corpora are different sizes and include different numbers of newspapers, a direct comparison of article counts makes little sense. Instead, we scale each country's line to show variation around its overall average for the entire period. In other words, the value of 1 on the vertical axis corresponds to the country's average daily article count in our corpus. The figure shows that the four countries' publication patterns follow one another closely. Indeed, the correlation coefficients between these smoothed averages range from .75 (Britain and Canada) to .90 (Australia and US). In addition to the obvious rise associated with 9/11, there are also notable increases associated with the 2005 London transportation bombings as well as the period between 2014 and 2016, due to increased activity by ISIS and the sharp uptick of refugees to Europe.[4]

Figure 5.2 shows the same comparison, but now for valence levels. The values in this figure are not scaled against their average, so we can clearly see how the actual degree of negativity compares across countries. Here, too, the degree to which the four countries' trajectories follow the same pattern is quite clear. Indeed, the mutual correlations are again high, ranging from .56 (Australia and Britain) to .77 (Canada and US). Perhaps surprisingly, the US media is comparatively *least* negative when covering Muslims and Islam, while the British media is the most negative.

It is important to remember that these values are all scaled against a representative sample of American newspaper articles. This allows for direct comparability across countries, but it also raises a question about the appropriate benchmark for comparison. For example, if all articles in the British papers we sample tend to be much more negative than those in the US newspapers, Muslim articles may seem very negative when compared to a US baseline, but much less negative when compared to a British one. To strengthen the confidence we have in our analyses, we assembled representative corpora for Britain, Canada, and Australia using the same methods of quasi-random

---

[3] We use a 180-day moving average, in which each day's count is averaged with a weighted combination of the values from previous days. The weighting is exponential, so that the most recent days are weighted most heavily. Specifically, the weighting factor for our 180-day average is $2/(180 + 1) \approx .011$. This means the previous day receives a weight of $1 - .011 \approx .989$, the one before that $(1 - .011)^2 \approx .978$, and so on. The final day included has a weight of just .135.

[4] The upward spike in Britain in mid-2016 is related to debates surrounding Muslim immigration during the Brexit vote of June 23, 2016.

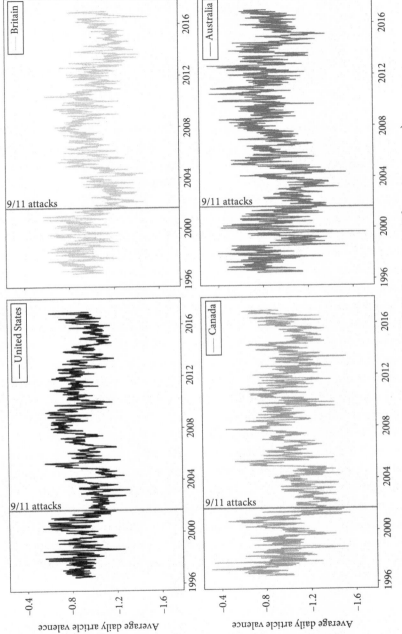

Figure 5.2 Daily average valence, four countries, 1996–2016 (180-day exponential moving average)

Table 5.1   Mean valence scores for Muslim corpora by country

	United States	Britain	Canada	Australia
Mean valence, US scaler	−.94	−1.07	−1.03	−.98
Mean valence, national scalers	−.94	−.87	−.95	−.98
Article count	256,963	318,437	121,588	88,419

sampling we used when generating the US representative corpus.[5] This allows us to tone-check Muslim articles in each country using multiple points of comparison. Table 5.1 shows the mean valence score for each individual country, scaled both against our US representative corpus and against each country's national representative corpus.

Whether measured purely against the US representative corpus or against each country's individual representative corpora, the results are clear: the United States is not exceptional. Coverage of Muslims is extremely negative across all four countries. British articles are modestly more negative than American articles when measured against the US baseline and are marginally less negative when measured against a domestic representative corpus. Nonetheless, British Muslim articles are strongly negative whether compared to representative sets of articles from United States or from Britain; the same is true for Canadian and Australian ones, whether measured against the US baseline or their national representative corpora. This gives us confidence that using either benchmark leads to the same conclusions. For the sake of simplicity and direct comparability, we use the US representative corpus as a common baseline in our analyses in this chapter.

Figure 5.3 shows valence distribution estimates for articles mentioning Muslims in each of our four countries calibrated to the US representative corpus.[6] When the valence of Muslim articles is positive, the difference between the four countries is minimal. However, when the valence is negative, articles tend to be somewhat less negative in the United States, and somewhat more negative in Britain, Canada, and Australia. All in all, however, this illustration of our data confirms that articles touching on Muslims are

---

[5] We assembled corpora of 59,404 British articles, 22,860 Canadian articles, and 24,114 Australian articles, following the same procedures used to collect the US representative corpus, and drawing from the same sources we used for our Muslim corpora for each country. See appendix I.A for more information about representative corpus selection.

[6] See appendix II.5 for a version of this figure using national representative corpora as benchmarks.

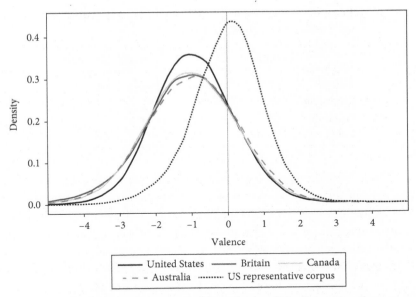

Figure 5.3 Kernel density estimates of the valence of Muslim national corpora scaled against and compared to the US representative corpus

extremely negative not just in the United States, but also in three other countries with different levels of global power, geographic locations, immigrant populations, and media markets.

Factors associated with negativity: Similar or different across countries?

In chapter 3, we explored the factors linked with negativity in our US Muslim corpus. Foreign settings and words related to violence were the most powerful predictors of negativity. Articles linked to extremism words or published in tabloids were also associated with substantial negativity. Newspapers in Britain, Canada, and Australia are comparably negative, but do these factors play a similar role outside of the United States? What if articles in Canada focused more centrally on women's rights, for example, or if those in Australia were principally about religious practices? Just because coverage in these four countries is extremely negative does not mean that it is negative for precisely the same reasons.

Table 5.2 Percentage of articles containing at least one word associated with each element

	United States	Britain	Canada	Australia
Violence	73	63	66	64
Extremism	45	47	47	39
Religiosity	53	49	53	50
Value clash	50	49	47	51

Table 5.2 lists the share of articles in each country containing words from our key categories; it shows that when newspapers write about Muslims in the United States, Britain, Canada, and Australia, they touch on relatively similar topics. The greatest spread within any category is only 10 percentage points, between a low of 63% of British articles and a high of 73% of US articles that contain violence words. But the United States is not a systematic outlier with respect to these four categories. Mentions of extremism range from a low of 39% in Australia to a high of 47% in Britain and Canada. The United States is tied for the highest percentage of religiosity words, but sits in between Canada and Australia with regard to articles that contain value-clash words. There are thus few notable differences—and a high degree of similarity—in the subjects journalists in these four countries touch on when writing articles about Muslims.

The most important way in which newspapers in the four countries differ is related to the prevalence of stories set exclusively abroad. In US papers, a mere 13% of articles mention a foreign location and no domestic locations. The corresponding amounts for British, Canadian, and Australian outlets are 34%, 49%, and 32%, respectively. It is not surprising that the United States is an outlier here, given that it is a global power with more extensive foreign entanglements, so that more events taking place outside the country will have some connection to actions or decisions at home. If we compare the frequency of articles that mention *any* foreign location (whether they mention a domestic setting or not), the countries appear much more similar. Ninety percent of all US articles mention a foreign location; the equivalent percentages for British, Canadian, and Australian newspapers are 83%, 89%, and 85%, respectively. Moreover, if we look at articles in each country that exclusively mention a domestic location with no references to foreign cities, countries, or regions, the figures for the United States, Britain, Canada, and Australia are 9%, 13%, 9%, and 11%. There are thus far more similarities than differences across newspapers in these four countries even with respect to foreign and domestic geographic references.

In addition to examining the prevalence of topics, we want to understand whether the relative negativity associated with each of these topics is similar across the four countries. Figure 5.4 displays coefficient plots from multivariate regressions for each location, allowing us to compare results from the United States to those from Britain, Canada, and Australia.[7] With a few nuances, they show clearly that the negativity present in Muslim articles in those countries is largely associated with the same factors that we identified in the US corpus.

Stories tagged for violence words and those set exclusively outside the home country are likely to be among the most negative in every location. Tabloids and extremism are also linked with significant negativity, while value clash and religiosity are associated with modestly less negativity than the average (strongly negative) article about Muslims in all locations, all else being equal. Right-leaning newspapers are slightly more positive in the US and slightly more negative elsewhere, but are not linked to substantively important tone differences in any country.

Among all of these variables, the greatest difference across the four locations is associated with tabloids. In Canada, tabloid coverage is predicted to be more negative than broadsheet coverage, but by a substantially lower degree than elsewhere, especially in contrast to Britain.[8] Britain's *Sun*, for example, at times touches on Islam or Muslims almost gratuitously within highly negative stories, including ones that are not set exclusively abroad and that are not explicitly linked to terrorism or extremism. For example, one article relays a convicted murderer's anger "at claims he planned to convert to Islam," and another suggests in passing that "an awful lot of recent child sexual abuse has been committed by gangs of Muslim men."[9] British tabloids are simply exceptionally negative when writing articles that touch on Muslims—so much so that tabloids are associated with the greatest amount of negativity of any variable in our British corpus.

---

[7] The figure is a direct analog to figure 3.2 in chapter 3, which displayed the same results for the United States only. All coefficients are statistically significant at the p < .001 level, except for right-leaning in Australia, which is not statistically significant.

[8] There is only one tabloid in our Canadian sample (the *Vancouver Sun*), which limits the generalizability of our finding in that country.

[9] The *Sun*, October 15, 2016; the *Sun*, October 20, 2016.

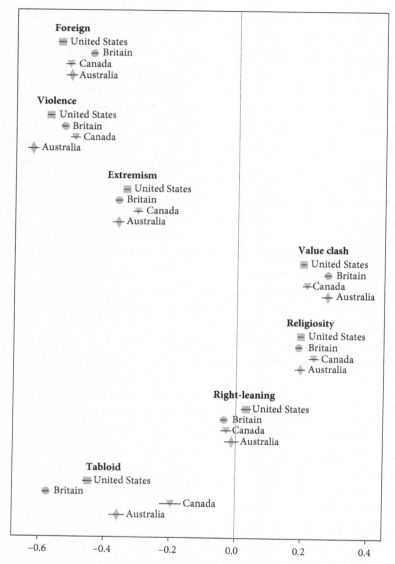

Figure 5.4 Factors associated with the tone of Muslim articles, by country

The words on the page: Describing Muslims and Islam

To assess whether similarities in reporting on Muslims in the Anglophone North extend beyond broad categories to specific word choice, we also conduct a collocation analysis, just as we did in chapter 4. We isolate the

Table 5.3 Top dozen descriptive words surrounding Muslim/Islam root words (L1R1 collocates) for each country

United States	Britain	Canada	Australia
radical	radical	radical	radical
fundamentalist	fundamentalism	militant	militant
militant	devout	devout	cleric
devout	militant	fundamentalist	devout
fundamentalism	fundamentalist	fundamentalism	fundamentalist
predominantly	militancy	predominantly	fundamentalism
extremism	cleric	extremist	populous
militancy	extremism	militancy	extremist
radicalism	convert	extremism	convert
extremist	predominantly	cleric	moderate
cleric	extremist	radicalism	predominantly
dietary	moderate	observant	extremism

words immediately to the left and to the right of the root words Muslim* and Islam* and compare the frequency of specific words within that window to their frequency in the rest that country's corpus.[10] This analysis reveals which words are most intensely connected to Muslims and Islam in each of the four countries, both as adjectives modifying our root words ("devout Muslims") and as nouns that our root words modify ("Muslim cleric").

Table 5.3 displays the top dozen words concentrated within a one-word window on each side of the root words Muslim* or Islam* for each country across the entire 21-year period of our study. This table shows both a striking degree of similarity and negativity. "Radical" is the word most strongly associated with Muslims in all four countries. Taken together, "radical/radicalism," "militant/militancy," "fundamentalist/fundamentalism," and "extremist/extremism" make up 8 of the top 12 words in the United States and Canada, 7 of the top 12 in Britain, and 6 of the top 12 in Australia.

Naturally, it is not only negative words that are commonly linked to Muslims or Islam. "Devout," "cleric," and "predominantly" also appear in all four country lists, for example. Evidently, when the press in the Anglophone

10 We filter out proper names and words that appear fewer than 100 times.

North writes about Muslims, it is prone to use the same sets of words concentrated in closest proximity to references to Muslims or Islam. Most of those words are strongly negative and amplify links to the small minority of the global Muslim population involved in radical fundamentalism, rather than the average Muslim's lived experiences and interpretation of Islam. Overall, there is remarkable consistency across newspapers in these four countries. This is true for the over-time patterns in article volume and tone, for the prevalence of presumptively negative topics like violence or extremism, for the factors most strongly associated with the tone of coverage, and for the specific words used to describe Muslims and Islam.

Is there a global media discourse about Muslims?

The striking similarities between the United States, Britain, Canada, and Australia raise the possibility that newspaper coverage of Muslims might be a global phenomenon rather than primarily a national one. Are world events linked to violence, extremism, and conflict associated with Islamist terrorism ineluctable drivers of negative coverage no matter which newspaper writes about Muslims? If such a "newsworthiness" explanation were valid, we would see minimal variation in the tone of coverage not only across these four countries, but also when surveying a wider array of locations.

So far, we have looked at dozens of newspapers in four countries on three continents. But these countries are all highly developed, immigrant Muslim-minority countries from the Global North. If we want to understand whether there is indeed a *global* element to media coverage of Muslims, we also need to examine newspapers from the Global South. The optimal way to do this involves collecting articles for the same 21-year period from a representative cross-section of newspapers from every region of the world. Unfortunately, this is simply not possible. Newspaper databases do not offer access to articles from earlier years for most countries of interest to us. Moreover, our methods are most directly comparable when assessing English-language sources. These two factors rule out a full analysis of Global South countries that parallels the one in the first part of this chapter. We can, however, test our core question by conducting a probe of major English-language newspapers from recent years. If there are close parallels between our Anglophone country outlets and those from the Global South, it is plausible that there may be a truly global discourse about Muslims. If not, it suggests that the similarities we found above may be limited to coverage of Muslims in the Global North.

To undertake our probe, we collected 79,397 articles from January 1, 2015 through December 31, 2019, from six countries representing three regions with significant English-language readership: South Asia, Southeast Asia, and Africa. We selected a Muslim-majority and a Muslim-minority country from each region and identified the largest English-language newspaper available through the Nexis Uni database. The countries (and newspapers) are: Pakistan (*Dawn*) and India (the *Times of India*); Malaysia (*New Straits Times*) and Singapore (the *Straits Times*); and Nigeria (the *Sun*) and Kenya (*Daily/Sunday Nation*).[11] We use "Global South" here simply as a shorthand, recognizing that Singapore is not typically classified in this category, given its level of economic development.[12] Naturally, no sample of English-language newspapers from a half-dozen countries can accurately capture patterns across the Global South, or even from any of the regions within it. But the variation across location and populations represented by these six newspapers allows us to explore the proposition that media coverage of Muslims follows a global pattern.

In fact, stories about Islam and Muslims vary widely across these six outlets. Table 5.4 illustrates the main axes of difference. The bottom right cell conveys the overall average tone of −.38. The equivalent average tone in the newspapers in our Anglophone North Muslim corpus is vastly different at −1.01. There is a small difference between Muslim-majority and Muslim-minority countries, which is eclipsed by the differences across regions. This regional spread is primarily a function of the notable negativity in Kenya and positivity in Malaysia. The Kenyan Muslim corpus establishes that a Global South newspaper can be just as negative as Global North newspapers, but the Malaysian Muslim corpus demonstrates that positive coverage of Islam and Muslims is indeed possible.

---

[11] According to the CIA *World Factbook*, the percent of the national Muslim population is as follows: Pakistan (96%), India (14%), Malaysia (61%), Singapore (14%), Nigeria (54%), and Kenya (11%). Within these countries, we identified the most widely circulating newspaper of record published in English with continuous availability across the five years from January 1, 2015 to December 31, 2019.

[12] We include Singapore because it is a Southeast Asian Muslim-minority country that has a major English-language newspaper available through Nexis Uni.

Table 5.4 Average tone of Muslim corpus articles from leading newspapers in six countries

	South Asia		Southeast Asia		Africa		
	Pakistan	India	Malaysia	Singapore	Nigeria	Kenya	Average
Muslim-majority country	−.45		+.15		−.42		−.30
Muslim-minority country		−.43		−.31		−.93	−.46
Region average		−.44		−.05		−.65	−.38
Article count	23,762	28,679	9,842		7,178	5,540	4,396

Table 5.5 Percentage of articles containing at least one word associated with each element

	Pakistan	India	Malaysia	Singapore	Nigeria	Kenya
Violence	22	15	22	33	32	40
Extremism	11	8	10	20	19	29
Religiosity	30	34	38	40	51	36
Value clash	22	24	22	30	29	29

These differences raise a question about what these six newspapers cover compared to their counterparts in the Anglophone countries. Table 5.5 shows a much lower prevalence of all of our four major topics than in our Anglophone North newspapers. In particular, the percentage of articles containing words related to violence or extremism is much lower than in the United States, Britain, Canada, or Australia. As we saw in table 5.2, 63–73% of articles in the Muslim corpora from those countries contain words related to violence; the same is true for 15–40% of our Global South newspapers. Similarly, 39–47% of articles in the Anglophone North newspapers contain words linked to extremism, but only 8–29% of articles in the Global South corpora do.

Even more than was the case for the four Anglophone North countries we examine, there is a disparity among our Global South countries in terms of the proportion of articles that exclusively mention foreign versus domestic locations. While newspapers from Kenya and Singapore touch on foreign places in 81% and 84% of all articles, respectively—similar to the range of 83–90% in the Anglophone North newspapers—newspapers in countries like India and Pakistan are far less likely to mention locations outside of their borders. Only 29% of all articles in the *Times of India* and 42% of those in *Dawn* name a foreign country.[13]

Articles that exclusively mention a domestic location ranged from 9 to 13% in the Anglophone North countries. Singapore and Kenya have similar percentages, at 11% and 14%. In Nigeria and Malaysia, 26% and 27% of articles exclusively touch on a domestic location, a proportion that rises to 32% and 46% in India and Pakistan. Two of our Global South newspapers thus resemble Anglophone North newspapers in their propensity to refer to foreign or domestic locations, but the other four do not. It is thus not the case that all newspapers around the world focus equally on foreign settings, on violence, or on extremism in their articles about Islam or Muslims. Perhaps given their relatively small domestic Muslim populations, US newspapers and their analogs in Britain, Canada, and Australia are simply much more likely to direct their readers' attention to conflict and to foreign locations when compared to newspapers from the Global South.

These conclusions are reinforced by looking at collocations within our six newspapers. Once again, we isolated words just to the left and right of the root words Muslim* and Islam*. Table 5.6 shows the notably different word choices evident in these newspapers compared to the Anglophone North newspapers. It also shows how much word choices vary across our six locations. The country whose word list is closest to that of Anglophone North newspapers is Kenya. As in all four Anglophone North countries, the top collocate in Kenya's *Daily Nation/Sunday Nation* is "radical;" the list also contains the words "predominantly," "cleric," and "militant," as well as several words linked to different forms of violence, such as "slain," "coup," and "insurgency." This helps us understand why the average Kenyan article has essentially the same valence (−.93) as the average article in the United States (−.94).

Apart from Kenya, however, the most prominent words in other countries are extremely varied. To be sure, "radical," "militant," and "extremism," appear on several other countries' lists. Yet they are nowhere near as

---

[13] Fifty percent of articles in the Malaysian newspaper and 69% of those in Nigeria touch on locations outside of those countries' borders. Appendix I.C provides further information about the geocoding analysis.

Table 5.6 Top dozen L1R1 collocates for each country

Pakistan	India	Malaysia	Singapore	Nigeria	Kenya
militant	brethren	finance	insulting	faithful	radical
banking	community	cemetery	boarding	radical	predominantly
jurisprudence	seminary	jurisprudence	community	devout	cleric
world	clergy	calendar	populous	cleric	calendar
radical	embrace	banking	moderate	scholar	mainly
modernism	devout	preacher	scholar	calendar	banking
brotherly	preacher	alike	predominantly	militant	preach
calendar	predominantly	convert	penal	preacher	militant
revolution	population	scholar	conservative	sect	faithful
scholar	jurisprudence	minority	militancy	ticket	slain
mode	radical	moderate	conservatism	predominantly	coup
welfare	ghetto	population	convert	extremism	insurgency

prevalent, nor are the lists as uniform as they are in the Anglophone North countries we examine. Looking closely at the top dozen collocates in the Malaysian newspaper, for example, reveals no single word associated with clear negativity.

What accounts for the overall positivity associated with Muslims and Islam in Malaysia? Using a keywords in context (KWIC) analysis of the top three words on the list helps us answer that question. Sentences about cemeteries and jurisprudence tend to include announcements of burials of prominent people, discussions about scholars who are experts in Islamic jurisprudence, or references to "Islamic political jurisprudence." By far the most common type of sentence, however, revolves around Islamic finance, an industry in which Malaysia excels. Some of these provide historical context, such as "Dr. Badawi was endeared to Malaya/Malaysia and contributed inter alia with others to the development of Islamic studies and Islamic finance in the decade after independence."[14] Others explicitly extol the country's success, with lines like this: "Malaysia is renowned as the leader in Islamic finance, says Najib."[15] In addition, some describe awards ceremonies that domestic banks have taken part in, such as "the GIFA 2017 awards ceremony, which

---

[14] *New Straits Times*, August 28, 2017.
[15] *New Straits Times*, November 6, 2017.

was attended by Islamic banking and finance professionals from around the world, are the most prestigious awards in the Islamic finance services industry."[16] In all of these cases, the tone of the sentences is positive. These kinds of stories help account for the overarching positivity of articles in the Malaysian newspaper.

If Kenya's *Daily/Sunday Nation* newspaper reflects a negativity with which we are familiar, and Malaysia's *New Straits Times* exhibits a positivity that is uncommon, what can we learn from a closer look at a newspaper that is more representative of the average tone of coverage in the Global South outlets we examine? Although India is very different from our Anglophone North countries on a number of important measures, it parallels them in being a democracy with a Muslim minority, even if that minority is indigenous and much larger. Because India has over 1.3 billion inhabitants, it is particularly useful to understand why *Times of India* coverage of Muslims is less than half as negative as a typical major American broadsheet such as the *New York Times*. This difference in average tone is particularly striking given that India has also suffered from Islamist terrorist attacks on its soil, and that it has a Hindu nationalist government that has taken steps to isolate Muslims through laws that risk stripping many of citizenship rights (Swami 2008; Chapparban 2020).

As with other Global South newspapers, the *Times of India* communicates less negativity because of its journalistic choice to make fewer references to conflict or extremism, and to focus less on foreign locations. What do *Times of India* articles cover instead? There is a much greater focus on domestic topics that may be related in part to the presence of Muslim political parties, and even more to the fact that Muslims are a significant factor in both national and many regional elections. Among the top three Indian collocates, the words "brethren" and "seminar" are rare outside of sentences that reference Muslims and Islam, but they are not widely used even within such sentences. The word "community" is much more frequent in our Indian corpus. Sentences mentioning community touch on all types of topics, including festivals, economics, sports, and gender equality.

Far and away the most common use of "community," however, revolves around politics and policy. One Muslim "community leader" complains, for example, of "how insensitive the government is to Muslims and their issues."[17] Another article discusses the voters of Gauripur constituency, "of which most hail from the Muslim community."[18] Others touch on varied issues such as the Muslim community's complex relationship with the ruling Bharatiya Janata Party (BJP); or public policy issues like the provision of a Muslim cemetery or reserved seats for Muslims in a medical college; or they argue that, "according to the constitution of India, both the Judiciary and the Parliament do not have any mandate to interfere in the religious affairs of the Muslim community."[19] Most of these sentences are negative, in keeping with the average article valence of −.43 in our Indian Muslim corpus. Yet they are not as strongly negative as are sentences drawn from US or other Anglophone North newspapers. Journalists in India simply make different decisions about how many column inches to allocate to various aspects of Islam and Muslim life.[20] While these are based in part on the different demographic and political situation in India, they have a cumulative effect of conveying much less negativity overall.

The six newspapers we have examined here are notably different both from one another and from those in the Anglophone North. Kenya's *Daily/ Sunday Nation* resembles papers from the United States, Britain, Canada, and Australia more than any of the other Global South newspapers we analyzed. Articles from Pakistan, India, Nigeria, and Singapore are approximately a third to a half as negative on average as those from the Anglophone North, while those from Malaysia are even modestly positive on average. These five countries' newspapers tend to focus more on domestic stories and less on violence and extremism. Articles about Muslims and Islam in these outlets cover a wider range of topics, including especially politics and business. Although we cannot draw sweeping conclusions about newspapers from the Global South from this brief probe, we can confidently say that there is no inevitable global newspaper discourse about Muslims and Islam.

---

[17] *Times of India*, March 7, 2015.

[18] *Times of India*, April 7, 2016.

[19] *Times of India*, September 21, 2018.

[20] Among the 17 American newspapers in our study, only one has an average valence less negative than India's. Muslim articles in the Minneapolis *Star Tribune* have an average valence of −.35. The newspaper publishes relatively fewer articles related to exclusively foreign news, violence, or extremism (respectively: 3%, 59%, and 30%, compared to 12%, 73%, and 45% for the US corpus as a whole). It also published only 237 articles per year (on average) mentioning Islam or Muslims.

Conclusions

All in all, our analysis shows a remarkable consistency in how newspapers cover Muslims across our four Anglophone countries from the Global North. If coverage is very negative in the United States, it is comparably negative in Britain, Canada, and Australia. This is due to a similar set of factors— principally stories set abroad, those linked to violence or extremism, and ones published in tabloid newspapers. This finding is reinforced through our identification of the core words most associated with Muslims, where "radical," "fundamentalist," "militant," and "extremist" feature as prominent collocates in all four countries. These similarities are notable given the unique characteristics of the United States as a global superpower and as a prominent target of Islamist violence. It appears that the structural similarities between these countries shape coverage of Muslims and Islam more than any differences among them.

We did not, however, find evidence of a uniform *global* discourse about Muslims. Our probe into six newspapers from South Asia, Southeast Asia, and Africa showed wide variation. The overall average tone ranged from −.93 in Kenya's *Nation* to +.15 in Malaysia's *New Straits Times*. By comparison, average tone in the Anglophone North papers ranged from −.94 in the United States to −1.07 in Britain. Newspapers in the Global South were much less likely to contain words related to violence or extremism. Instead, they focus more on domestic politics or business, or other topics that, while negative, are not nearly as negative as those related to extremism or fundamentalism. We cannot draw broad conclusions about coverage of Muslims in the Global South as a whole from our probe into these six newspapers. Nonetheless, it is clear that media producers have a choice about what topics to cover and how to cover them. The lack of a global news discourse about Muslims reflects the diversity of demographic, historical, and cultural backgrounds of differently situated countries.

This point, however, reinforces the distinctiveness of the parallels between the United States, Britain, Canada, and Australia. The striking similarities we found in these four countries are not the result of uniform global journalistic standards of newsworthiness. Rather they are the product of a particular gatekeeping process that tends to select stories about Muslims that emphasize forms of conflict. In the next chapter, we use inductive topic modeling techniques to delve even more deeply into the varieties of themes that are prevalent in American newspapers. We use this approach not only to look more closely at what topics are most common, but also to explore nuances in reporting that may temper the overwhelming negativity we have seen in our corpus of Muslim articles.

6

What do newspapers talk about when they talk about Muslims?

In previous chapters, we looked at patterns in newspaper coverage across groups, over time, and across countries. In this chapter, we take a closer look at patterns *within* our Muslim corpus; specifically, at the topics of the individual articles in the corpus. To do so, we draw on a powerful inductive approach called *topic modeling*. Topic modeling serves as an invaluable complement to the more deductive approach we have followed so far, both because articles containing specific feature words are not necessarily *about* those words and because, conversely, articles that do not contain those same words might nonetheless be about the topic they are associated with. By letting texts speak for themselves, we get a more refined and nuanced look at what the articles in our corpus are actually about. This is particularly valuable for two reasons.

First, it provides an independent method of assessing the content of articles in our corpus by breaking down the elements identified by the theoretical literature into more nuanced categories. For example, earlier we examined the tone of the relatively small subset of our articles that exclusively mention foreign locations, while also noting that a much larger proportion contained at least one reference to a foreign location, alongside at least one reference to a domestic location. But these figures do not reveal the proportion of articles that are primarily *about* foreign coverage, nor do they illustrate the specific locations most often covered, nor whether there are meaningful differences in tone or word choice across types of locations within our corpus. Topic modeling allows us to highlight distinctive aspects of articles that focus on specific geographic locations. In particular, we take advantage of this to zero in on places where Muslims are more likely to be victims of systematic violence and oppression to see if the negativity associated with those locations is more intense or of a different nature than it is elsewhere.

In a similar vein, our topic modeling analysis reveals that not all of our articles that mention religiosity keywords are necessarily about Islam as

Covering Muslims. Erik Bleich and A. Maurits van der Veen, Oxford University Press. © Oxford University Press 2022.
DOI: 10.1093/oso/9780197611715.003.0006

a religion. In fact, some articles concentrate on topics associated with Christianity by including words like "church" and "pope." Stories that link across faiths are not extremely common in our corpus, but they tend to be more positive than the average article mentioning Muslims, and thus help account for the relative positivity associated with religiosity. In addition, our topic modeling analysis shows that articles focused on conflict come in two varieties. Consistent with the approach we have taken so far, a certain proportion is linked to topics of political violence. Yet our inductive approach also illustrates the importance of "law and order" topics within Muslim articles. These articles sometimes revolve around terrorism, but they also concentrate on policing, prosecutions, and everyday forms of lawbreaking.

As a second main advantage, our topic modeling analysis allows us to identify themes within our corpus that have not been the subject of extensive research. For example, approximately 13% of US Muslim articles revolve primarily around topics related to politics, and another 9% are linked to culture. Articles primarily about family, business, and education make up a further 13%. These topics have not received attention from most scholars studying media coverage of Muslims, even though together they account for over a third of the corpus. While there are many avenues for further research suggested by these findings, here we concentrate on one closely linked to our focus on tone-checking: we investigate which sets of articles are comparatively most *positive*, thus offering insights into which topics offset—at least to some degree—the negativity so strongly present in coverage of Muslims.

The first section of the chapter introduces the topic modeling technique, explaining our inductive approach. Next, we take a closer look at the largest single category of topics emerging from our analysis: foreign locations. The topic model reveals which locations are most widely covered, and also what types of locations are most prominent in US newspaper articles. We analyze these differences with a specific focus on contexts where Muslims have been the victims of oppression. We then turn to an exploration of the other major categories of articles highlighted in previous chapters. Topic modeling analysis offers new insights into two of these categories: religiosity and events linked to violence. We explore the presence and effect of subsets of articles that touch on Christianity and law and order to gain a deeper understanding of how newspapers cover these subjects. We also discuss the seeming absence in the topic model of specific clusters of words related to extremism, and identify key differences in coverage that set right-leaning papers apart from the other papers in our corpus. Finally, we delve into topics not frequently discussed by scholars of Muslims and the media: politics, culture, family, business, and education. Rather than providing an exhaustive review of each type of story, we focus on the extent to which these categories are likely to provide a counterweight to the strongly negative tone that dominates other topics, highlighting the particular importance of stories about education and the arts.

What newspapers talk about: An inductive approach

Until now, we have tested numerous propositions from the scholarly literature about what drives negative coverage of Muslims. This has allowed us to build on existing expertise to advance our understanding of how geography, events, and real or perceived cultural differences shape the tone of stories in our Muslim corpus. But a deductive, hypothesis-testing method also has limitations. If we want to look beyond the straightforward presence or absence of known elements, we need an inductive approach. Topic modeling algorithms inductively identify sets of words that often occur together within a text across all texts in a corpus. Such clusters of words usually indicate specific topics common within the corpus. These, in turn, can be amalgamated into broader themes comprising multiple, logically related topics.[1]

Applying a topic model to our Muslim corpus produced 36 topics. Of these, 34 topics were substantively meaningful, and those are the focus of our analysis here.[2] Each topic is represented by a set of words, but not every word associated with a topic has the same strength of association: the algorithm assigns each word a weight within the topic. At times, the same word is associated with multiple topics, albeit with different weights. One way to visualize these different weights is to look at the top words in a word cloud, with their size scaled by their weight. Figure 6.1 shows examples of two such visualizations, for topics we label Afghanistan/Taliban and the Islamic State, respectively, based on the words the algorithm identifies as most strongly associated with each topic. The second image features several words also associated, more strongly, with other topics in our model: Iraq/Iraqi and Syria/ Syrian, in particular.

---

[1] A useful way to think of topic modeling algorithms is that they attempt to reduce the complexity of texts by identifying a specified number of semantic features: they summarize texts, in a way. For additional details about our topic modeling methodology, see appendix II.6.

[2] See appendix II.6 for details.

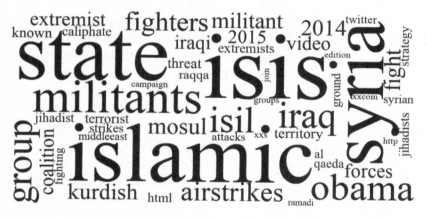

Figure 6.1 Word clouds for two topics in our model: Afghanistan/Taliban and ISIS

In addition to the word-to-topic mapping, our topic modeling algorithm also produces a document-to-topic mapping: a weighted list of the topics present in each newspaper article. For most articles in our corpus, about a dozen topics are present, though only a few of them are prominent. Scaling topic weights so that they sum to 1 for each article, the average weight of the most prominent topic is .36; the second topic has an average weight of .20, and the third .13. Our analyses here focus on the most prominent topic in each article: the topic we can most confidently say the article is *about*.[3]

---

[3] An alternative approach would be to look at articles in which a topic's weight exceeds a particular threshold. We experimented with thresholds of .5, .33, and .25; while specific numbers change, the

Not all negativity is the same: Variation in foreign settings

For each of the 34 substantive topics from our model, we look at the top words to determine the most appropriate name, or label, for the topic. More than half (18) refer to specific foreign locations. This analysis adds important contours to our earlier discussion of stories set exclusively abroad. Recall that while 13% of our articles contain one or more mentions of foreign regions, countries, or cities but zero references to geographic locations in the United States, an additional 77% mention both a foreign and a domestic location. While these figures communicate just how often the stories in our corpus mention foreign places, they cannot tell us what fraction of articles is largely about foreign countries, nor which foreign locations are most prominently covered.

Table 6.1 shows the top five words associated with each topic representing a geographic location, and the proportion of articles for which it is the most prominent topic in the article. The topic model allows us to say with confidence that just under two-fifths of the articles in our corpus are largely about foreign locations. Looking at the specific distribution of countries is also revealing, as we can see that stories about Muslims set abroad are not all the same.

The greatest number of articles are set in states where an overwhelming majority of the population is Muslim. Next most numerous are stories set in three locations where there is no preponderant majority religion and where different religions have their own geographic strongholds: Israel and Palestine, Pakistan and India, and Lebanon. A third group features countries where the Muslim population is a clear minority: France, Russia, and the Philippines. Finally, two topics center on areas with large Muslim populations, but where Muslims long did not control government and were victimized by those with political and/or military power: Bosnia and Kosovo. This differentiation raises questions about whether coverage of foreign locations varies based on the relative demographic and political position of Muslims in different regions.

We know from our analysis in chapter 3 that articles linked primarily to foreign locations are likely to be even more negative than the average article

substantive findings remain the same. We use the "most salient topic" metric here because it makes intuitive sense.

Table 6.1 Geographic topics

Category/Topic	Top five words	%
All foreign locations		*39.1*
Muslims majority		*22.3*
Iraq	Iraqi, Iraq, Baghdad, Shiite, Sunni	3.7
Iran	Iran, Iranian, Tehran, nuclear, Ahmadinejad	3.1
Afghanistan	Taliban, Afghan, Afghanistan, Kabul, Karzai	2.8
Egypt	Egypt, Egyptian, Brotherhood, Mubarak, Cairo	2.2
Somalia	Somalia, Somali, Africa, Mogadishu, African	2.1
Syria	Syrian, Syria, Assad, Bashar, Damascus	1.9
ISIS	ISIS, Islamic, State, Syria, militants	1.7
Turkey	Turkey, Turkish, Erdogan, Istanbul, Ankara	1.7
Saudi Arabia	Saudi, Arabia, Saudis, Riyadh, kingdom	1.6
Indonesia	Indonesia, Indonesian, Jakarta, Bali, Suharto	1.4
No clear majority		*9.6*
Palestine-Israel	Palestinian, Israeli, Israel, Palestinians, Gaza	5.8
Pakistan-India	Pakistan, India, Pakistani, Kashmir, Musharraf	2.5
Lebanon	Lebanon, Hezbollah, Lebanese, Beirut, Israel	1.3
Muslims minority		*4.5*
France	France, French, Europe, European, Paris	1.8
Russia	Russian, Russia, Moscow, Chechnya, Putin	1.7
Philippines	Philippines, Sayyaf, Philippine, hostages, Abu	1.0
Muslims victim		*2.7*
Bosnia	Bosnian, Bosnia, Serb, Serbs, tribunal	1.7
Kosovo	Kosovo, Milosevic, Albanians, Serbia, Serbian	1.0

in the US Muslim corpus, which has a tone of −.94. Figure 6.2, which shows valence by type of foreign location, confirms that the average article in all four foreign subsets is more negative than that. Articles linked with Muslim-minority countries are the most negative, with an average valence of −1.41. These articles tend to focus on the often-fraught relations between Muslim minorities and the national government. For example, in the France topic—in which France dominates, but other Western European countries such as Germany or Belgium are also prominent—the emphasis is on immigrants and migration. In the Russia topic, the focus is on the struggle for autonomy/independence in Chechnya, and to a lesser degree the neighboring regions of Ingushetia and Dagestan. In the Philippines, finally, the rebel group Abu

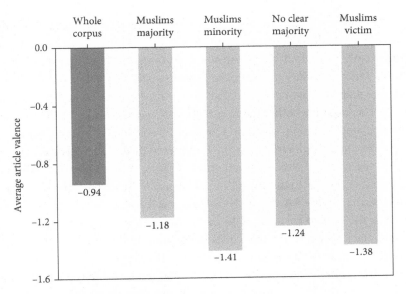

Figure 6.2 Valence levels by type of foreign location

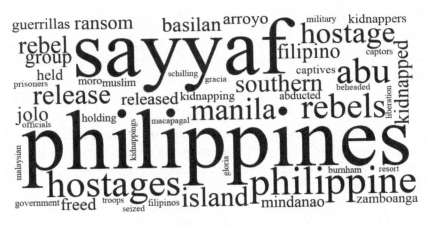

Figure 6.3 Word cloud for the Philippines topic

Sayyaf and its notorious practice of hostage-taking are central, as shown in the word cloud for that topic in figure 6.3, which includes the words "kidnappers," "kidnapped," "hostage(s)," and "release(d)," among others. In sum, articles set in countries where Muslims are the minority thus primarily focus on them as threats to varying degrees.

Yet negative articles featuring Muslims in foreign settings need not be negative *about* Muslims. Looking more closely at locations where Muslims are numerically important but politically less powerful draws our attention to stories where Muslims are more likely cast as *victims* of violence and oppression. In chapter 2, we raised the question of how prevalent such articles are in our corpus and whether the negativity in these articles was more likely to be associated with non-Muslims. Our topic model analysis draws our attention to two such topics in our corpus, both set in the former Yugoslavia in the 1990s: the war in Bosnia between ethnic Croats, ethnic Serbs, and Bosnian Muslims; and the struggle by ethnic Albanians in Kosovo for independence from Serbia. Figure 6.4 shows the word cloud for each. While this set of articles is the second most negative of the four types of foreign topics (with an average tone of −1.38), the word clouds indicate that these topics are different from many of the others: in addition to the proper names in each, there are words such as "tribunal," "massacre," and "genocide" in the Bosnia topic (referring to the genocide in Srebrenica); and "refugees," "liberation," and "independence" in the Kosovo topic. While these are not the most prominent words in each topic, they are distinct and noteworthy compared to those found in the other foreign location topics.

The word clouds convey the outlines of the different topics, but for systematic comparisons across topics, it is more helpful to conduct a collocation analysis. Table 6.2 shows, for each of the four types of foreign location, which words are most strongly associated with the context immediately to the left and right of our corpus word roots. We exclude proper nouns, such as "Kosovo" or "Albanians," so as to focus our comparison not on the locations themselves, but on what is written about those locations. As before, the strength of association is measured by how much more common particular words are in this immediate context than they are throughout our entire corpus.[4]

The table makes clear that there are real differences in the types of stories newspapers tell about Muslims in each of these different contexts. In countries where Muslims have a clear majority, words associated with religion and religiosity are more prominent than in the other categories: "heterodox,"

---

[4] Specifically, the table includes only words that occur at least 25 times immediately to the left or right of Muslim* or Islam* in the subset of articles in each topic (excluding proper nouns), and that occur with a frequency at least twice that of the word's frequency in the rest of our corpus. Note: the presence of "revolution" at the top of the Muslim majority column is driven by frequent references to Iran's Islamic Revolution.

Figure 6.4 Word clouds for topics where Muslims were victims: Bosnia and Kosovo

"holiest," "strict," and "cleric(s)." In Muslim-minority contexts, the emphasis is on separatism and internal war, with words such as "separatists," "liberation," "rebels," and "guerrillas." The intermediate category, which includes the topics for Israel and Palestine, Pakistan and India, and Lebanon, displays characteristics of the two categories on either side, with "holiest" and "holy" on the one hand, and "guerrillas" and "resistance" on the other hand.

Interestingly, the words most strongly associated with the victim topics are noticeably less negative than those in the other columns, and with a greater focus on people suffering from, rather than actively pursuing,

Table 6.2 Top collocates, by foreign subcategory

Muslim majority	Muslim minority	No clear majority	Victim
revolution	separatists	jihad	enclave
ultraconservative	liberation	militant	unarmed
populous	radical	resistance	fundamentalists
heterodox	separatist	militants	dominated
radical	extremists	radical	men
fundamentalist	radicals	guerrillas	led
holiest	rebels	militancy	refugees
strict	militants	holiest	expelled
clerics	radicalism	fundamentalist	civilians
extremists	guerrillas	fundamentalists	fundamentalist
fundamentalists	militancy	radicals	nationalist
cleric	extremism	holy	radical

conflict: "enclave," "unarmed," "dominated," "refugees," and "civilians" all
stand out. This is not to say that the sentences in which these words appear
are also less negative: after all, as the word clouds in figure 6.4 make clear,
they also include words such as "massacre," "genocide," and "atrocities."

One caveat for these findings is that both of the victim topics relate to
conflicts in the former Yugoslavia that largely played out prior to 9/11. To
see whether this may have biased which words appear in the final column
in table 6.2, we expanded the category to include all articles mentioning
Uighurs and Rohingya, broadening both the geographic range and the time
periods involved. Uighurs are a predominantly Muslim ethnic group mostly
living in China who have been persecuted by the Chinese central government for years. The Rohingya are a mostly Muslim ethnic group originally
living in Myanmar, although much of the population has fled to Bangladesh
in recent years, following systematic persecution and genocide. While our
topic model did not generate separate topics for these two groups, we can
use references to them as a proxy. When we combine those articles with
our two victim topics, the basic findings remain the same: "enclave," "unarmed," and "dominated" remain in the list. So does the focus on people
rather than aggressors: "civilians" and "refugees" disappear from the list, but
"inhabitants" appears in their stead.

Overall, these results give the lie to the suggestion that newspaper
readers will encounter only one type of foreign news story about Muslims.

Instead, different contexts elicit different types of stories: some focus on Muslims as religious practitioners, some highlight Muslims as politically violent actors, and some emphasize Muslims as people on the receiving end of political violence. These findings are important because they highlight that negative news featuring Muslims is not always negative about Muslims *as Muslims.*

At the same time, it is important to remember that these more sympathetic portrayals of Muslims constitute only a small fraction of all articles. Even adding articles mentioning Uighurs and Rohingya to the ones focused on Bosnia and Kosovo, this type of article makes up only 3.5% of our Muslim corpus.[5] Moreover, although such articles may elicit sympathy for Muslims, the short- and long-term effects of exposure to them are not clear. These types of stories tend to appear within a broader negative context, so that readers are exposed to articles that remain highly negative overall. As we noted in chapter 2, this is problematic, because there is evidence to suggest that media consumers are unlikely to remember such stories as challenging negative stereotypes they may hold about Muslims (Mastro and Tukachinsky 2014). One study even found that readers developed *more* negative attitudes towards stereotyped groups portrayed as victims (Bos et al. 2016).

Religion and violence: Nuances and extensions

Among the remaining 16 topics, seven are related to elements already identified in the theoretical literature and analyzed in previous chapters: two are associated with religiosity, and another five revolve around violence, often linked to specific events. Table 6.3 shows these topics, along with the thematic category and additional information about topic words and corpus proportions, as in table 6.1.

Our topic modeling results reveal a distinction between religion articles primarily focused on Islam and those that contain a substantial concentration of words related to Christianity. These sets of articles differ significantly in their average tone, with those in the Islam topic at $-.80$, compared to those in the Christianity topic at .00 (exactly neutral). These topics map closely on to the religiosity variable we used in earlier analyses: 91% of articles with

[5] Articles that mention Islamophobia—which are also likely to identify Muslims as victims of discrimination or violence—only constitute 0.5% of our overall corpus.

Table 6.3 Religious and violence-related topics

Category/Topic	Top five words	%
Religion		6.3
Christianity	church, Christian, Catholic, pope, Christians	3.4
Islam	Muslims, mosque, Islam, Muslim, community	2.9
Violence		6.0
Killings/attacks	killed, police, attack, wounded, killing	2.2
Al Qaeda	Laden, Bin, Osama; Qaeda, al	2.1
Military	military, troops, forces, army, soldiers	1.7
Law and order		7.7
Judiciary	court, trial, judge, prosecutors, charges	4.0
Law enforcement	police, officials, intelligence, terrorist, information	3.7

Islam and 97% of articles with Christianity as the main topic are flagged for our religiosity variable. While it may seem puzzling that there are enough articles focusing on Christianity for it to emerge as its own topic in our corpus, we have encountered instances of such articles earlier. In chapter 2, for instance, an article about the history of Christianity in Iraq served to illustrate what the average tone for our corpus sounds like. In chapter 4, meanwhile, we saw that articles discussing the passing of Pope John Paul II produced a noticeable positive valence spike in 2005.

The average Islam-focused religious article is slightly less negative than our corpus average, but the Christianity-focused articles help explain why the broader religion category from our topic model is comparatively even less negative overall (the average tone is $-.37$), and thus why our religiosity variable was associated with more positive valences in the analyses in chapter 3. The religion theme is also one where right-leaning papers stand out from the other papers in our corpus: they are more than twice as likely to feature articles that focus on Islam and close to twice as likely to publish articles where Christianity is the dominant topic. Thus, while 2.6% of articles in the non-right-leaning papers in our corpus focus on Islam, this rises to 5.7% for right-leaning papers; the analogous figures for Christianity are 3.2% and 5.7%, respectively. This comparative emphasis on religion partially accounts for our finding in chapter 3 that the overall tone of articles in right-leaning papers is slightly less negative than the corpus average.[6]

[6] While right-leaning papers are slightly more negative in articles about Islam (average tone $-.88$, compared to $-.78$ for non-right-leaning papers), this is still less negative than the overall corpus

Violence, too, emerges as an important focus of coverage here, as it did in our earlier analyses. Table 6.3 lists three topics that are directly linked to violent events such as terrorism and military operations. As was the case for the religion topics, these violence topics map closely onto the violence variable we used in previous chapters. Among the top four topics whose articles are most likely to feature violence words are two that refer to a specific geographic location and two of the three listed under the violence theme in table 6.3: ISIS (fully 99% of all articles), Afghanistan (98%), al Qaeda (97%), and the military (95%). The first topic classified under violence, Killings/attacks, appears further down the list of topics featuring violence words, but still comes before all other thematic topics except for the Bush presidency topic (discussed later in this chapter, where "war" is one of the top words) and the law enforcement topic (which includes "terrorism"). In other words, our "violence" variable captures both topics that are specifically centered around violence and those where violence is a significant component.

The category listed next, law and order, links to violence both explicitly—"terrorist" is one of the top words for the law enforcement topic—and implicitly, by including many words associated with violence or its aftermath. For example, prominent words in the judiciary topic are "trial," "convicted," "guilty," "sentenced," and "prison." Moreover, many of these trials and convictions are directly linked to terrorism. Consider five randomly selected headlines from this category: "Terrorism Defendant Returns to Court"; "I Will Never Leave Guantanamo"; "Malaysia Ousted Deputy Premier Found Guilty of Corruption"; "Guilty Plea, Apology in 1982 Double Murder in Philadelphia"; and "Closing Arguments Begin in Trial of Men Charged in Plot to Destroy the Sears Tower."[7] The first and fifth are explicitly about terrorism, while the second is about an innocent man swept up in the US government's "war on terror." Of the remaining two, one is about nonpolitical violence. Only the third headline, about a major corruption trial in Malaysia, is not directly associated with violence. Even this article, however, contains violence, as the corruption verdict led to protests and necessitated

---

average, so more articles in this category helps make right-leaning papers less negative. For articles about Christianity, right-leaning papers are not only more likely to publish them, but they are also slightly more positive (+.04 vs. −.01), compounding the positive impact on overall average tone.

[7] Sources and dates, respectively: *Richmond Times-Dispatch*, February 16, 2006; *Boston Globe*, December 3, 2007; *New York Times*, April 14, 1999; *Philadelphia Inquirer*, March 17, 2011; *New York Times*, November 30, 2007.

"several hundred riot policemen" to protect the court building. In sum, the law and order category is suffused with reporting on violent events and their consequences.

Perhaps surprisingly, there are no topics uniquely related to extremism. Of course, we know that "extremism," "fundamentalism," "radicalism," etc. are mentioned frequently in our corpus. Yet they do not emerge as identifiable clusters of co-occurring words that constitute a separate topic. This is because references to extremism often appear in the context of an article that is about a specific location or about law and order. For example, 80% of articles where ISIS is the most prominent topic contain references to extremism, as do 75% of articles where the Egypt topic dominates and 74% of Pakistan-India articles. Among geographic locations, the topics least associated with extremism words are Bosnia (16%) and Kosovo (30%), which makes sense for two reasons. First, as we saw in chapter 4, extremism words became far more common after 9/11, while the conflicts in Bosnia and Kosovo largely ended before that time. Second, to reinforce the point we made earlier, in neither of these two conflicts were Muslim actors strongly associated with extremism. That being said, Muslims *were* victims of extremist actors on the other side of the conflict. The fact that the latter—Christians rather than Muslims—were not frequently referenced as being extremist offers an important reminder that the use of such terms is always a choice.

Finally, writing about extremism is another area where right-leaning papers stand out. The two topics most closely linked to extremist groups in our model, ISIS and al Qaeda, are about twice as likely to feature in the reporting of such papers. Al Qaeda is the main topic of 1.9% of the articles in our corpus published in non-right-leaning papers, compared to 4.0% of the articles published in right-leaning papers. For ISIS, the figures are 1.6% and 3.0%, respectively. As we saw in chapter 4, right-leaning papers tend to use words directly referencing extremism less than do other papers. However, we now see that they write about extremist groups much more than do other papers; they simply do it without explicitly using the keywords we flagged in our corpus as referencing extremism.[8]

---

[8] The same goes for tabloid papers, which are even more likely to write about al Qaeda and ISIS than is the case for right-leaning papers.

Underexplored topics: Sources of positivity?

Most scholarship about media portrayals of Muslims has focused on negative coverage. This is understandable, given the pervasive and intense negativity associated with Islam and Muslims that we and others have identified. However, using an inductive topic modeling approach reveals a set of articles that do not fit neatly within the main categories already identified by existing research. As Table 6.4 shows, more than a third of all articles in our corpus are predominantly associated with topics other than foreign coverage, violence, extremism, or religiosity. While none of these categories contains articles that are, on average, positive, each one tends to be more positive than the average article in our overall corpus.

Figure 6.5 displays the average valence of articles whose main topic falls into each of the broad themes we have identified, juxtaposed with the overall corpus valence. Unsurprisingly, articles about topics in the foreign, violence, and law and order themes are among the most negative, while those primarily grounded in religion are much more positive than average. The remaining five thematic categories are also more positive than the corpus average. Articles focused on politics have an overall average tone of −.79, which is still comparatively close to the corpus average. Yet those focused on family, business, culture, and education are substantially less negative than the average Muslim article in US newspapers.

Table 6.4 Other thematic topics

Category/Topic	Top five words	%
Politics		*13.1*
Trump campaign	Trump, Republican, Clinton, Obama, Donald	4.5
Bush presidency	Bush, administration, war, states, president	4.1
Rights	rights, law, human, women, court	2.5
Elections	elections, party, election, vote, political	2.1
Culture		*9.2*
Entertainment	book, story, film, world, life	7.6
Arts	museum, art, paintings, gallery, NW	1.6
Family	family, home, father, mother, children	*5.7*
Business	dollar, companies, money, business, oil	*4.4*
Education	school, students, schools, education, student	*2.6*

Note: Categories may not exactly match the sum of components due to rounding.

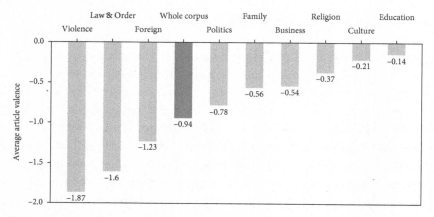

Figure 6.5 Average article valence by topic theme

Interestingly, these additional categories also tend to contain topics that are among those most likely to contain words we flagged for our "value clash" variable. Even though the fit is imperfect, over 70% of all articles associated with the family, education, and the two culture topics contain such words.[9] This may help account for some of the relative positivity linked to stories tagged for our value-clash feature. The topic that most closely approximates the literature's notion of a value clash, however, is that of "rights" in the politics category. As the word cloud in figure 6.6 shows, this topic focuses on human, civil, religious, and constitutional rights, with an emphasis on women and freedom. Yet because the focus here is as much on rights themselves as it is on the people whose rights might be in question, our value-clash variable is "only" flagged in 58% of the articles in this category, well behind its levels in the family, education, and culture categories.

Education articles are the most positive thematic category in our Muslim corpus, with an average valence of −.14, even if only 2.6% of all articles have education as their main topic. Rather than focusing on incompatible approaches to raising and educating children, as existing scholarship might suggest, these articles cover a much wider array of education-related stories, as this random sample of five headlines indicates: "South Africa Gives Denver Visitors Valuable Lessons"; "In Season of Protest, Haverford Speaker Is the Latest to Bow Out"; "Asians Promote Political Power"; "Board

---

[9] The next topic most strongly associated with value-clash words is Christianity, for which fewer than 60% of all articles contain such words.

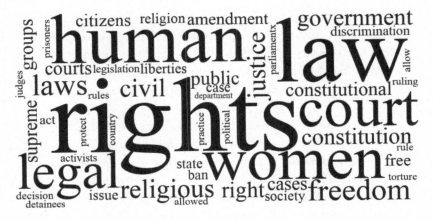

Figure 6.6 Word cloud for the "rights" topic

Votes to Require Recitation of Pledge at Public Schools"; and "Nomads Give Children a Chance at Settled Life."[10] None of these articles are about clashing approaches to education; indeed, none are specifically about education and Islam. On the other hand, all address the value and importance of education, helping explain the comparatively positive average tone of articles in this topic.

While education is the least negative of our categories, it is not the most positive individual topic; that distinction belongs to the arts. As a small subset of the culture theme, the 1.6% of all articles most strongly associated with the arts topic are the most positive articles in our Muslim corpus. Indeed, arts is the only topic whose average valence is well above neutral, at +.56.[11] Articles where this topic is central often feature listings of museum and gallery exhibits, along with discussions of the same. The language in such articles is generally quite positive. Consider this description of an exhibit at New York's Metropolitan Museum of Art:

> Sultans of Deccan India, 1500–1700, Opulence and Fantasy, through July 26. This beautiful, evocative exhibition sheds new light on the miniature paintings, calligraphies, luxurious metalwork and breathtaking jewels

[10] *Denver Post*, November 8, 1998; *New York Times*, May 14, 2014; *San Jose Mercury News*, November 5, 2002; *New York Times*, October 18, 2001; *USA Today*, May 8, 2007.

[11] The Christianity topic is the second most positive. As we saw earlier, its average valence is right at the neutral point (.00).

that remain from the succession of cosmopolitan Muslim kingdoms and their turbulent 200-year golden age on the Deccan Plateau of south-central India. It also presents the paintings in new ways. Most strikingly, they are relieved of the white mats favored by Western museums and collections. Their decorative borders and patterned album pages are a revelation.[12]

Naturally, there are articles in this topic with a negative tone. Yet even these often contain positive segments. Consider, for example, an article titled "Triage for Treasures after a Bomb Blast," published in the *New York Times* on February 1, 2014. The article describes the aftermath of a truck bomb aimed at Cairo's police headquarters, which also hit the Museum of Islamic Art. While negative about the bomb and the damage to the art, the article is simultaneously very positive about the art itself: "precious glass . . . from exquisite medieval lamps," "beautiful brass details, marble plaques and wood inlays from some of the city's most splendid mosques," "exquisite pieces of woodwork that stayed together simply because the pieces fit so perfectly," and so on. The article quotes the Islamic art historian Shahira Mehrez on the museum's collection: "Not only are there beautiful artifacts . . . but there's also the first manifestation of the arabesque design, the first dated lusterware, the first geometric star pattern. These objects are invaluable not just for their unique artistic value, but as a documentary of artistic development of the Islamic world." Even though this article's overall valence is negative, such glowing descriptions convey an undeniable positivity associated with Islamic art.

Overall, articles in these more positive categories of family, culture, and education offer powerful testimony that shared values—an appreciation of the beauty of art, the importance of family, and the value of education—are at the heart of more positive coverage of Muslims and Islam. The fact that these values are associated with many of the same words and ideas that are sometimes highlighted as markers of a "value clash" helps explain why our values variable was associated with comparatively more positive coverage in chapter 3. In addition, it points to a way that newspapers, and the journalists who produce their content, can work to balance the negative coverage associated with foreign, violence, and law and order topics.

[12] *New York Times*, July 17, 2015.

Conclusions

This final empirical chapter lets the articles in our corpus speak for themselves, to show the range of different topics they cover. Some of these were expected; some less so. Together, they underscore that although it sometimes appears that media coverage of Muslims and Islam is always negative in the same way, or that readers encounter only one type of story, there is in fact substantial variation across topics. For example, even within a theme we captured with a single variable in earlier chapters—foreign locations—we identified important variations by type of location. Specifically, we showed that the words most strongly associated with Muslims and Islam vary considerably depending on the type of context. In particular, reporting on locations where Muslims have been victims of systematic political violence features many more words identifying them as victims and also simply as people: "unarmed," "civilians," etc.

Other results similarly added nuance and provided new insights to our findings in previous chapters. We found that articles about religiosity can be divided into two topics: Christianity and Islam. Both are more positive, on average, than the overall corpus, but the former is especially so. Moreover, right-leaning papers are comparatively much more likely to publish articles on both of these topics. Articles about violence include both those about political violence and those about "regular" criminal violence. In addition, many articles not directly about violence are about its aftermath in the legal system. Extremism did not emerge as a separate topic, because it tends to be linked to specific contexts and locations. Here, too, right-leaning papers stand out: while they use extremism words less often than do other papers, they are much more likely to write about extremist groups such as al Qaeda and ISIS.

Finally, the topic model highlighted a number of topics that are comparatively much less negative: the arts and education, but also family, business, and entertainment. Articles that focus on these topics are often about values that are shared across cultures instead of those leading to perceived clashes. Reporting on these topics thus has the greatest potential to mitigate the strongly negative coverage frequently associated with Muslims and Islam more generally.

7

Conclusions and extensions

Islamophobia, constructing boundaries, and tone-checking the media

The media play a central role in helping people understand the wider world. They are a key source of information about groups, events, places, and topics with which we have limited contact in our daily lives. In the United States and in other Western societies, media representations shape attitudes toward Muslims and Islam, which in turn have been shown to influence policy preferences and even individual actions. Feeling warmly toward a group encourages trust and cooperation. Conversely, negative attitudes can lead to aversion, discrimination, or even hate crimes. Negative media coverage also affects Muslims themselves, undermining young people's identification as American and their trust in government. For all of these reasons, it is vital to develop a thorough understanding of how such a highly stigmatized group is represented in the American and international media.

In this chapter, we briefly summarize the main findings of our study. We then explore how our methods can help readers grasp not only American media representations of Muslims, but those of many more groups in a wide variety of locations as well. In this book, for example, we have discussed US newspaper coverage of Catholics, Jews, Hindus, African Americans, Latinos, Mormons and atheists, as well as British, Canadian, Australian, and Global South newspaper coverage of Muslims. As we have demonstrated, our approach facilitates the study of media portrayals of *any* group in virtually *any* geographic location, and especially comparative studies across groups and locations.

We conclude our investigation by broadening our lens to examine three extensions to our findings. First, we assess the degree of overt Islamophobia in newspapers. Is the pervasive and enduring negativity we identify a function of sweeping hostility toward Islam and Muslims as a whole? We then reflect on how the media influence perceived social boundaries even in the

Covering Muslims. Erik Bleich and A. Maurits van der Veen, Oxford University Press. © Oxford University Press 2022.
DOI: 10.1093/oso/9780197611715.003.0007

absence of outright Islamophobia. How might the newspaper reporting we investigate—and the media more broadly—lead to the stigmatization of Muslims and other marginalized groups, even if there is no conscious intent by journalists to reinforce social boundaries or hierarchies? Finally, we emphasize how important it is for journalists and citizens alike to tone-check the media. Articles touching on Muslims are intensely negative. Being aware of that fact can help raise consciousness among readers of their reactions and interpretations not only of Muslims, but of all marginalized groups in our societies.

What we have learned

Our principal finding bears emphasizing once more: newspaper articles that mention Muslims or Islam are overwhelmingly negative. The vast majority of Muslim articles are more negative than the average article in US newspapers. And Muslim articles are not just a little bit negative, they are intensely negative. The average Muslim story is more negative than over 84% of all articles published in a large representative sample drawn from a wide variety of American outlets. Muslim articles are negative not just with respect to this random sample, but also compared to those about other world religious groups like Catholics, Jews, and Hindus, and compared to domestic outgroups such as African Americans, Latinos, Mormons, and atheists.

Some skeptics might wonder if such intense negativity is natural, given the amount of Islamist terrorism that has occurred in the early 21st century. If that is the case, the prevalence of stories linked to extremist actions might be a straightforward explanation for the observed negativity. In a similar vein, given that Muslims are the predominant population in a number of foreign conflict zones, stories about war, rebellion, or other forms of violence could also generate substantial negativity for reasons simply related to newsworthiness.

Our analysis shows that articles touching on violent conflict or extremism, and those set uniquely in a foreign location, do account for a significant portion of the negativity in articles touching on Muslims or Islam. Taken together, over 80% of all articles are related to one or more of these factors. Even so, articles *not* associated with these factors are *still* negative. They are negative even compared to our pool of representative US newspaper articles that *do* contain stories set exclusively in foreign locations, that cover conflict, and that cover terrorism and extremism. Stories about Muslims unrelated to these highly negative variables are also substantially more negative than comparable stories about Catholics, Jews, or Hindus.

Other factors commonly associated with negativity also cannot explain our findings. Coverage in tabloids is indeed notably more negative, on average, than are stories published in broadsheets. But articles in right-leaning newspapers, those that touch on religious practices, and even those that mention words related to a supposed clash of values over women's or LGBTQ+ rights are not associated with more negativity than the average Muslim article. In other words, there is something particular about how the media cover Muslims. The negativity cannot easily be explained away as a function of the media simply reporting newsworthy stories. In short, it is impossible to account for the extent of negativity in Muslim articles through any obvious explanation.

Looking at change over time, we found that 9/11 affected the amount and the topics of coverage more than the tone of coverage. There was an enormous spike in the number of articles in the wake of that day's tragedy, and the American media have maintained a higher baseline level of coverage of Muslims and Islam in the post-9/11 era. They have also covered terrorism and extremism to a greater extent than in the pre-9/11 years. Yet the average tone in the years before and after 2001 has been essentially the same. In general, terrorist acts and other conflict-laden events typically lead to a short-term increase in negativity, but article valence reverts to previous levels before long. Significantly, positive events have a much smaller effect on article amounts and tone. Events thus matter for coverage, but they have a bigger effect on the quantity of articles than on their tone, and these effects tend to fade fairly quickly rather than to endure.

As a global power, the United States has distinctive interactions with Muslim countries around the world, yet US coverage of Muslims is not unique. Examining a similarly diverse array of newspapers in Britain, Canada, and Australia reveals common patterns in the quantity, tone, and themes of coverage. Reporting on Muslims and Islam rose following 9/11; it is just as negative—if not more so—in those three countries as in the United States; and there is a significant presence of stories about foreign locations, violence, and extremism. At the same time, as we have shown, this is an editorial choice in these countries rather than an outcome dictated by world events. Our probe into six newspapers drawn from South Asia, Southeast Asia, and Africa revealed much less attention to these negative topics. The average Muslim articles in most of these newspapers were simply much less negative than their counterparts in the Anglophone North countries. There is thus no global newspaper discourse about Muslims and Islam that can be accounted for by the inherent newsworthiness of negative stories.

Finally, we use an inductive topic modeling approach to reveal nuances in coverage of Muslims in US newspapers that were not previously known. This strategy allows us to identify more precisely the proportion of articles focused primarily on foreign locations, as well as variation in the countries that have been the subject of coverage. In particular, we demonstrate that a very small percentage of articles revolve principally around locations where Muslims are the victims of violence; we also show that those articles are still extremely negative, even if their negativity is less likely to focus on Muslims as perpetrators of violence. Our topic modeling analysis also reveals that over a third of all articles about Muslims focus on themes not previously highlighted by researchers. Several of these themes—most notably education and culture—are associated with some of the least negative coverage of Muslims that we have identified. While articles heavily loaded for these topics are a small percentage of all coverage of Muslims, they highlight the fact that story selection is itself a choice that journalists make as they assemble their news coverage every day.

What our approach contributes

Our book provides a new and independent way to confirm that media coverage of Muslims is negative, but our approach allows us to do much more than that. The system we develop enables us to say not only that coverage is negative on the whole, but also exactly how negative (or positive) each individual article is relative to the average tone of a representative sample of American newspaper articles. For the first time, scholars and citizens can refer to a common baseline for comparing articles about any group or topic.

We provide precise measures of the negativity inherent in Muslim articles in a way that has not been possible before, and trace the ebbs and flows of this negativity across time measured in years, months, or even day-by-day. We compare coverage of Muslims to that of world religious groups such as Catholics, Jews, or Hindus, and to domestic identity groups like African Americans, Latinos, Mormons and atheists. In other work, we have applied the same scale and approach to analyze coverage of additional groups, such as Asian Americans, Native Americans, and UK atheists (Media Portrayals of Minorities Project 2019, 2020, 2021; van der Veen and Bleich 2021a), as well as US media coverage of Africa (Bleich et al. 2020). Using this common tool for media analysis, we are able to examine coverage of the widest array of groups, geographic locations, or even topics such as sexual harassment, freedom of speech, or mass shootings, all compared against the same common benchmark.[1]

Our approach relies on a combination of deductive and inductive analysis. Together, these provide insights into the nearly 1.7 million articles we assembled for this book. In the case of our Muslim corpus, deductive analysis offers support for theories of the media that emphasize the negativity that is common in foreign coverage, the appeal of covering violence, the dynamics surrounding "media storms," and the differences between tabloid and broadsheet publications. It allows us to specify with precision which factors theorized to be linked to negative coverage of Muslims are in fact associated with the greatest degree of negativity—and which are far less likely to be associated with strong negativity than commonly presumed. Our inductive approach helps us identify elements present in the coverage that were previously seldom recognized, and enables us to pinpoint those rare instances in which coverage of Muslims and Islam is likely to be positive. We supplement these approaches by human analysis of samples of our texts to make sure that real readers would interpret our articles in ways that are consistent with our big-data conclusions.

Our methods are powerful, but perhaps more importantly, they are replicable. Any researcher that has access to a newspaper database can specify search terms, download articles, and use the same approach we use to examine coverage of their topic. We base our analysis on newspapers because they produce a large quantity of texts about a variety of topics on a daily basis, but the logic of our approach can be extended to investigate television or radio transcripts, social media data, and online news platforms. Given that newspapers tend to be factually rather than emotionally oriented (Nisbet, Ostman, and Shanahan 2009, 174–76), we believe that our findings of significant negativity are likely to be amplified on other platforms, a hypothesis that future research can explore. Crucially, by providing a common metric against which the tone of texts can be gauged, our method enables researchers to understand how any individual medium portrays a topic relative to all the other

---

[1] See mediaandminorities.org.

media. While our approach certainly does not answer every question media researchers may have, it allows for a vastly richer understanding of how the media represent the widest variety of groups, regions, and topics.

Islamophobia and constructing boundaries

The empirical findings presented in this book raise important questions about whether American newspapers are influenced by and perhaps even help foster Islamophobia. Scholars have long asserted that the media convey substantial and overt anti-Muslim sentiment (Mortimer 1981; Runnymede Trust 1997; Said 1997; Ahmed and Matthes 2017). Islamophobia in its clearest form involves "indiscriminate negative attitudes or emotions directed at Islam or Muslims" (Bleich 2011, 1585). This definition captures sweeping generalizations that denigrate the entire faith or group, but excludes targeted critiques of specific aspects of Islam or of individuals or subsets of the Muslim population. Fortunately, we find little evidence of overt Islamophobia in the US or wider Anglophone press. Some tabloids stoke emotions to sell newspapers, but only the rare newspaper article explicitly condemns Islam or Muslims as a whole. Moreover, a portion of the negativity present in our articles involves stories of Muslims as victims of attacks, natural disasters, wars, or poverty. Coverage of Bosnia and Kosovo in the 1990s and more recent stories about Myanmar's Rohingya and China's Uighurs contain many negative words, but do not attribute the negativity to Muslims—quite the opposite.

Still, the near relentlessness of negative words in close proximity to Muslims and Islam in American, British, Canadian, and Australian newspapers is cause for concern. Whether or not journalists intend to associate Muslims with negativity, media consumers are bombarded with negative words almost whenever they read the words "Muslims" or "Islam." This is not part of any grand plan. Reporters write stories day-by-day, and editors review those stories with an eye to improving their quality. Our own interactions with journalists suggest that they are sometimes harried and may rely on internalized assumptions when pressed by a deadline, but most are simply trying to get today's story right. There is no coordinated plan to perpetuate negative images of Muslims.

At the same time, by providing a long-term overview of coverage, our research suggests that American journalists and their Anglophone press counterparts are communicating a great deal of negativity in stories that touch on Islam or Muslims. Moreover, our comparison to newspapers in South Asia, Southeast Asia, and Africa reveals that story choice is not entirely dictated by world events. The balance of US coverage tilts toward topics that associate Muslims with violence and extremism, a finding that is consistent with research demonstrating that the media are disproportionately drawn to report expressions of fear and anger conveyed by anti-Muslim fringe organizations (Bail 2012). The negativity conveyed by US newspapers is substantially stronger than that communicated by the *Times of India*, for example, even though India has experienced domestic terrorism and is much closer to the geographic base of Islamist radicals. Moreover, taking American newspapers on their own terms, there is still a "Muslim penalty" inherent in their reporting—articles not mentioning violence or extremism and not set in foreign locations are more negative when they touch on Muslims than when they cover Catholics, Jews, or Hindus.

This means that even if there is not much overt Islamophobia in American newspapers, the media still play a central role in defining the presumptively meaningful differences between "us" and "them." Anthropologists, sociologists, and social psychologists have aptly described the symbolic and social boundaries that distinguish ingroups and outgroups within our societies (Barth 1969; Lamont and Molnár 2002; Dovidio and Gaertner 2010). They highlight the significance of the conscious or unconscious defining, reinforcing, or effacing of divisions between groups. Studies of "aversive racism" emphasize the effect that subtle, repeated cues can have on attitudes and actions even of individuals who consider themselves egalitarian and not prejudiced (Dovidio, Gaertner, and Pearson 2017). Several prominent scholars have focused particular attention on how Muslims are excluded through processes like these, especially in European countries (Zolberg and Long 1999; Alba 2005). We view the media as a key site of boundary-making, and one that affects Muslims not only in Europe, but also in North America and Australia, and quite likely across the entire Global North. If the "Muslim penalty" is not a function of conscious Islamophobia, it may nonetheless both reflect and contribute to subconscious forms of aversive racism.

The media emphasize the features of Muslims and Islam that resonate with the public, both through their story selection and through their choice of words. At times, this is because journalists explicitly connect Muslims or Islam to foreign locations, conflict, or extremism when they need not do so. One prominent example is the frequent use by American newspapers of the term "Islamic State," instead of alternatives such as IS, ISIS, ISIL, or Daesh/ Da'ish. This distinction may strike some as superficial. Yet granting Abu Bakr al-Baghdadi the status to speak on behalf of an "Islamic" state was both gratuitous and prejudicial, when ISIS represented far less than 1% of the global Muslim population. United Nations Secretary-General Ban Ki-moon (2014) noted that it was roundly condemned for its name: "As Muslim leaders around the world have said, groups like ISIL—or Da'ish—have nothing to do with Islam, and they certainly do not represent a state. They should more fittingly be called the 'Un-Islamic Non-State.'"

At other times, story selection simply fits a well-worn narrative of a clash of civilizations. One of the sentences we cite in chapter 3, for example, reads: "But their differences have implications for all the big issues the West grapples with in considering the Muslim world."[2] This suggests that there are "big issues" between "the West" and "the Muslim world," as if sweeping generalizations about billions of people living in dozens of countries could be accurate or insightful. As is true for the members of any large religion, Muslims vary widely in their views on faith, politics, and values, just as Muslim-majority countries differ significantly in levels of political violence, social inequality, and political openness (Fish 2011). Terms like "the Muslim world" diminish these complexities and contribute to simplistic views of Muslims.

Boundary-making can also happen even in spite of sympathetic coverage. Muslims often explicitly reject violence and are themselves victims of discrimination or attacks. Reporting these stories is, of course, critical. The *New York Times*, for example, ran the article we quoted in chapter 3 about Hunter College senior Ferida Osman in the wake of the November 2015 Paris attacks.[3] It focused on Muslims coping with the stress of an Islamophobic backlash. At the same time, these stories implicitly reinforce a notion that Muslims are at their most newsworthy in the context of violence. The media in the United States and elsewhere simply run relatively fewer stories about the arts, about Muslims contributing to their local communities, or about family life than they do about violence. Harkening back to the epigram that opened chapter 1, comedian Maz Jobrani is right: there are almost no stories about Muslims simply "baking cookies," even though US

[2] *New York Times*, April 27, 2008.
[3] *New York Times*, November 25, 2015.

newspapers commonly write about festivals, cultural contributions, and religious celebrations when they touch on other groups, such as Hindus.

Through their choices, media outlets thus help define and reinforce boundaries that distinguish Muslims and Islam as culturally different and distant, and often associated with conflict or violence. Given that most people in the United States do not interact with Muslims on a daily basis, this coverage undoubtedly contributes to the startling survey results we reported in our opening chapter: 50% of respondents believe Islam is not part of mainstream American society, and over 40% agree that there is a "natural conflict" between Islam and democracy, and that Islam encourages violence more than other religions. These beliefs are understandable given the prevalence of an oversimplified media portrayal of Muslims that regularly associates them with violence. The media help draw and reinforce boundaries that can lead not only to aversion or to subtle discrimination, but also to anti-Muslim hate crimes against Ferida Osman or against the many other victims tracked by civil society groups or FBI data (Kishi 2017; FBI 2019; CAIR, n.d.; New America, n.d.).

Tone-checking the media

Most media consumers have learned to be skeptical of perspectives conveyed via social media outlets that spread half-truths, rumors, or extreme interpretations based on questionable facts or outright falsehoods. They also know that outlets like Fox News are hardly "fair and balanced," and that their left-leaning counterparts such as MSNBC present the world filtered through an ideological lens. But many people look to major US newspapers for impartial information. Readers are likely to think of them as among the most even-handed, fact-based sources of news available.

Yet our research shows that US newspapers—and those in other countries—systematically associate some groups with negativity. Journalists may agree that Muslims are vulnerable outgroups in national or global settings, and some openly regret that stories about Islam (too) often contain references to terrorism.[4] Yet even if the media do not set out to stigmatize

---

[4] The tendency of the media to inject mentions of terrorism into stories about Muslims and Islam that otherwise have nothing to do with terrorism has been noted by a number of journalists, as we saw earlier (Haberman 2004; Walsh 2016).

Muslims, as we showed in chapter 4, words like "radical," "fundamentalist," "militant," and "extremist" are strongly linked to Muslims and Islam in US newspapers. It is therefore hardly surprising that when Americans were asked for one-word impressions of Islam, three of the top responses were "fanatic," "radical," and "terror" (Pew Research Center 2007).

What might journalists do differently? Clearly, they cannot simply stop reporting negative stories associated with Muslims and Islam, nor should they. Violent extremism and Islamophobic incidents are inherently newsworthy. At the same time, media outlets *can* pay much closer attention to the types of articles they run and to the word selection within them. They can consciously decrease the habitual mentions of terrorism or extremism that rose dramatically following 9/11, as well as think pieces that offer sweeping generalizations about the Muslim world. They can ramp up coverage of Muslims in domestic settings, in particular in stories about the arts, entertainment, sports, education, economics, and interfaith cooperation. These are all topics linked with substantially less negativity than the average Muslim article, and provide a fuller perspective on Muslims and Islam both within the United States and around the world.

Ultimately, though, the media as an institution is unlikely to change dramatically or suddenly. As media consumers, however, readers, viewers, and listeners can actively become more conscious of media tone. Tone-checking as we consume media is especially important when it comes to stories about marginalized communities. What are the topics and specific words most commonly associated with Muslims, Jews, African Americans, Latinos, or any other group that faces stigmatization? What is the tone of articles, television reports, radio shows, or social media posts touching on these communities? What are the words or concepts that we most naturally connect with different groups of people, social movements, neighborhoods, or regions of the country or world, and how have the media influenced those associations?

Decades of research reveal that implicit biases affect decision-making (Dovidio, Gaertner, and Pearson 2017). Overcoming these biases is difficult, but developing the conscious habit of tone-checking the media can help limit the subconscious effect of the negativity on our attitudes and assumptions. Scholarship on media literacy suggests that more positive, counter-stereotypical portrayals of Muslims by journalists, especially when combined with readers becoming increasingly conscious of the inherent negativity conveyed by the media, may help reduce stigmatization (Scharrer and Ramasubramanian 2015). As our research has shown, most individuals can discern which texts are more positive or negative, even when tone differences are relatively small. Recognizing the relative tone of reporting on marginalized groups is possible, and counteracting it through conscious processing is critical, given the dramatic negativity conveyed by major US newspapers. We hope that our analysis encourages journalists and readers alike to recognize how Muslims and marginalized groups are portrayed, and to understand how we can all be more proactive in promoting equality, respect, and dignity for everyone in our societies.

Appendix

This appendix is divided into two main parts. Part I discusses the corpora we use and the generation of variables for each text in each corpus. This part is divided into three subsections. The first outlines the construction of the various corpora. Next, we discuss our sentiment analysis method, including its validation. The third section elaborates on our geocoding approach. Part II of the appendix supplies additional data for the analyses conducted in chapters 2–6, along with some further information about our topic modeling approach.

Corpus collection and methodology

I.A. Corpus creation

All of our corpora were created by manually downloading articles from one of three online databases: LexisNexis Academic (now Nexis Uni), Factiva, and ProQuest. Here we discuss, in turn, the data collection process for the representative corpora, the American group corpora, and the Muslim corpora from other countries.

Representative corpus—United States

For the representative corpus, we aimed to assemble a random selection of newspaper articles from the same sources we use for our substantive corpora. Unfortunately, most online databases do not offer the option to select a random sample of articles. To get a representative set of articles through a directed search, we undertook the following steps:

1. We selected three dates at random per calendar year, making sure to include at least one from each half year (first and second six months of the year). We began by selecting two random dates in each calendar year. For years in which those two dates fell within the same half of the year (January–June or July–December), we selected the third randomly from the other half. For all other years, the third date was selected randomly from the whole year. A chronological listing of all selected dates appears in table I.A.1. Each day of the week is represented (although Sundays appear only three times among the 60 dates).
2. To approximate a random sampling, we searched for words that do not have any valence themselves, under the assumption that the valence distribution across articles containing those words will mirror that of the distribution across all articles. Specifically, we first selected from the labMT lexicon (see lexicon descriptions below) those words with a valence exactly at the midpoint of the lexicon's scale. From those, we chose only those that are also among the 4,000 most common words in the English language. This produced a list of 18 words: because, per, standard, situation, carbon, assess, throw, liver, plain, supervisor, something, throat, whereas, boot, fourth, stir, price, and odds. LexisNexis/Nexis Uni does not permit a search for the word "because," leaving us with 17 words. There is no reason to believe that articles in which these words appear are systematically biased toward positive or negative valences, nor that they are more or less distant from neutrality (cf. van der Veen and Bleich 2021b)

The final column in table I.A.3 shows the breakdown by newspaper of the number of articles in the representative sample.

Table I.A.1 Publication dates of articles in representative corpus

1996/2/27	1996/3/25	1996/12/9	2006/2/24	2006/8/24	2006/10/5
1997/1/30	1997/8/18	1997/12/3	2007/2/24	2007/6/5	2007/10/12
1998/6/5	1998/9/13	1998/10/27	2008/6/2	2008/7/2	2008/8/12
1999/3/11	1999/3/17	1999/9/9	2009/5/18	2009/7/3	2009/10/27
2000/3/29	2000/5/1	2000/10/16	2010/1/6	2010/5/25	2010/9/18
2001/4/4	2001/10/3	2001/11/16	2011/5/14	2011/7/27	2011/8/7
2002/3/21	2002/7/14	2002/8/21	2012/3/1	2012/4/28	2012/8/3
2003/1/22	2003/2/15	2003/12/20	2013/3/1	2013/4/29	2013/12/16
2004/5/14	2004/8/24	2004/12/18	2014/1/14	2014/3/13	2014/12/17
2005/3/5	2005/5/9	2005/7/2	2015/3/26	2015/5/25	2015/7/28

Representative corpus—Britain, Canada, Australia

In chapter 5, we note that we calibrated the British, Canadian, and Australian corpora not only against the main (US) representative corpus, but also against their own national representative corpora. These corpora were collected using the same process described earlier for the United States, and from the same sets of newspapers we use for our Muslim corpora for each country. Their respective sizes were 59,404 (Britain), 22,860 (Canada), and 24,114 (Australia) articles.

Group corpora—United States

For the substantive corpora, we selected all articles that met search criteria presented in table I.A.2 (the wildcard character * indicates we accepted any word that began with the specified letters).

For the Muslim corpus, we filtered out any articles that were captured only because they included Islamabad (a city), Islamorada (an island), or the proper names Islami or al-Islam. The search criteria for Jews are slightly more complex because of the need to avoid accidentally capturing references to jewelry, in particular. For the Mormon corpus, we filtered out any references to the last name Mormont, associated with some characters in the *Game of Thrones* books and movies.

Table I.A.2 Search criteria

Muslim	muslim* or moslem* or islam*
Catholic	catholic*
Jew	jew or jews or jewish* or jewry or judai* or jewess*
Hindu	hindu*
African American	african-american* or african american*
Latino	latino* or latina* or latinx* or hispanic*
Mormon	mormon*
Atheist	atheis*

Table I.A.3 Article counts by paper and group: Part 1

Source	Muslim	Catholic	Jewish	Hindu	Representative
Arizona Republic	4,923	39,529	5,770	446	3,041
Atlanta Journal-Constitution	10,737	15,834	14,875	1,197	3,608
Boston Globe	17,096	31,948	20,796	1,417	2,982
Daily News (New York)	9,477	10,483	15,736	543	2,368
Denver Post	6,104	12,173	7,760	484	1,904
Las Vegas Review-Journal	2,324	7,994	4,943	240	1,318
New York Post	9,315	6,422	11,932	375	2,089
New York Times	59,693	40,039	66,624	5,850	5,799
Philadelphia Daily News	3,980	10,423	3,648	182	1,250
Philadelphia Inquirer	15,317	41,459	15,691	995	2,571
Richmond Times Dispatch	6,412	11,511	6,404	450	2,131
San Jose Mercury News	13,752	21,143	11,827	1,480	3,481
Star-Tribune (Minneapolis)	4,978	11,065	6,438	583	1,603
Tampa Bay Times	11,094	47,456	11,913	938	3,237
USA Today	8,749	6,536	5,230	476	1,993
Wall Street Journal	23,581	7,489	10,441	1,588	3,437
Washington Post	49,431	43,558	36,426	3,222	5,471
Total	256,963	365,062	256,454	20,466	48,283

In addition, we applied two deduplication filters to the articles we collected. First, if two (or more) articles were published on the same date and were identical for the first 250 characters, we kept only the article processed first. This will not capture duplicates where, for instance, the first sentence is prefixed by a single word (e.g., "today") but the article is otherwise identical. The second deduplication filter, accordingly, uses Levenshtein string comparison (which measures how many characters need to be changed to go from one text string to another) to filter out those articles whose first 300 characters are exceedingly similar. Manual verification of both deduplication filters established that both functioned as intended. Table I.A.3 lists the final article counts by newspaper across the four substantive corpora used in the first part of chapter 3, as well as the representative corpus. Newspapers are listed in alphabetical order.

Table I.A.4 lists the tallies for the second set of four groups considered in chapter 3. For the African American and Latino corpora, we draw only from the four national newspapers in our sample, in order to keep corpus size manageable. For the other two groups, we draw on the same set of newspapers as for our main Muslim corpus, with the exception of the *Denver Post*, which as of 2020 was no longer available through any of the electronic databases we had access to.

We code newspapers as right-leaning if they endorsed Republican candidates four or five times during the five presidential election cycles included in our corpus. The four

Table I.A.4 Article counts by paper and group: Part 2

Source	African American	Latino	Mormon	Atheist
Arizona Republic			2,990	416
Atlanta Journal-Constitution			936	734
Boston Globe			1,638	1,022
Daily News (New York)			652	269
Las Vegas Review-Journal			1,874	260
New York Post			675	292
New York Times	25,027	27,252	3,365	2,462
Philadelphia Daily News			334	227
Philadelphia Inquirer			660	592
Richmond Times Dispatch			618	490
San Jose Mercury News			1,105	608
Star-Tribune (Minneapolis)			410	386
Tampa Bay Times			909	745
USA Today	6,970	6,011	886	509
Wall Street Journal	6,254	7,200	846	653
Washington Post	39,374	25,494	2,611	1,740
Total	77,625	65,957	20,510	11,405

papers in question are the *Arizona Republic*, *Las Vegas Review-Journal*, *Richmond Times-Dispatch*, and *New York Post*.[1] The United States does not have a major tabloid newspaper presence—supermarket tabloids do not qualify as newspapers—but our corpus nonetheless contains three tabloid titles: the New York *Daily News*, the *New York Post*, and the *Philadelphia Daily News*.

Muslim corpora—Britain, Canada, Australia

The Muslim corpora for the cross-national comparison in chapter 5 were generated in the same way as the US corpus: we used the same search strings, processing, and deduplication filters. For Britain, we selected the major nationwide papers, producing a corpus comparable in size to the US corpus. The other two countries have smaller populations, and accordingly also smaller media markets. Here we selected the

[1] The *Wall Street Journal*, often seen as a right-leaning paper, does not generally endorse presidential candidates; to be consistent with our coding rule, we do not classify it as right-wing. However, including the *Wall Street Journal* as a right-leaning paper makes no substantive difference in our results.

Table I.A.5 Article counts by paper: Britain

Source	Right-leaning	Tabloid	Count
Daily Mail & Mail on Sunday	√	√	19,611
Daily Record & Sunday Mail		√	8,184
Daily Star & Sunday Star	√	√	7,181
Daily Telegraph & Sunday Telegraph	√		32,229
Evening Standard		√	13,883
Express & Sunday Express	√	√	11,422
Financial Times			30,586
Guardian			48,210
i (published by the *Independent*)			6,570
Independent			39,717
Mirror & Sunday Mirror		√	16,058
News of the World	√	√	1,430
Observer			9,457
People		√	1,634
Sun	√	√	17,526
Times & Sunday Times	√		54,739
Total			318,437

six top-circulation papers available on LexisNexis. These newspapers were classified as right-leaning based on published information and consultation with country experts, and as tabloids based on their traditional publication format.[2] Tables I.A.5, I.A.6, and I.A.7 display the article counts by source in each country.

Table I.A.6 Article counts by paper: Canada

Source	Right-leaning	Tabloid	Count
Gazette			25,052
Globe and Mail			25,764
National Post	√		24,067
Toronto Star			29,006
Vancouver Province	√	√	6,276
Vancouver Sun			11,423
Total			121,588

[2] For Australia, we relied in part on Gans and Leigh (2011).

Table I.A.7 Article counts by paper: Australia

Source	Right-leaning	Tabloid	Count
The Age & Sunday Age			19,218
Courier Mail & Sunday Mail	√	√	17,058
Daily Telegraph & Sunday Telegraph	√	√	21,591
Herald Sun & Sunday Herald Sun		√	15,198
Sun-Herald			1,860
Sydney Morning Herald			10,816
West Australian	√	√	2,678
Total			88,419

Muslim corpora—Global South (India, Kenya, Malaysia, Nigeria, Pakistan, Singapore)

The Muslim corpora for the cross-national comparison of Global South papers in chapter 5 were generated in the same way as the US corpus: we used the same search strings, processing, and deduplication filters. For each country, we selected the highest-circulation or most-sold English-language paper, and downloaded articles for the years 2015–2019. Table I.A.8 displays article counts by paper and country.

Table I.A.8 Article counts by paper and country: Global South

Country	Source	Count
India	*Times of India*	28,679
Kenya	*Daily Nation & Sunday Nation*	4,396
Malaysia	*New Straits Times*	9,842
Nigeria	*Sun*	5,540
Pakistan	*Dawn*	23,762
Singapore	*Straits Times*	7,178
Total		79,397

Text preprocessing

Each of the corpora used in the book was subjected to the same preprocessing steps. We took the title (headline) and text body of each article and combined them to form the raw text. Next, we performed a number of basic cleaning operations on each text. We converted sentence break punctuation such as question marks or exclamation points to periods; other forms of punctuation, such as commas, parentheses, etc., as well as special characters, were surrounded by spaces to set them off from words they might be attached to. Periods not marking sentence breaks (such as Mr., or U.S.) as well as possessives (the 's in "George's book") were removed and contractions were spelled out. Finally, we expanded some common abbreviations, such as those for months (Feb. becomes February).

Because a number of important names have variant spellings (e.g., Mohammed/ Mohamad/Mohammad), in the preprocessing stage we combined all such variant spellings into a single spelling. This prevents us from underestimating the frequency of references to key figures such as the Prophet Mohammad, Osama bin Laden, al Qaeda, etc.

Translating texts into American English

Most of the sentiment lexica we use were constructed from American English word lists. This means that some will overlook the same word spelled slightly differently: favour as opposed to favor; criticise as opposed to criticize, etc. In order to address this issue, we "translated" non-US newspaper articles into American English in several steps. First, we convert "-our" words to their American "-or" version, as appropriate. Next, we do the same for verb forms, from "-is" (-ise, -ising, -isation, etc.) to "-iz" and from "-lys" to "-lyz." Finally, we take all the words in an extensive list of spelling variants available online that are not covered by the first two steps and convert them to American English as well.[3]

I.B. Sentiment analysis

We introduce our sentiment analysis approach in chapter 2. Here we provide additional details on the sentiment lexica we use, our handling of intensifiers such as negation words, and our validation of the method.

---

[3] The list is at http://www.tysto.com/uk-us-spelling-list.html. It was last updated May 8, 2014, and accessed April 2, 2020.

Each sentiment analysis dictionary has its own idiosyncrasies, shaped by the method used to generate the dictionary and the original application. This is true for domain-specific dictionaries as well as for general-purpose ones, although the latter can perform well across a range of applications (Blitzer, Dredze, and Pereira 2007; González-Bailón and Paltoglou 2015). Rather than rely on any single dictionary, we use an average of sentiment scores produced by eight different, widely used, and individually validated dictionaries: the lexicon produced by Liu and collaborators (Hu and Liu 2004); labMT, produced by Dodds and collaborators (Dodds et al. 2011); lexicoderSD, produced by Young and Soroka (2012); MPQA, produced by Wilson, Wiebe, and Hoffman (2005); NRC, developed at the Canadian National Research Council (Mohammad and Yang 2011); SentiWordNet, based on WordNet (Baccianella, Esuli, and Sebastiani 2010); SO-CAL, developed by Taboada and collaborators (Taboada et al. 2011); and WordStat, constructed by Provalis Research (Provalis, n.d.).

Of these eight lexica, the two that have been in use longest were produced in the early 2000s by computer scientists developing new tools for automated sentiment analysis (Hu and Liu 2004; Wilson, Wiebe, and Hoffmann 2005). Interestingly, each contains roughly twice as many negative as positive words. One simply contains lists of positive and negative words (all positive/negative words are equally positive/negative); the other ranks sentiment intensity from ±.175 to ±1.

The other six lexica are newer, and provide even more diversity. Two of them assign valence levels to words by relying on human coders recruited through Amazon's Mechanical Turk. One automatically propagates valences through a semantic and syntactic network, WordNet, starting with paradigmatically positive and negative words ("good," "bad," etc.). For the other three, the constructors of the lexicon assign valences themselves. Two of them include not just words but also word stems, or roots: "abhor*" will capture "abhor," but also "abhors," "abhorred," "abhorrent," etc. Two rank sentiment intensity; the other four simply identify words as positive or negative. While most were developed by computer scientists and computational linguists, one was produced by political scientists, and one by a commercial company selling text analysis software. All contain more negative than positive terms, and they range in size from under 4,000 to over 24,000 total terms included. Table I.B.1 offers more information about each of them.

Significantly, for all their differences, each is intended as a general-purpose lexicon, not targeted at specific topics or types of texts. Yet only 135 positive words and 196 negative words are captured by all eight lexica: less than 10% of even the smallest lexicon. This illustrates just how difficult it is to construct a single lexicon that can capture sentiment across a wide range of texts. On any given sentiment analysis application, one of these dictionaries will perform best. However, it is impossible to know *ex ante* which dictionary that will be. Rather than try to second-guess the decisions that went into the construction of each lexicon, we instead average across them, thus drawing on all their strengths while minimizing the impact of any particular lexicon that might be ill-suited to a particular text or topic. Taking the average score, in other words, will produce a robust measure that is far less vulnerable to the particularities of a given corpus of texts than any single dictionary would be.

Table I.B.1 Sentiment analysis lexica used

Name	Positive terms	Negative terms	Notes on lexicon construction
HuLiu	2,003 (+1)	4,783 (−1)	Constructed at the University of Illinois in Chicago, based on WordNet (Miller 1995). Developed for social media; contains terms such as "f*ck."
labMT	2,668 (range from 1 to 3.5)	1,063 (range from −1 to −3.5)	Mechanical Turk coders coded the "happiness level" of the most frequent 5,000 words from four separate sources: Twitter, Google Books (English), music lyrics (1960 to 2007), and the *New York Times* (1987 to 2007). Full lexicon has 10,222 entries. We filter out words with low valence scores (absolute value < 1), as recommended by the lexicon's creators.
LexicoderSD	1,615 (+1), of which 1,043 stems	2,768 (−1), of which 1,971 stems	All words from the General Inquirer (GI) (Stone and Hunt 1963), the Regressive Imagery Dictionary (RID) (Martindale 1975), and *Roget's Thesaurus* with the same valence in all three dictionaries (or same in two and omitted from the third). Includes wildcards to accept any endings for a given stem.
MPQA	2,299 (range from 0.175 to 1)	4,150 (range from −0.175 to −1)	Used words from GI (from Hatzivassiloglou and McKeown 1997), and from their own prior work (Riloff and Wiebe 2003). We use only single-word entries (no phrases), and average valence for words with multiple entries. "Strong" polarity is given a value of 1, "weak" polarity gets ½.
NRC	2,312 (+1)	3,243 (−1)	All words from *Roget's Thesaurus* that occur at least 120,000 times in Google's n-gram corpus, coded using five different MT coders for each word.
SentiWordNet	11,116 (range from 0.1 to 1)	13,106 (range from −0.1 to −1)	Assigns valences to the synonym sets (synsets) in the online semantic dictionary WordNet. Starting from "paradigmatically" positive or negative words, propagated valence across WordNet using the network structure implied by synsets sharing words. Full lexicon has 29,436 entries; we filter out words with low aggregate valence (absolute value < 0.1). For words with multiple valences (e.g., in multiple synsets), averaged the values.
SOCAL	3,716 (range from 0.5 to 5.0)	6,341 (range from −0.5 to −5.0)	"Sentiment Orientation CALculator," manually constructed from all words in a 400-text corpus of Epinions reviews, movie reviews (Pang, Lee, and Vaithyanathan 2002), and GI.
WordStat	5,539 (+1), of which 337 stems	9,539 (−1), of which 578 stems	Constructed by Provalis (makers of WordStat), by combining word lists from GI, RID, and the Linguistic Inquiry and Word Count (LIWC) dictionary (Tausczik and Pennebaker 2010) and searching WordStat's internal dictionary for potential synonyms. Includes wildcards to specify any ending acceptable for a given stem.

Intensifiers

Benamara et al. (2006) offer a broad survey of ways to extend a basic bag of words approach to take into account the order in which words appear. The most common approach has been to take into account intensifiers, including negators, that directly precede sentiment words (Benamara et al. 2006; Kennedy and Inkpen 2006). Doing so is relatively straightforward and makes intuitive sense. Accordingly, we adopt the method proposed by Taboada et al. (2011), adjusting a word's value in the lexicon by tracking intensifiers that directly precede the word in the text. Specifically, we use a list of 216 different intensifiers they develop, and apply the modifying factor associated with each such intensifier to any positive or negative word that immediately follows. Some of these modifying factors intensify the strength of a word, some weaken it, and some change the polarity. We handle multiple consecutive intensifiers (including negation) simply by combining their individual intensification effects.

The default multiplier for a valence word is 1. Intensifier values are added to this default, and the result is multiplied by the valence. For example, "slightly" has a multiplier of −0.5, which means that a subsequent word's valence is multiplied by (1 + −0.5) = 0.5. We handle negation in a parallel fashion by identifying words that shift polarity, such as "not," "no," "nor," "nothing," "never," and "nowhere," and add them to the list of polarity-shifting words in Taboada et al. (2011), such as "hardly." To get a polarity shift, we need a multiplier below −1. We assign our negation and polarity-shifting words a multiplier of −1.5, so that the valence is multiplied by (1 + −1.5) = −0.5.[4] The intensification multiplier is applied to the next valence word; it resets upon encountering a word that is not either another intensifier, a valence word, or one of a small list of words we skip over ("a," "an," "the," "and," "to," and "as").

Validation

We have tested our approach—along with the relative performance of the eight individual lexica—on a widely used dataset of 50,000 movie reviews (Maas et al. 2011). Even though our approach is calibrated against newspaper articles and not against user reviews, it successfully classifies individual reviews as positive or negative over 75% of the time. Not insignificantly, this success rate compares favorably with some widely used machine learning algorithms.[5] As we would expect, our method has a more difficult time classifying reviews that are closer to neutral. If, instead of averaging across our eight lexica, we look at the performance of each of those lexica individually, the best performing lexicon—not coincidentally, a lexicon specifically tailored for classifying reviews—outperforms our eight-lexicon average by just under 3 percentage points, while the worst-performing lexicon does less well by about 7.5 percentage points. This illustrates the value of averaging: we

---

[4] The intuition here is that "not good" is generally not as bad as "bad" (nor is "not bad" the same as "good"), so simply reversing polarity is not the appropriate adjustment.

[5] For more information, see van der Veen and Bleich (2021b). Our approach also performs slightly above average compared to published results obtained using a range of machine learning and lexical methods on the even more widely used Cornell movie review dataset (Khan, Qamar, and Bashir 2016, table 9). Most importantly for our purposes, we obtain this accuracy level with no domain-specific knowledge or training.

gain most of the benefits of the best-performing lexicon without becoming vulnerable to domain specificity.[6]

We have also validated our method's performance on three datasets that are more social science–focused: tweets made during a political debate, comments posted on the BBC website, and sentences from *New York Times* op-eds. On each of these, our method outperforms all or nearly all of 24 different state-of-the-art sentiment analysis approaches tested in a wide-ranging benchmark comparison of different methods (Ribeiro et al. 2016). On two of the three, the best-performing single lexicon we use slightly outperforms our method; on the third, our averaging method actually outperforms each individual lexicon. Further confirming the value of averaging across multiple lexica, the best-performing lexicon differs in each of these three tests.[7]

While it is important to perform well at classifying individual articles, we are actually much more interested in correctly identifying patterns and trends across sets of texts (cf. Hopkins and King 2010). To test this, we ran bootstrapping simulations in which we randomly selected small sets of movie reviews with the same polarity (positive or negative), averaged their valence as calculated by our method, and compared this to the "true" polarity. In order to eliminate the possibility that strong performance on identifying positive reviews hides weak performance on identifying negative reviews, or vice versa, we separated the two categories. For each simulation we selected 1,000 sets of reviews (each set composed of the same number of reviews randomly drawn without replacement), and we repeated each simulation 1,000 times. With just 6 articles per set, our overall performance is 95% (95.6% correct for sets of negative articles; 94.55% for positive). With 12 articles, performance reaches 99%; and for sets of 25 articles, accuracy is at 100% (with the lower bound of the 95% confidence intervals at 99.8%).[8]

I.C. Geocoding

In order to identify whether an article is set domestically or abroad, we apply a straightforward geocoding method: we look for location names of the major cities, as well as states, provinces, and prominent counties at home, as well as for names of countries or capital cities abroad.

For the United States, we include the names of all fifty states and their capital cities, plus all cities with a population over 100,000 (as of 2016), including any cities that previously had populations that size but have shrunk. In addition, we add smaller cities (population 15,000–100,000 as of 2016) in each of the home states of the papers in our corpus: Arizona, California, Colorado, Florida, Georgia, Massachusetts, Maryland (for the *Washington Post*), Minnesota, Nevada, New York, Pennsylvania, and Virginia. For Britain, Canada, and Australia, we use an analogous approach, identifying key provinces, districts, urban areas, etc., as well as large cities.

In each country, we remove any location names that are more likely to be used to refer to something other than the location. For example, the city of Reading (Pennsylvania) is written the same way as "reading" (a book, for example). A number of location names are

---

[6] Indeed, across a number of validation tests, the eight different lexica we use rank differently each time.

[7] For additional details, see van der Veen and Bleich (2021b).

[8] Details in van der Veen and Bleich (2021b).

also common person names, and we removed those too. Finally, some location names are more likely to refer to a foreign location than to an American location, such as Rome (there is a Rome, New York, but Rome, Italy, is the more likely target).

For the Global South newspapers, we include each country's name as well as its capital city and largest cities (those with a population of a million or more). These lists are much less detailed than those for the Anglophone North countries, so our Global South results likely undercount the proportion of articles referencing a domestic location. This only strengthens our finding that papers in our selection of Global South countries include more purely domestic reporting on Muslims and Islam than do the United States, Britain, Canada, or Australia.

To identify foreign locations, we search for the names of all other countries and capital cities, except for those that are identical to domestic location names (in which case both are removed from the list, so as to avoid misinterpreting a location). A sizable majority of articles in our corpus contains both domestic and foreign location names. In order to isolate those articles exclusively set abroad, we specify a "foreign only" variable that has a value of 1 only if the article in question contains foreign location names but no domestic location names.

Supplementary materials for the analyses in chapters 2–6

Here we present supplementary data for the empirical text chapters. In order to keep the numbering aligned with chapter numbers, the first section in this appendix is numbered II.2 (for chapter 2).

II.2. Chapter 2—Supplementary material

Chapter 2 introduced our corpus of articles mentioning Muslims or Islam in the US print media. We noted that there is a fair amount of variation across newspapers in the average valence of such articles (albeit not enough to recommend against pooling all articles together into a corpus). Table II.2.1 breaks down average article valence by newspaper.

Chapter 2 also showed that coverage mentioning Islam tends to be somewhat more negative than coverage mentioning only Muslims. Here, we dig more deeply into the corpus to get a broad overview of the substantive contents of the texts in our corpus. Table II.2.2 displays the most common unambiguously positive and negative words in the corpus. To get this list, we first identified all words present in at least six of our eight sentiment lexica;[1] 957 positive and 1,638 negative words meet this criterion. Next, we created a frequency dictionary for our corpus, tallying the number of occurrences of each word throughout the entire corpus. We then simply went down the list (past the most common words such as "the", "and", etc.) and identified the first 10 words from the positive and negative word sets, respectively.

While the positive words are all fairly generic and anodyne, the negative words strongly point to a specific type of discussion regarding Muslims, involving conflict, violence, and terrorism. Moreover, these words are more negative than the positive words are positive: an article containing equal numbers of words from these two lists will almost certainly leave a negative impression on a reader. It is also worth remembering that "terror," in the negative column, was one of the top three negative words Americans offered when asked in a Pew survey for a one-word impression of Islam, as shown in the epigram opening chapter 2. Similarly, "peace," in the positive column, maps onto "peaceful," one of the top three positive words (Pew Research Center 2007). This underscores the powerful link between how the media cover and how people think about Muslims and Islam.

---

[1] We eliminate a few words that have opposing signs (positive, negative) in different lexica.

Table II.2.1 Average article valence, by newspaper, in our Muslim corpus

Newspaper	Average valence
New York Times	−0.945
USA Today	−0.965
Wall Street Journal	−1.018
Washington Post	−0.932
Arizona Republic	−0.670
Atlanta Journal-Constitution	−0.741
Boston Globe	−0.819
Denver Post	−0.856
Las Vegas Review-Journal	−0.786
Philadelphia Inquirer	−1.108
Richmond Times Dispatch	−0.686
San Jose Mercury News	−0.912
Star-Tribune (Minneapolis)	−0.346
Tampa Bay Times	−0.826
Daily News (New York)	−1.244
New York Post	−1.408
Philadelphia Daily News	−1.089

Table II.2.2 Top 10 most common positively- and negatively-valenced words in the corpus.

Positive words	Negative words
like	war
support	attack
well	terrorism
peace	death
free	hard
right	opposition
good	terror
intelligence	threat
great	bomb
top	dead

II.3. Chapter 3—Supplementary material

In chapter 3 we presented a number of regression results using our key independent variables. To be confident of the results, we need to be sure these variables are not highly correlated. Table II.3.1 confirms this is the case by showing a correlation matrix among the variables. Most correlations are very low; even the highest, between right-leaning and tabloid papers—the *New York Post* is classified as both—is just .349, well below a level that would raise concerns about multicollinearity.

Figures 3.2 and 3.7 in chapter 3 display the estimated regression coefficients associated with these key explanatory variables, as well as with a dummy variable for Muslims. Models 1 and 2 in table II.3.2 list the estimated coefficients corresponding to those figures. Model 3 shows the results for the same analysis, but with additional dummies for two of the other three groups. In addition, we investigate (model 4) whether the effect of particular variables is specific to the Muslim corpus. We do this by adding interaction effects for each of our variables. As the data show, this does little to change the overall story. Still, it is worth noting that references to violence are associated with even greater negativity for Muslims than is the case for the other groups; conversely, references to extremism are associated with comparatively less negativity for Muslims. In addition, while tabloids are associated with negative valence across all groups, right-leaning papers cover other religious groups more positively.

Table II.3.3 provides three additional robustness checks for our findings. In model 5 we replace our binary variable for right-leaning papers by the left-right slant scores calculated by Gentzkow and Shapiro (2010). These scores were calculated for the year 2005—in the middle of the time period we include—and are based on the relative frequency with which newspapers use phrases closely identified with the Democratic and Republican parties. For our papers, the scores range from the *Philadelphia Daily News* on the left at 0.32 through the *Las Vegas Review-Journal* on the right at 0.50. We were unable to find a slant score for the *San Jose Mercury News*, so this title is omitted in model 4. Due to the smaller range of possible values (0.32 through 0.45, rather than 0 and 1), the coefficient estimate is greater than in the other models. Nevertheless, the basic finding that right-leaning papers are slightly more positive overall remains. Nor are any of the other estimates substantively changed.

Table II.3.1 Correlation matrix among key independent variables

	Foreign	Violence	Extremism	Value clash	Religiosity	Right-leaning
Violence	−.044					
Extremism	.055	.269				
Value clash	−.041	−.052	−.045			
Religiosity	−.035	−.064	−.031	.214		
Right-leaning	−.033	−.040	−.046	−.025	−.004	
Tabloid	−.020	−.046	−.044	−.037	−.018	.349

Table II.3.2 Regression results

	Model 1	Model 2	Model 3	Model 4
Muslim		−.534	−.491	−.511
Catholic			.026	
Jewish			.063	
Foreign setting	−.543	−.564	−.565	−.592
Muslim * Foreign				.049
Violence	−.575	−.459	−.463	−.408
Muslim * Violence				−.167
Extremism	−.340	−.458	−.460	−.577
Muslim * Extremism				.237
Religiosity	.196	.158	.158	.146
Muslim * Religiosity				.050
Value clash	.202	.205	.205	.203
Muslim * Value clash				−.001
Right-leaning	.031	.161	.164	.189
Muslim * Right-leaning				−.158
Tabloids	−.450	−.459	−.463	−.446
Muslim * Tabloids				−.004
Constant	−.457	.056	.017	.054
Adjusted R^2	.154	.236	.236	.238
Observations	256,963	898,945	898,945	898,945

Note: All coefficients are statistically significant at the p < .001 level, except for the Muslim interaction effects for Value clash and Tabloids, which are not significant. Model 1 is run on the Muslim corpus only; models 2–4 are run on the pooled four-group corpus.

In model 6, we return to using our original measure of right-leaning papers, but add circulation weights.[2] We assign a value of 1 to the weight for each article in the lowest-circulation paper (the *Philadelphia Daily News*, at 97,694), and increase the weights for the other papers proportionally to their total circulation. Accordingly, the largest value is 24.35, for the *Wall Street Journal*, with a circulation of 2,378,827. Naturally, the circulation of all papers in our corpus has varied over the course of the 21 years included, so we use these weights as an imperfect proxy. Model 5 shows that our findings again remain the same in substantive terms. Finally, model 7 adds fixed effects for each year and each paper in our corpus. We do not show the estimated coefficients for the year and paper dummies, but the substantive findings again remain the same.

[2] We use circulation data from 2013 for the larger papers (obtained from http://auditedmedia.com/news/blog/top-25-us-newspapers-for-march-2013; accessed in 2015, no longer available online), supplemented by figures obtained from *Wikipedia*.

Table II.3.3 Regression results (continued)

	Model 5 (slant scores)	Model 6 (circulation weights)	Model 7 (source & year dummies)
Muslim	−.542	−.544	−.527
Foreign setting	−.544	−.608	−.556
Violence	−.464	−.441	−.439
Extremism	−.462	−.510	−.452
Religiosity	.151	.180	.164
Value clash	.199	.234	.202
Right-leaning	1.549	.171	.077
Tabloids	−.328	−.346	−.298
Constant	−.590	.026	.036
Adjusted R^2	.236	.226	.248
Observations	850,743	898,945	898,945

Note: All coefficients are statistically significant at the p < .001 level, except for the year dummies for 2000 and 2005 (not significant), and the publication dummies for the Denver Post (p = .066). Dummy coefficient estimates available from the authors upon request.

II.4. Chapter 4—Supplementary material

The discussion in chapter 4 mentioned in broad terms how long it takes article counts and valences to return to their pre-event levels (the four-week average prior to the event) following major events. Tables II.4.1, II.4.2, and II.4.3 provide more specific information for 9/11 along with five additional events among the top 10 volume spikes listed in table 4.3. We selected these events because they are each linked most clearly to a single specific starting date. Table II.4.1 shows how long it takes article volume to return to the four-week average prior to the event. The table shows just how exceptional the 9/11 attacks were in this respect.

Table II.4.2 takes an analogous look at the impact on average article valence after each of these events. As we noted in the chapter, the effect on valence systematically lasts less long than the increase in article volume. In this table, too, the longest shock is associated with 9/11, but here it is only slightly longer than those associated with some of the other events.

Finally, we show the impact of Ramadan/Eid on the number of articles published and their average tone. The first two rows of table II.4.3 present the data corresponding to the discussion in the chapter. The third row adds some additional information, looking at the valence of only those sentences within an article that explicitly mention our corpus keyword roots of Muslim* or Islam*. Here, we see a difference both for Ramadan as compared to the rest of the year—not visible in the overall article valence data—and for the end of Ramadan and Eid compared to the rest of Ramadan. For both of these periods, average sentence-level valence is clearly less negative than it is during the rest of the year.

Table II.4.1 Impact of 9/11 and other major events on average daily article count (events in chronological order)

Event	4-week daily avg. pre-event	First week after	Peak week	# weeks to return to pre-event level
USS Cole bombing (Oct. 12, 2000)	22.20	36.46	37.50	7
9/11 attacks (Sep. 11, 2001)	19.12	50.17	138.90	638
9/11 anniversary (Sep. 11, 2002)	40.84	58.47	58.47	16
US invasion of Iraq (Mar. 20, 2003)	49.99	67.31	76.48	9
Benghazi attacks (Sep. 11, 2012)	25.20	32.71	41.98	15
Obama speech on ISIS (Sep. 10, 2014)	44.02	56.97	61.54	8

Table II.4.2 Impact of 9/11 and other major events on article valence, averaged weekly (events in chronological order)

Event	4-week avg. pre-event	First week after	Lowest weekly value after	# weeks to return to pre-event level
USS Cole bombing (Oct. 12, 2000)	−0.94	−1.09	−1.10	3
9/11 attacks (Sep. 11, 2001)	−0.95	−1.35	−1.35	9
9/11 anniversary (Sep. 11, 2002)	−0.97	−1.02	−1.34	7
US invasion of Iraq (Mar. 20, 2003)	−1.09	−1.39	−1.50	2
Benghazi attacks (Sep. 11, 2012)	−0.91	−1.32	−1.32	7
Obama speech on ISIS (Sep. 10, 2014)	−1.05	−1.08	−1.17	3

Table II.4.3 Comparison of publication rate and valence, Ramadan vs. rest of year

	Not Ramadan/Eid	All Ramadan/Eid	End of Ramadan/Eid
Articles/day	33.25	36.03	38.55
Article valence	−0.939	−0.941	−0.904
Sentence valence	−1.216	−1.095	−0.980

II.5.   Chapter 5—Supplementary material

Figure 5.4 in chapter 5 displays the estimated coefficients associated with our key explanatory variables, across four country corpora. Table II.5.1 lists the regression results that produced those figures.

For the analyses reported in table II.5.1, we compare the different national corpora to one another after calibrating all against the same US representative corpus. As we show in table 5.1 in chapter 5, benchmarking each national corpus against a representative corpus drawn from its own national media market does not produce substantively different results. To confirm this observation, figure II.5.1 shows a kernel density estimate for the corpora when each is calibrated against its own representative corpus. This figure is the analogue to figure 5.3 in the chapter, and differs only marginally from that figure. In particular, we see that the four corpora now resemble each other even more closely, with the United States less of an outlier in the center of the distribution. Meanwhile, the British corpus shifts in a more positive direction when compared to its own national media market, suggesting that the general tenor of newspaper language in Britain is slightly more negative compared to that in the other three countries.[3] The figure confirms that the US calibration benchmark we use does not affect our overall substantive conclusion: the tone of media coverage (and its distribution) is strikingly similar across these four national corpora.

Table II.5.1   Regression results

	United States	Britain	Canada	Australia
Foreign setting	−.543	−.445	−.517	−.513
Violence	−.575	−.533	−.500	−.628
Extremism	−.340	−.364	−.306	−.365
Religiosity	.196	.190	.236	.194
Value clash	.202	.277	.214	.275
Right-leaning	.031	−.036	−.030	−.011
Tabloids	−.450	−.576	−.195	−.359
Constant	−.457	−.448	.514	−.274
Adjusted R^2	.154	.146	.147	.187
Observations	256,963	318,437	121,588	88,419

Note: All coefficients are statistically significant at the p < .001 level, except right-leaning paper for Australia, which is not statistically significant.

---

[3] One factor likely contributing to this effect is the substantial presence of tabloid papers on the British market.

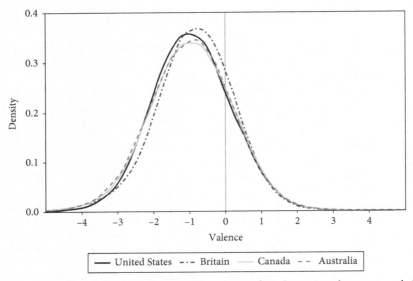

Figure II.5.1. Kernel density estimates of the valence of Muslim national corpora, scaled against their national representative corpora

II.6. Chapter 6—Supplementary material

In chapter 6, we present and analyze the results of applying a topic model to our Muslim corpus. Here, we offer additional methodological details. A number of different topic modeling algorithms are widely used; of these, Latent Dirichlet Allocation (LDA) and Non-negative Matrix Factorization (NMF) are perhaps best known (Blei 2012; Lee and Seung 1999). Each algorithm has strengths and weaknesses, but generally they produce similar results. Here, we use NMF, which has the attractive feature of producing topics that are fairly stable: if a topic is found when the algorithm is asked to identify 35 different topics, it will generally be present in the same form also when the algorithm identifies 36 different topics. This is not always the case with LDA.

In addition, NMF tends to outperform LDA on measures of average topic coherence for the same number of topics when that number is below 100, as is the case here (Stevens et al. 2012). This matters because coherent topics are topics that make sense to human beings as well as to the algorithm computing them. A topic is coherent when the words most strongly associated with it fit meaningfully together. To assess topic coherence, we rely on an algorithm that calculates how close a topic's top words are to one another when all words are projected into a multidimensional semantic space. A number of such algorithms exist; we use word2vec, which is the best known and most widely used (Mikolov et al. 2013). Using the information this algorithm produces about how closely words are associated with other words, we can automatically calculate how coherent the top words in each topic are and produce an average coherence measure for the topic model as a whole.[4] We choose the number of topics for which average topic coherence is highest (cf. Greene and Cross 2017).

One particular feature of NMF is that it will often generate a few "junk" topics, to accommodate words that do not fit neatly into other topics (Stevens et al. 2012). As we noted in chapter 6, while for our Muslim corpus the best number of topics is 36, two of these are not meaningful, and we ignored them in our analyses. One of these two topics collects words associated with schedules and locations (addresses, times of day, etc.), and the other collects words associated with the electronic databases we used to compile our corpus: Factiva, Dow Jones (the owner of Factiva), etc.

[4] Specifically, we calculate average mutual coherence (as measured by cosine distance) of the top 10 words in the topic.

References

Abrahamian, Ervand. 2003. "The US Media, Huntington and September 11." *Third World Quarterly* 24 (3): 529–44. https://doi.org/10.1080/0143659032000084456.

Adida, Claire L., David D. Laitin, and Marie-Anne Valfort. 2016. *Why Muslim Integration Fails in Christian-Heritage Societies*. Cambridge, MA: Harvard University Press.

Ahmed, Saifuddin, and Jörg Matthes. 2017. "Media Representation of Muslims and Islam from 2000 to 2015: A Meta-Analysis." *International Communication Gazette* 79 (3): 219–44. https://doi.org/10.1177/1748048516656305.

Alba, Richard. 2005. "Bright vs. Blurred Boundaries: Second-Generation Assimilation and Exclusion in France, Germany, and the United States." *Ethnic and Racial Studies* 28 (1): 20–49. https://doi.org/10.1080/0141987042000280003.

Ali, Wajahat, Eli Clifton, Matthew Duss, Lee Fang, Scott Keyes, and Faiz Shakir. 2011. "Fear, Inc.: The Roots of the Islamophobia Network in America." Washington, DC: Center for American Progress.

Allen, Christopher. 2010. *Islamophobia*. Farnham, UK: Ashgate.

Alsultany, Evelyn. 2012. *Arabs and Muslims in the Media: Race and Representation after 9/11*. New York: NYU Press.

American National Election Studies. 2020. "ANES Continuity Guide." https://electionstudies.org/resources/anes-continuity-guide/.

Arendt, Florian, and Temple Northup. 2015. "Effects of Long-Term Exposure to News Stereotypes on Implicit and Explicit Attitudes." *International Journal of Communication* 9: 2370–90.

Aust, Philip Jerold. 2004. "Communicated Values as Indicators of Organizational Identity: A Method for Organizational Assessment and Its Application in a Case Study." *Communication Studies* 55 (4): 515–34. https://doi.org/10.1080/10510970409388636.

Axt, Jordan R., Charles R. Ebersole, and Brian A. Nosek. 2014. "The Rules of Implicit Evaluation by Race, Religion, and Age." *Psychological Science* 25 (9): 1804–15. https://doi.org/10.1177/0956797614543801.

Baccianella, Stefano, Andrea Esuli, and Fabrizio Sebastiani. 2010. "SENTIWORDNET 3.0: An Enhanced Lexical Resource for Sentiment Analysis and Opinion Mining." In *Proceedings of the Seventh International Conference on Language Resources and Evaluation (LREC'10)*, 2200–4.

Bail, Christopher A. 2012. "The Fringe Effect: Civil Society Organizations and the Evolution of Media Discourse about Islam since the September 11th Attacks." *American Sociological Review* 77 (6): 855–79. https://doi.org/10.1177/0003122412465743.

Baker, Paul, Costas Gabrielatos, and Tony McEnery. 2013. *Discourse Analysis and Media Attitudes: The Representation of Islam in the British Press*. Cambridge: Cambridge University Press.

Balzacq, Thierry. 2019. "Securitization Theory: Past, Present, and Future." *Polity* 51 (2): 331–48.

Balzacq, Thierry, Sarah Léonard, and Jan Ruzicka. 2016. "'Securitization' Revisited: Theory and Cases." *International Relations* 30 (4): 494–531. https://doi.org/ 10.1177/0047117815596590.

Barth, Fredrik. 1969. *Ethnic Groups and Boundaries: The Social Organization of Culture Difference*. Bergen: Universitetsforlaget.

Baumeister, Roy F., Ellen Bratslavsky, Catrin Finkenauer, and Kathleen D. Vohs. 2001. "Bad Is Stronger Than Good." *Review of General Psychology* 5 (4): 323–70. https:// doi.org/10.1037/1089-2680.5.4.323.

Benamara, Farah, Carmine Cesarano, Antonio Picariello, Diego Reforgiato, and V. S. Subrahmanian. 2006. "Sentiment Analysis: Adjectives and Adverbs Are Better Than Adjectives Alone." In *Proceedings of the International Conference on Weblogs and Social Media (ICWSM)*, Vol. 7. Boulder, CO.

Blei, David M. 2012. "Probabilistic Topic Models." *Communications of the ACM* 55 (4): 77. https://doi.org/10.1145/2133806.2133826.

Bleich, Erik. 2011. "What Is Islamophobia and How Much Is There? Theorizing and Measuring an Emerging Comparative Concept." *American Behavioral Scientist* 55 (12): 1581–1600. https://doi.org/10.1177/0002764211409387.

Bleich, Erik, James P. Callison, Georgia Grace Edwards, Mia Fichman, Erin Hoynes, Razan Jabari, and A. Maurits van der Veen. 2018. "The Good, the Bad, and the Ugly: A Corpus Linguistics Analysis of US Newspaper Coverage of Latinx, 1996–2016." *Journalism* 22 (6): 1522–39. https://doi.org/10.1177/1464884918818252.

Bleich, Erik, Mira Chugh, Adrienne Goldstein, Amelia Pollard, Varsha Vijayakumar, and A. Maurits van der Veen. 2020. "Afro-Pessimist or African Rising? US Newspaper Coverage of Africa, 1994–2018." *Journalism Studies* 22 (13): 1775–94. https://doi.org/ 10.1080/1461670X.2020.1790027.

Bleich, Erik, Hasher Nisar, and Rana Abdelhamid. 2016. "The Effect of Terrorist Events on Media Portrayals of Islam and Muslims: Evidence from *New York Times* Headlines, 1985–2013." *Ethnic and Racial Studies* 39 (7): 1109–27. https://doi.org/10.1080/ 01419870.2015.1103886.

Bleich, Erik, Hasher Nisar, and Cara Vazquez. 2018. "Investigating Status Hierarchies with Media Analysis: Muslims, Jews, and Catholics in the *New York Times* and the *Guardian* Headlines, 1985–2014." *International Journal of Comparative Sociology* 59 (3): 239–57. https://doi.org/10.1177/0020715218775142.

Bleich, Erik, Julien Souffrant, Emily Stabler, and A. Maurits van der Veen. 2018. "Media Coverage of Muslim Devotion: A Four-Country Analysis of Newspaper Articles, 1996–2016." *Religions* 9 (8): 247. https://doi.org/10.3390/rel9080247.

Bleich, Erik, Hannah Stonebraker, Hasher Nisar, and Rana Abdelhamid. 2015. "Media Portrayals of Minorities: Muslims in British Newspaper Headlines, 2001–2012." *Journal of Ethnic and Migration Studies* 41 (6): 942–62. https://doi.org/10.1080/ 1369183X.2014.1002200.

Blitzer, John, Mark Dredze, and Fernando Pereira. 2007. "Biographies, Bollywood, Boom-Boxes and Blenders: Domain Adaptation for Sentiment Classification." In *Proceedings of the 45th Annual Meeting of the Association of Computational Linguistics*, 440–47.

Bolce, Louis, and Gerald De Maio. 2008. "A Prejudice for the Thinking Classes: Media Exposure, Political Sophistication, and the Anti-Christian Fundamentalist." *American Politics Research* 36 (2): 155–85. https://doi.org/10.1177/1532673X07309601.

Boomgaarden, Hajo G., and Rens Vliegenthart. 2009. "How News Content Influences Anti-immigration Attitudes: Germany, 1993–2005." *European Journal of Political Research* 48 (4): 516–42. https://doi.org/10.1111/j.1475-6765.2009.01831.x.

Bos, Linda, Sophie Lecheler, Moniek Mewafi, and Rens Vliegenthart. 2016. "It's the Frame That Matters: Immigrant Integration and Media Framing Effects in the Netherlands." *International Journal of Intercultural Relations* 55 (November): 97–108. https://doi.org/ 10.1016/j.ijintrel.2016.10.002.

Bouma, Gerlof. 2009. "Normalized (Pointwise) Mutual Information in Collocation Extraction." In *From Form to Meaning: Processing Texts Automatically*, edited by Christian Chiarcos, 31–40. Tübingen: Narr.

Bowe, Brian J., Shahira Fahmy, and Jorg Matthes. 2015. "U.S. Newspapers Provide Nuanced Picture of Islam." *Newspaper Research Journal* 36 (1): 42–57. https://doi.org/ 10.1177/0739532915580312.

Boydstun, Amber E., Anne Hardy, and Stefaan Walgrave. 2014. "Two Faces of Media Attention: Media Storm versus Non-storm Coverage." *Political Communication* 31 (4): 509–31. https://doi.org/10.1080/10584609.2013.875967.

Brown, Katherine E. 2010. "Contesting the Securitization of British Muslims: Citizenship and Resistance." *Interventions* 12 (2): 171–82. https://doi.org/10.1080/ 1369801X.2010.489690.

Brubaker, Rogers. 2009. "Ethnicity, Race, and Nationalism." *Annual Review of Sociology* 35 (1): 21–42. https://doi.org/10.1146/annurev-soc-070308-115916.

Brubaker, Rogers. 2017. "Between Nationalism and Civilizationism: The European Populist Moment in Comparative Perspective." *Ethnic and Racial Studies* 40 (8): 1191–1226. https://doi.org/10.1080/01419870.2017.1294700.

Buzan, Barry, Ole Wæver, and Jaap de Wilde. 1998. *Security: A New Framework for Analysis.* Boulder, CO: Lynne Rienner.

CAIR (Council on American-Islamic Relations). n.d. "Counter-Islamophobia Project." http://islamophobia.org/.

Casanova, José. 2006. "The Long, Difficult, and Tortuous Journey of Turkey into Europe and the Dilemmas of European Civilization." *Constellations* 13 (2): 234–47.

Cesari, Jocelyne. 2007. "The Muslim Presence in France and the United States: Its Consequences for Secularism." *French Politics, Culture & Society* 25 (2). https://doi.org/ 10.3167/fpcs.2007.250204.

Cesari, Jocelyne. 2012. "Securitization of Islam in Europe." *Die Welt Des Islams* 52 (3/4): 430–49.

Chagnon, Nicholas J. 2017. "Racialized Culpability: Victim Blaming and State Violence." In *Sociology of Crime, Law and Deviance*, edited by Mathieu Deflem, 22:199–219. Bingley, UK: Emerald Publishing Limited. https://doi.org/10.1108/ S1521-613620170000022016.

Chapparban, Sajaudeen Nijamodeen. 2020. "Religious Identity and Politics of Citizenship in South Asia: A Reflection on Refugees and Migrants in India." *Development* 63 (1): 52.

Cheney, Richard. 2003. "Remarks by the Vice President." December 22, 2003. https://georgewbush-whitehouse.archives.gov/news/releases/2003/12/print/ 20031223-1.html.

Cherif, Feryal M. 2010. "Culture, Rights, and Norms: Women's Rights Reform in Muslim Countries." *Journal of Politics* 72 (4): 1144–60. https://doi.org/10.1017/ S0022381610000587.

CIA (Central Intelligence Agency). 2020. *World Fact Book.* https://www.cia.gov/library/ publications/the-world-factbook/geos/us.html.

Conboy, Martin. 2005. *Tabloid Britain: Constructing a Community through Language.* New York: Routledge.

Conway, Mike. 2006. "The Subjective Precision of Computers: A Methodological Comparison with Human Coding in Content Analysis." *Journalism & Mass Communication Quarterly* 83 (1): 186–200. https://doi.org/10.1177/107769900608300112.

Creighton, Mathew J., and Amaney Jamal. 2015. "Does Islam Play a Role in Anti-immigrant Sentiment? An Experimental Approach." *Social Science Research* 53 (September): 89–103. https://doi.org/10.1016/j.ssresearch.2015.04.001.

DiMaggio, Paul J., and Walter W. Powell. 1983. "The Iron Cage Revisited: Institutional Isomorphism and Collective Rationality in Organizational Fields." *American Sociological Review* 48 (2): 147–60.

Dodds, Peter Sheridan, Kameron Decker Harris, Isabel M. Kloumann, Catherine A. Bliss, and Christopher M. Danforth. 2011. "Temporal Patterns of Happiness and Information in a Global Social Network: Hedonometrics and Twitter." *PLoS ONE* 6 (12). https://doi.org/10.1371/journal.pone.0026752.

Dovidio, John F., and Samuel L. Gaertner. 2010. "Intergroup Bias." In *The Handbook of Social Psychology*, 5th ed., edited by Susan T. Fiske, Daniel T. Gilbert, and Gardner Lindzey, 2:1084–1121. New York: Wiley.

Dovidio, John F., Samuel L. Gaertner, and Adam R. Pearson. 2017. "Aversive Racism and Contemporary Bias." In *The Cambridge Handbook of the Psychology of Prejudice*, edited by Chris G. Sibley and Fiona Kate Barlow, 267–94. Cambridge: Cambridge University Press. https://doi.org/10.1017/9781316161579.012.

Dunaway, Johanna. 2013. "Media Ownership and Story Tone in Campaign News." *American Politics Research* 41 (1): 24–53. https://doi.org/10.1177/1532673X12454564.

Eberl, Jakob-Moritz, Christine E. Meltzer, Tobias Heidenreich, Beatrice Herrero, Nora Theorin, Fabienne Lind, Rosa Berganza, Hajo G. Boomgaarden, Christian Schemer, and Jesper Strömbäck. 2018. "The European Media Discourse on Immigration and Its Effects: A Literature Review." *Annals of the International Communication Association* 42 (3): 207–23. https://doi.org/10.1080/23808985.2018.1497452.

Edkins, Brett. 2016. "Washington Post to Expand Newsroom in Aftermath of 2016 Election." *Forbes*, December 29, 2016. https://www.forbes.com/sites/brettedkins/2016/12/29/washington-post-to-expand-newsroom-in-aftermath-of-2016-election/.

Edwards, Frank, Hedwig Lee, and Michael Esposito. 2019. "Risk of Being Killed by Police Use of Force in the United States by Age, Race–Ethnicity, and Sex." *Proceedings of the National Academy of Sciences* 116 (34): 16793. https://doi.org/10.1073/pnas.1821204116.

Erisen, Cengiz, Milton Lodge, and Charles S. Taber. 2014. "Affective Contagion in Effortful Political Thinking: Affective Contagion." *Political Psychology* 35 (2): 187–206. https://doi.org/10.1111/j.1467-9221.2012.00937.x.

Esposito, John L., and İbrahim Kalin. 2011. *Islamophobia: The Challenge of Pluralism in the 21st Century*. Oxford: Oxford University Press.

Fairclough, Norman. 2013. *Language and Power*. 2nd ed. New York: Routledge.

FBI (Federal Bureau of Investigation). 2019. "2018 Hate Crime Statistics." https://ucr.fbi.gov/hate-crime/2018/topic-pages/victims.

Firth, J. R. 1957. "A Synopsis of Linguistic Theory 1930–1955." In *Studies in Linguistic Analysis*, 1–32. Oxford: Philological Society.

Fish, M. Steven. 2011. *Are Muslims Distinctive?: A Look at the Evidence*. Oxford: Oxford University Press. https://www.amazon.com/Are-Muslims-Distinctive-Look-Evidence/dp/0199769214.

Galtung, Johan, and Mari Holmboe Ruge. 1965. "The Structure of Foreign News: The Presentation of the Congo, Cuba and Cyprus Crises in Four Norwegian Newspapers." *Journal of Peace Research* 2 (1): 64–90. https://doi.org/10.1177/002234336500200104.

Gans, Joshua S., and Andrew Leigh. 2011. "How Partisan Is the Press? Multiple Measures of Media Slant." IZA Discussion Paper 6156. Bonn, Germany: Forschungsinstitut zur Zukunft der Arbeit. http://ftp.iza.org/dp6156.pdf.

Gentzkow, Matthew, and Jesse M. Shapiro. 2010. "What Drives Media Slant? Evidence from U.S. Daily Newspapers." *Econometrica* 78 (1): 35–71.

Gilliam, Franklin D., and Shanto Iyengar. 2000. "Prime Suspects: The Influence of Local Television News on the Viewing Public." *American Journal of Political Science* 44 (3): 560. https://doi.org/10.2307/2669264.

Golan, Guy. 2006. "Inter-Media Agenda Setting and Global News Coverage: Assessing the Influence of the *New York Times* on Three Network Television Evening News Programs." *Journalism Studies* 7 (2): 323–33. https://doi.org/10.1080/14616700500533643.

González-Bailón, Sandra, and Georgios Paltoglou. 2015. "Signals of Public Opinion in Online Communication: A Comparison of Methods and Data Sources." *ANNALS of the American Academy of Political and Social Science* 659 (1): 95–107. https://doi.org/10.1177/0002716215569192.

Greene, Derek, and James P. Cross. 2017. "Exploring the Political Agenda of the European Parliament Using a Dynamic Topic Modeling Approach." *Political Analysis* 25 (1): 77–94. https://doi.org/10.1017/pan.2016.7.

Greste, Peter. 2018. "The War on Journalism: How 9/11 Changed Everything." In *Sydney Writers' Festival*. Sydney, Australia: PEN International Sydney. https://pen.org.au/blogs/news/the-war-on-journalism-how-9-11-changed-everything.

Güney, Ülkü. 2010. "'We See Our People Suffering': The War, the Mass Media and the Reproduction of Muslim Identity among Youth." *Media, War & Conflict* 3 (2): 168–81. https://doi.org/10.1177/1750635210360081.

Haberman, Clyde. 2004. "A Little Late, but a Stand against Hate." *New York Times*, November 16, 2004, sec. New York. https://www.nytimes.com/2004/11/16/nyregion/a-little-late-but-a-stand-against-hate.html.

Hackett, Robert A. 1989. "Coups, Earthquakes and Hostages? Foreign News on Canadian Television." *Canadian Journal of Political Science* 22 (4): 809–26. https://doi.org/10.1017/S0008423900020266.

Hagendoorn, L. 1995. "Intergroup Biases in Multiple Group Systems: The Perception of Ethnic Hierarchies." *European Review of Social Psychology* 6 (1): 199–228. https://doi.org/10.1080/14792779443000058.

Hamilton, James T. 2000. *Channeling Violence: The Economic Market for Violent Television Programming*. Princeton, NJ: Princeton University Press.

Hamilton, James T. 2004. *All the News That's Fit to Sell: How the Market Transforms Information into News*. Princeton, NJ: Princeton University Press.

Harcup, Tony, and Deirdre O'Neill. 2017. "What Is News?: News Values Revisited (Again)." *Journalism Studies* 18 (12): 1470–88. https://doi.org/10.1080/1461670X.2016.1150193.

Harder, R.A., J. Sevenans, and P. Van Aelst. 2017. "Intermedia Agenda Setting in the Social Media Age: How Traditional Players Dominate the News Agenda in Election Times." *International Journal of Press/Politics* 22 (3): 275–93. https://doi.org/10.1177/1940161217704969.

Hardy, Anne. 2018. "The Mechanisms of Media Storms." In *From Media Hype to Twitter Storm*, edited by Peter Vasterman, 133–48. Amsterdam: Amsterdam University Press.

Hatzivassiloglou, Vasileios, and Kathleen R. McKeown. 1997. "Predicting the Semantic Orientation of Adjectives." In *ACL '98/EACL '98: Proceedings of the 35th Annual Meeting of the Association for Computational Linguistics and Eighth Conference of the European Chapter of the Association for Computational Linguistics*, 174–81. https:// doi.org/10.3115/976909.979640.

Helbling, Marc. 2012. *Islamophobia in the West: Measuring and Explaining Individual Attitudes*. London: Routledge.

Helbling, Marc, and Richard Traunmüller. 2018. "What Is Islamophobia? Disentangling Citizens' Feelings toward Ethnicity, Religion and Religiosity Using a Survey Experiment." *British Journal of Political Science* 50 (3): 811–28. https://doi.org/10.1017/ S0007123418000054.

Hilton, James L., and William von Hippel. 1996. "Stereotypes." *Annual Review of Psychology* 47 (1): 237–71. https://doi.org/10.1146/annurev.psych.47.1.237.

Hoewe, Jennifer, and Brian J. Bowe. 2021. "Magic Words or Talking Point? The Framing of 'Radical Islam' in News Coverage and Its Effects." *Journalism* 22 (4): 1012–30. https:// doi.org/10.1177/1464884918805577.

Holsti, Ole R. 1964. "An Adaptation of the 'General Inquirer' for the Systematic Analysis of Political Documents." *Behavioral Science* 9 (4): 382–87.

Hopkins, Daniel J., and Gary King. 2010. "A Method of Automated Nonparametric Content Analysis for Social Science." *American Journal of Political Science* 54 (1): 229– 47. https://doi.org/10.1111/j.1540-5907.2009.00428.x.

Hopkins, P. D., and N. J. Shook. 2017. "Development of an Intergroup Anxiety toward Muslims Scale." *International Journal of Intercultural Relations* 61: 7–20. https:// doi.org/10.1016/j.ijintrel.2017.08.002.

Hu, Minqing, and Bing Liu. 2004. "Mining and Summarizing Customer Reviews." In *Proceedings of the Tenth ACM SIGKDD International Conference on Knowledge Discovery and Data Mining*, 168–77. Seattle, WA.

Hussain, Yasmin, and Paul Bagguley. 2012. "Securitized Citizens: Islamophobia, Racism and the 7/7 London Bombings." *Sociological Review* 60 (4): 715–34. https://doi.org/ 10.1111/j.1467-954X.2012.02130.x.

ICM Unlimited. 2015. "ICM Unlimited Survey for Channel 4." https:// www.icmunlimited.com/polls/icm-muslims-survey-for-channel-4/.

Imhoff, Roland, and Julia Recker. 2012. "Differentiating Islamophobia: Introducing a New Scale to Measure Islamoprejudice and Secular Islam Critique." *Political Psychology* 33 (6): 811.

Inglehart, Ronald, and Pippa Norris. 2003. "The True Clash of Civilizations." *Foreign Policy* 135 (March): 62. https://doi.org/10.2307/3183594.

Islam, Roumeen, ed. 2008. *Information and Public Choice: From Media Markets to Policy Making*. Washington, DC: World Bank.

Ivandic, Ria, Tom Kirchmaier, and Stephen Machin. 2019. "Jihadi Attacks, Media and Local Hate Crime." CEP Discussion Paper DP1615. London: Centre for Economic Performance.

Jackson, Liz. 2010. "Images of Islam in US Media and Their Educational Implications." *Educational Studies* 46 (1): 3–24. https://doi.org/10.1080/00131940903480217.

Jamal, Amaney. 2009. "The Racializaton of Muslim Americans." In *Muslims in Western Politics*, edited by Abdulkader H. Sinno, 200–215. Bloomington: Indiana University Press.

Jones, Robert P., Daniel Cox, William A. Galston, and E. J. Dionne Jr. 2011. "What It Means To Be American: Attitudes in an Increasingly Diverse America Ten Years after 9/11." Washington, DC: Public Religion Research Institute.

Kahn, Kim Fridkin, and Patrick J. Kenney. 2002. "The Slant of the News: How Editorial Endorsements Influence Campaign Coverage and Citizens' Views of Candidates." *American Political Science Review* 96 (02): 381–94. https://doi.org/10.1017/S0003055402000230.

Kalkan, Kerem Ozan, Geoffrey C. Layman, and Eric M. Uslaner. 2009. "'Bands of Others'? Attitudes toward Muslims in Contemporary American Society." *Journal of Politics* 71 (3): 847–62. https://doi.org/10.1017/S0022381609090756.

Kearns, Erin, Allison Betus, and Anthony Lemieux. 2019. "Why Do Some Terrorist Attacks Receive More Media Attention Than Others?" *Justice Quarterly* 236 (6): 985–1022. https://doi.org/10.2139/ssrn.2928138.

Kennedy, Alistair, and Diana Inkpen. 2006. "Sentiment Classification of Movie Reviews Using Contextual Valence Shifters." *Computational Intelligence* 22 (2): 110–25. https://doi.org/10.1111/j.1467-8640.2006.00277.x.

Kepplinger, Hans Mathias, and Johanna Habermeier. 1995. "The Impact of Key Events on the Presentation of Reality." *European Journal of Communication* 10 (3): 371–90. https://doi.org/10.1177/0267323195010003004.

Khan, Farhan Hassan, Usman Qamar, and Saba Bashir. 2016. "SentiMI: Introducing Point-Wise Mutual Information with SentiWordNet to Improve Sentiment Polarity Detection." *Applied Soft Computing* 39 (February): 140–53. https://doi.org/10.1016/j.asoc.2015.11.016.

King, Gary, and Will Lowe. 2003. "An Automated Information Extraction Tool for International Conflict Data with Performance as Good as Human Coders: A Rare Events Evaluation Design." *International Organization* 57 (3): 617–42. https://doi.org/10.1017/S0020818303573064.

Kishi, Katayoun. 2017. "Assaults against Muslims in U.S. Surpass 2001 Level." Washington, DC: Pew Research Center, November 15. https://www.pewresearch.org/fact-tank/2017/11/15/assaults-against-muslims-in-u-s-surpass-2001-level/.

Koopmans, Ruud. 2015. "Religious Fundamentalism and Hostility against Out-Groups: A Comparison of Muslims and Christians in Western Europe." *Journal of Ethnic and Migration Studies* 41 (1): 33–57. https://doi.org/10.1080/1369183X.2014.935307.

Kroon, Anne C., Toni G. L. A. van der Meer, and Dana Mastro. 2021. "Confirming Bias without Knowing? Automatic Pathways between Media Exposure and Selectivity." *Communication Research* 48 (2): 180–202. https://doi.org/10.1177/0093650220905948.

Kumar, Deepa. 2010. "Framing Islam: The Resurgence of Orientalism during the Bush II Era." *Journal of Communication Inquiry* 34 (3): 254–77. https://doi.org/10.1177/0196859910363174.

Kunst, Jonas R., David L. Sam, and Pål Ulleberg. 2013. "Perceived Islamophobia: Scale Development and Validation." *International Journal of Intercultural Relations* 37 (2): 225–37. https://doi.org/10.1016/j.ijintrel.2012.11.001.

Kunst, Jonas R., Hajra Tajamal, David L. Sam, and Pål Ulleberg. 2012. "Coping with Islamophobia: The Effects of Religious Stigma on Muslim Minorities' Identity Formation." *International Journal of Intercultural Relations* 36 (4): 518–32.

Lajevardi, Nazita. 2019. "The News Media and Portrayals of Muslims Foreign and Domestic." *Maydan*, May 9, 2019. https://themaydan.com/2019/05/the-news-media-and-portrayals-of-muslims-foreign-and-domestic/.

Lajevardi, Nazita. 2020. *Outsiders at Home: The Politics of American Islamophobia.* Cambridge: Cambridge University Press.

Lamont, Michèle, and Virág Molnár. 2002. "The Study of Boundaries in the Social Sciences." *Annual Review of Sociology* 2: 167–95.

Lee, Daniel D., and H. Sebastian Seung. 1999. "Learning the Parts of Objects by Non-negative Matrix Factorization." *Nature* 401 (6755): 788–91. https://doi.org/10.1038/44565.

Lee, S. A., C. A. Reid, S. D. Short, J. A. Gibbons, R. Yeh, and M. L. Campbell. 2013. "Fear of Muslims: Psychometric Evaluation of the Islamophobia Scale." *Psychology of Religion and Spirituality* 5 (3): 157–71. https://doi.org/10.1037/a0032117.

Lewis, Valerie A., and Ridhi Kashyap. 2013. "Piety in a Secular Society: Migration, Religiosity, and Islam in Britain." *International Migration* 51 (3): 57–66. https://doi.org/10.1111/imig.12095.

Lichtblau, Eric. 2016. "Hate Crimes against American Muslims Most since Post-9/11 Era." *New York Times*, September 18, 2016. https://www.nytimes.com/2016/09/18/us/politics/hate-crimes-american-muslims-rise.html.

Loughran, Tim, and Bill McDonald. 2011. "When Is a Liability Not a Liability? Textual Analysis, Dictionaries, and 10-Ks." *Journal of Finance* 66 (1): 35–65. https://doi.org/10.1111/j.1540-6261.2010.01625.x.

Lovejoy, Jennette, Brendan R. Watson, Stephen Lacy, and Daniel Riffe. 2016. "Three Decades of Reliability in Communication Content Analyses: Reporting of Reliability Statistics and Coefficient Levels in Three Top Journals." *Journalism & Mass Communication Quarterly* 93 (4): 1135–59. https://doi.org/10.1177/1077699016644558.

Lupia, Arthur, Logan S. Casey, Kristyn L. Karl, Spencer Piston, Timothy J. Ryan, and Christopher Skovron. 2015. "What Does It Take to Reduce Racial Prejudice in Individual-Level Candidate Evaluations? A Formal Theoretic Perspective." *Political Science Research and Methods* 3 (1): 1–20. https://doi.org/10.1017/psrm.2014.12.

Maas, Andrew L., Raymond E. Daly, Peter T. Pham, Dan Huang, Andrew Y. Ng, and Christopher Potts. 2011. "Learning Word Vectors for Sentiment Analysis." In *Proceedings of the 49th Annual Meeting of the Association for Computational Linguistics: Human Language Technologies*, Vol. 1, 142–50. Stroudsburg, PA: Association for Computational Linguistics.

Martin, Patrick, and Sean Phelan. 2002. "Representing Islam in the Wake of September 11: A Comparison of US Television and CNN Online Messageboard Discourses." *Prometheus* 20 (3): 263–69. https://doi.org/10.1080/08109020210141371.

Martindale, Colin. 1975. *Romantic Progression: The Psychology of Literary History.* Washington, DC: Hemisphere.

Mastro, Dana, and Riva Tukachinsky. 2011. "The Influence of Exemplar versus Prototype-Based Media Primes on Racial/Ethnic Evaluations." *Journal of Communication* 61 (5): 916–37. https://doi.org/10.1111/j.1460-2466.2011.01587.x.

Mastro, Dana, and Riva Tukachinsky. 2014. "The Influence of Media Exposure on the Formation, Activation, and Application of Racial/Ethnic Stereotypes." In *The International Encyclopedia of Media Studies.* Vol. 5, edited by Angharad N. Valdivia and Erica Scharrer. Chichester, UK: Wiley Blackwell. https://learning.oreilly.com/library/view/the-international-encyclopedia/9781118733561/190_vol-05-chapter-13.html.

McCombs, Maxwell. 2005. "A Look at Agenda-Setting: Past, Present and Future." *Journalism Studies* 6 (4): 543–57. https://doi.org/10.1080/14616700500250438.

McManus, John H. 1994. *Market-Driven Journalism: Let the Citizen Beware?* Thousand Oaks, CA: SAGE.

Media Portrayals of Minorities Project. 2019. "Report on Media Portrayals: 2018 Newspaper Coverage of African Americans, Asian Americans, Latinos, Jews, and Muslims." Middlebury, VT: Media Portrayals of Minorities Project. https://www.mediaandminorities.org/reports/.

Media Portrayals of Minorities Project. 2020. "Report on Media Portrayals: 2019 Newspaper Coverage of African Americans, Asian Americans, Native Americans, Latinos, Jews, and Muslims." Middlebury, VT: Media Portrayals of Minorities Project. https://www.mediaandminorities.org/reports/.

Media Portrayals of Minorities Project. 2021. "Report on Media Portrayals: 2020 Newspaper Coverage of African Americans, Asian Americans, Native Americans, Latinos, Jews, and Muslims." Middlebury, VT: Media Portrayals of Minorities Project. https://www.mediaandminorities.org/reports/.

Mertens, Stefan. 2016. "European Media Coverage of Islam in a Globalizing World." In *Representations of Islam in the News: A Cross-Cultural Analysis*, 59–74. Lanham, MD: Lexington Books.

Meyer-Gutbrod, Joshua, and John Woolley. 2020. "New Conflicts in the Briefing Room: Using Sentiment Analysis to Evaluate Administration-Press Relations from Clinton through Trump." *Political Communication* 38 (3): 241–59.

Mikolov, Tomas, Kai Chen, Greg Corrado, and Jeffrey Dean. 2013. "Efficient Estimation of Word Representations in Vector Space." *ArXiv:1301.3781 [Cs]*, January. http://arxiv.org/abs/1301.3781.

Miller, Charles. 2017. "Australia's Anti-Islam Right in Their Own Words: Text as Data Analysis of Social Media Content." *Australian Journal of Political Science* 52 (3): 383–401. https://doi.org/10.1080/10361146.2017.1324561.

Miller, George A. 1995. "WordNet: A Lexical Database for English." *Communications of the ACM* 38 (11): 39–41. https://doi.org/10.1145/219717.219748.

Mohammad, Saif M., and Tony Wenda Yang. 2011. "Tracking Sentiment in Mail: How Genders Differ on Emotional Axes." In *Proceedings of the 2nd Workshop on Computational Approaches to Subjectivity and Sentiment Analysis*, 70–79. Stroudsburg, PA: Association for Computational Linguistics. https://aclanthology.org/W11-1709.pdf.

Moore, Kerry, Paul Mason, and Justin Lewis. 2008. "Images of Islam in the UK: The Representation of British Muslims in the National Print News Media 2000–2008." Cardiff: Cardiff School of Journalism, Media and Cultural Studies.

Morey, Peter, and Amina Yaqin. 2011. *Framing Muslims: Stereotyping and Representation after 9/11*. Cambridge, MA: Harvard University Press.

Morgan, M. 2009. *The Impact of 9/11 on the Media, Arts, and Entertainment: The Day That Changed Everything?* Cham, Switzerland: Springer.

Mortimer, Edward. 1981. "Islam and the Western Journalist." *Middle East Journal* 35 (4): 492–505.

Mullainathan, Sendhil, and Andrei Shleifer. 2005. "The Market for News." *American Economic Review* 95 (4): 1031–53. https://doi.org/10.1257/0002828054825619.

Nacos, Brigitte L., and Oscar Torres-Reyna. 2003. "Framing Muslim-Americans before and after 9/11." In *Framing Terrorism: The News Media, the Government and the Public*, edited by Pippa Norris, Montague Kern, and Marion Just, 133–58. New York: Routledge.

Nacos, Brigitte L., and Oscar Torres-Reyna. 2007. *Fueling Our Fears: Stereotyping, Media Coverage, and Public Opinion of Muslim Americans*. Lanham, MD: Rowman & Littlefield.

National Centre for Social Research. 2010. "British Social Attitudes Survey, 2008." http://www.brin.ac.uk/2010/british-social-attitudes-survey-2008/.

New America. n.d. "Anti-Muslim Activities in the United States: Violence, Threats, and Discrimination at the Local Level." Washington, DC: New America. Accessed July 23, 2020. https://www.newamerica.org/in-depth/anti-muslim-activity/.

Nisar, Hasher, and Erik Bleich. 2020. "Group Status, Geographic Location, and the Tone of Media Coverage: Jews and Muslims in *New York Times* and *Guardian* Headlines, 1985–2014." *Comparative Migration Studies* 8 (1): 3. https://doi.org/10.1186/s40878-019-0153-3.

Nisbet, Eric C., Ronald Ostman, and James Shanahan. 2009. "Public Opinion toward Muslim Americans: Civil Liberties and the Role of Religiosity, Ideology, and Media Use." In *Muslims in Western Politics*, edited by Abdulkader H. Sinno, 161–99. Bloomington: Indiana University Press.

Norris, Pippa, and Ronald Inglehart. 2002. "Islam & the West: Testing the Clash of Civilizations Thesis." Kennedy School of Government Faculty Research Working Paper RWP02-015. Cambridge, MA: Harvard University. http://www.ssrn.com/abstract=316506.

Nossek, Hillel. 2004. "Our News and Their News: The Role of National Identity in the Coverage of Foreign News." *Journalism* 5 (3): 343–68. https://doi.org/10.1177/1464884904044941.

Obama, Barack. 2009. "Remarks by the President at Cairo University, 6-04-09." https://obamawhitehouse.archives.gov/the-press-office/remarks-president-cairo-university-6-04-09.

Ogan, Christine, Lars Willnat, Rosemary Pennington, and Manaf Bashir. 2014. "The Rise of Anti-Muslim Prejudice: Media and Islamophobia in Europe and the United States." International Communication Gazette 76 (1): 27–46. https://doi.org/10.1177/1748048513504048.

Oskooii, Kassra A. R., Karam Dana, and Matthew A. Barreto. 2019. "Beyond Generalized Ethnocentrism: Islam-Specific Beliefs and Prejudice toward Muslim Americans." *Politics, Groups, and Identities*, May, 1–28. https://doi.org/10.1080/21565503.2019.1623053.

Pang, Bo, Lillian Lee, and Shivakumar Vaithyanathan. 2002. "Thumbs up? Sentiment Classification Using Machine Learning Techniques." In *EMNLP-2002*. http://arxiv.org/abs/cs/0205070.

Park, Alison, John Curtice, Katarina Thomson, Miranda Phillips, Elizabeth Clery, and Sarah Butt. 2010. *British Social Attitudes: The 26th Report*. London: SAGE.

Park, Jaihyun, Karla Felix, and Grace Lee. 2007. "Implicit Attitudes toward Arab-Muslims and the Moderating Effects of Social Information." *Basic and Applied Social Psychology* 29 (1): 35–45. https://doi.org/10.1080/01973530701330942.

Peake, Jeffrey S. 2007. "Presidents and Front-Page News: How America's Newspapers Cover the Bush Administration." *Harvard International Journal of Press/Politics* 12 (4): 52–70. https://doi.org/10.1177/1081180X07307378.

Pérez, Efrén O. 2016. *Unspoken Politics: Implicit Attitudes and Political Thinking*. Cambridge: Cambridge University Press.

Perloff, Richard M. 2010. *The Dynamics of Persuasion: Communication and Attitudes in the Twenty-First Century*. 6th ed. New York: Routledge. https://www.routledge.com/The-Dynamics-of-Persuasion-Communication-and-Attitudes-in-the-Twenty-First/Perloff/p/book/9781138100336.

Peterson, Sophia. 1981. "International News Selection by the Elite Press: A Case Study." *Public Opinion Quarterly* 45 (2): 143. https://doi.org/10.1086/268647.

Pew Research Center. 2007. "Public Expresses Mixed Views of Islam, Mormonism." Washington, DC: Pew Research Center. https://www.pewforum.org/2007/09/26/public-expresses-mixed-views-of-islam-mormonism/.

Pew Research Center. 2009. "Conciliation in Cairo Drives the News Agenda." Washington, DC: Pew Research Center. https://www.journalism.org/2009/06/08/pej-news-coverage-index-june-1-7-2009/.

Pew Research Center. 2011. "Global Christianity: A Report on the Size and Distribution of the World's Christian Population." Washington, DC: Pew Research Center.

Pew Research Center. 2014a. "How Americans Feel about Religious Groups." Washington, DC: Pew Research Center.

Pew Research Center. 2014b. "Religious Landscape Study." Washington, DC: Pew Research Center. https://www.pewforum.org/religious-landscape-study/.

Pew Research Center. 2015. "The Future of World Religions: Population Growth Projections, 2010–2050." Washington, DC: Pew Research Center.

Pew Research Center. 2017. "U.S. Muslims Concerned about Their Place in Society, but Continue to Believe in the American Dream." Washington, DC: Pew Research Center. https://www.pewforum.org/2017/07/26/demographic-portrait-of-muslim-americans/.

Pew Research Center. 2018. "Being Christian in Western Europe." Washington, DC: Pew Research Center. https://www.pewforum.org/2018/05/29/being-christian-in-western-europe/.

Pew Research Center, Alan Cooperman, and Anna Schiller. 2017. "The Changing Global Religious Landscape." Washington, DC: Pew Research Center. https://www.pewforum.org/2017/04/05/the-changing-global-religious-landscape/.

Pew Research Center, and Michael Lipka. 2017. "Muslims and Islam: Key Findings in the U.S. and around the World." Washington, DC: Pew Research Center. https://www.pewresearch.org/fact-tank/2017/08/09/muslims-and-islam-key-findings-in-the-u-s-and-around-the-world/.

Phillips, Angela. 2014. *Journalism in Context: Practice and Theory for the Digital Age*. London: Routledge.

Powell, Kimberly A. 2011. "Framing Islam: An Analysis of U.S. Media Coverage of Terrorism since 9/11." *Communication Studies* 62 (1): 90–112. https://doi.org/10.1080/10510974.2011.533599.

Poynting, Scott, and Barbara Perry. 2007. "Climates of Hate: Media and State Inspired Victimisation of Muslims in Canada and Australia since 9/11." *Current Issues in Criminal Justice* 19 (2): 151–71. https://doi.org/10.1080/10345329.2007.12036423.

Provalis. n.d. "Sentiment Analysis with WordStat." https://provalisresearch.com/products/content-analysis-software/wordstat-dictionary/sentiment-dictionaries/.

Putnam, Robert, Thomas Sander, and David Campbell. 2007. "Faith Matters Survey." University Park, PA: Association of Religion Data Archives.

Putnam, Robert, Thomas Sander, and David Campbell. 2011. "Faith Matters Survey." University Park, PA: Association of Religion Data Archives.

Ribeiro, Filipe N., Matheus Araújo, Pollyanna Gonçalves, Marcos André Gonçalves, and Fabrício Benevenuto. 2016. "SentiBench—a Benchmark Comparison of State-of-the-Practice Sentiment Analysis Methods." *EPJ Data Science* 5 (1). https://doi.org/10.1140/epjds/s13688-016-0085-1.

Riffe, Daniel, and Alan Freitag. 1997. "A Content Analysis of Content Analyses: Twenty-Five Years of *Journalism Quarterly*." *Journalism Quarterly* 74 (4): 873–82.

Riloff, Ellen, and Janyce Wiebe. 2003. "Learning Extraction Patterns for Subjective Expressions." In *Proceedings of the 2003 Conference on Empirical Methods in Natural Language Processing*, 10:105–12. Stroudsburg, PA: Association for Computational Linguistics. https://doi.org/10.3115/1119355.1119369.

Rosenberg, Stanley D., Paula P. Schnurr, and Thomas E. Oxman. 1990. "Content Analysis: A Comparison of Manual and Computerized Systems." *Journal of Personality Assessment* 54 (1–2): 298–310. https://doi.org/10.1080/00223891.1990.9673995.

Ross, Michael L. 2008. "Oil, Islam, and Women." *American Political Science Review* 102 (1): 107–23. https://doi.org/10.1017/S0003055408080040.

Roy, Olivier. 2016. "Rethinking the Place of Religion in European Secularized Societies: The Need for More Open Societies." Fiesole, Italy: European University Institute.

Runnymede Trust. 1997. "Islamophobia: A Challenge for Us All." Runnymede Trust.

Said, Edward W. (1981) 1997. *Covering Islam: How the Media and the Experts Determine How We See the Rest of the World*. New York: Vintage.

Saleem, Muniba, Sara Prot, Craig A. Anderson, and Anthony F. Lemieux. 2017. "Exposure to Muslims in Media and Support for Public Policies Harming Muslims." *Communication Research* 44 (6): 841–69. https://doi.org/10.1177/0093650215619214.

Saleem, Muniba, Magdalena E Wojcieszak, Ian Hawkins, Miao Li, and Srividya Ramasubramanian. 2019. "Social Identity Threats: How Media and Discrimination Affect Muslim Americans' Identification as Americans and Trust in the U.S. Government." *Journal of Communication* 69 (2): 214–36. https://doi.org/10.1093/joc/jqz001.

Saleem, Muniba, Grace S. Yang, and Srividya Ramasubramanian. 2016. "Reliance on Direct and Mediated Contact and Public Policies Supporting Outgroup Harm." *Journal of Communication* 66 (4): 604–24. https://doi.org/10.1111/jcom.12234.

Scharrer, Erica, and Srividya Ramasubramanian. 2015. "Intervening in the Media's Influence on Stereotypes of Race and Ethnicity: The Role of Media Literacy Education." *Journal of Social Issues* 71 (1): 171–85. https://doi.org/10.1111/josi.12103.

Schemer, Christian. 2012. "The Influence of News Media on Stereotypic Attitudes toward Immigrants in a Political Campaign: Influence of News Media on Stereotypes." *Journal of Communication* 62 (5): 739–57. https://doi.org/10.1111/j.1460-2466.2012.01672.x.

Schlueter, Elmar, and Eldad Davidov. 2013. "Contextual Sources of Perceived Group Threat: Negative Immigration-Related News Reports, Immigrant Group Size and Their Interaction, Spain 1996–2007." *European Sociological Review* 29 (2): 179–91. https://doi.org/10.1093/esr/jcr054.

Schlueter, Elmar, Anu Masso, and Eldad Davidov. 2020. "What Factors Explain Anti-Muslim Prejudice? An Assessment of the Effects of Muslim Population Size, Institutional Characteristics and Immigration-Related Media Claims." *Journal of Ethnic and Migration Studies* 46 (3): 649–64. https://doi.org/10.1080/1369183X.2018.1550160.

Semati, Mehdi. 2010. "Islamophobia, Culture, and Race in the Age of Empire." *Cultural Studies* 24 (2): 256–75. https://doi.org/10.1080/09502380903541696.

Shapiro, Adam Hale, Moritz Sudhof, and Daniel J. Wilson. 2020. "Measuring News Sentiment." *Journal of Econometrics*. https://doi.org/10.1016/j.jeconom.2020.07.053.

Shaver, John H., Chris G. Sibley, Danny Osborne, and Joseph Bulbulia. 2017. "News Exposure Predicts Anti-Muslim Prejudice." Edited by Michiel van Elk. *PLoS ONE* 12 (3): e0174606. https://doi.org/10.1371/journal.pone.0174606.

Sheikh, Kashif Z., Vincent Price, and Hayg Oshagan. 1996. "Press Treatment of Islam: What Kind of Picture Do the Media Paint?" *International Communication Gazette* 56 (2): 139–54. https://doi.org/10.1177/001654929605600204.

Shoemaker, Pamela J. 1996. "Hardwired for News: Using Biological and Cultural Evolution to Explain the Surveillance Function." *Journal of Communication* 46 (3): 32–47. https://doi.org/10.1111/j.1460-2466.1996.tb01487.x.

Sidanius, Jim, and Felicia Pratto. 1999. *Social Dominance: An Intergroup Theory of Social Hierarchy and Oppression*. Cambridge: Cambridge University Press. https://doi.org/10.1017/CBO9781139175043.

Sides, John, and Dalia Mogahed. 2018. "Muslims in America: Public Perceptions in the Trump Era." Washington, DC: Democracy Fund Voter Study Group. https://www.voterstudygroup.org/publication/muslims-in-america.

Silk, Mark. 1998. *Unsecular Media: Making News of Religion in America*. Urbana: University of Illinois Press.

Silva, Derek M. D. 2017. "The Othering of Muslims: Discourses of Radicalization in the *New York Times*, 1969–2014." *Sociological Forum* 32 (1): 138–61.

Simon, Adam F., and Jennifer Jerit. 2007. "Toward a Theory Relating Political Discourse, Media, and Public Opinion." *Journal of Communication* 57 (2): 254–71. https://doi.org/10.1111/j.1460-2466.2007.00342.x.

Singer, J. David. 1965. "Data-Making in International Relations." *Behavioral Science* 10 (1): 68–80.

Sjøvaag, Helle, and Eirik Stavelin. 2012. "Web Media and the Quantitative Content Analysis: Methodological Challenges in Measuring Online News Content." *Convergence* 18 (2): 215–29. https://doi.org/10.1177/1354856511429641.

Sniderman, Paul M., and Louk Hagendoorn. 2007. *When Ways of Life Collide: Multiculturalism and Its Discontents in the Netherlands*. Princeton, NJ: Princeton University Press.

Soroka, Stuart. 2012. "The Gatekeeping Function: Distributions of Information in Media and the Real World." *Journal of Politics* 74 (2): 514–28. https://doi.org/10.1017/S002238161100171X.

Soroka, Stuart. 2014. *Negativity in Democratic Politics: Causes and Consequences*. New York: Cambridge University Press.

Soroka, Stuart, Patrick Fournier, and Lilach Nir. 2019. "Cross-National Evidence of a Negativity Bias in Psychophysiological Reactions to News." *Proceedings of the National Academy of Sciences* 116 (38): 18888–92. https://doi.org/10.1073/pnas.1908369116.

Soroka, Stuart, and Stephen McAdams. 2015. "News, Politics, and Negativity." *Political Communication* 32 (1): 1–22. https://doi.org/10.1080/10584609.2014.881942.

Stern, Samuel, Giacomo Livan, and Robert E. Smith. 2020. "A Network Perspective on Intermedia Agenda-Setting." *Applied Network Science* 5 (1): 31. https://doi.org/10.1007/s41109-020-00272-4.

Stevens, Keith, Philip Kegelmeyer, David Andrzejewski, and David Buttler. 2012. "Exploring Topic Coherence over Many Models and Many Topics." In *Proceedings of the 2012 Joint Conference on Empirical Methods in Natural Language Processing and Computational Natural Language Learning, Jeju Island, South Korea*, 952–61. Stroudsburg, PA: Association for Computational Linguistics.

Stohl, Michael. 2012. "US Homeland Security, the Global War on Terror and Militarism." In *The Marketing of War in the Age of Neo-Militarism*, edited by Kostas Gouliamos and Christos Kassimeris, 107–23. New York: Routledge.

Stohl, Michael. 2018. "Might There Be an After, After 9/11?" *Global-E* (UC Santa Barbara) 11 (10). https://www.21global.ucsb.edu/global-e/february-2018/might-there-be-after-after-911.

Stone, Philip J., and Earl B. Hunt. 1963. "A Computer Approach to Content Analysis: Studies Using the General Inquirer System." In *AFIPS '63: Proceedings of the May 21–23, 1963, Spring Joint Computer Conference*, 241–56. New York: Association for Computing Machinery. https://doi.org/10.1145/1461551.1461583.

Strawson, John. 2003. "Holy War in the Media: Images of Jihad." In *Media Representations of September 11*, edited by Steven Chermak, Frankie Y. Bailey, and Michelle Brown, 17–28. Westport, CT: Praeger.

Stritzel, Holger. 2007. "Towards a Theory of Securitization: Copenhagen and Beyond." *European Journal of International Relations* 13 (3): 357–83. https://doi.org/10.1177/1354066107080128.

Subramanian, Samanth. 2018. "One Man's (Very Polite) Fight against Media Islamophobia." *Guardian*, October 18, 2018, sec. News. https://www.theguardian.com/news/2018/oct/18/miqdaad-versi-very-polite-fight-against-british-media-islamophobia.

Swami, Praveen. 2008. "The Well-Tempered Jihad: The Politics and Practice of Post-2002 Islamist Terrorism in India." *Contemporary South Asia* 16 (3): 303–22. https://doi.org/10.1080/09584930802271331.

Taboada, Maite, Julian Brooke, Milan Tofiloski, Kimberly Voll, and Manfred Stede. 2011. "Lexicon-Based Methods for Sentiment Analysis." *Computational Linguistics* 37 (2): 267–307. https://doi.org/10.1162/COLI_a_00049.

Tausczik, Yla R., and James W. Pennebaker. 2010. "The Psychological Meaning of Words: LIWC and Computerized Text Analysis Methods." *Journal of Language and Social Psychology* 29 (1): 24–54. https://doi.org/10.1177/0261927X09351676.

Terman, Rochelle. 2017. "Islamophobia and Media Portrayals of Muslim Women: A Computational Text Analysis of US News Coverage." *International Studies Quarterly* 61 (3): 489–502. https://doi.org/10.1093/isq/sqx051.

Trevino, Melina, Ali M. Kanso, and Richard Alan Nelson. 2010. "Islam through Editorial Lenses: How American Elite Newspapers Portrayed Muslims before and after September 11, 2001." *Journal of Arab & Muslim Media Research* 3 (1): 3–17. https://doi.org/10.1386/jammr.3.1-2.3_1.

Trussler, Marc, and Stuart Soroka. 2014. "Consumer Demand for Cynical and Negative News Frames." *International Journal of Press/Politics* 19 (3): 360–79. https://doi.org/10.1177/1940161214524832.

Uenal, Fatih, Robin Bergh, Jim Sidanius, Andreas Zick, Sasha Kimel, and Jonas R Kunst. 2021. "The Nature of Islamophobia: A Test of a Tripartite View in Five Countries." *Personality & Social Psychology Bulletin* 47 (2): 275–92. https://doi.org/10.1177/0146167220922643.

United Nations Secretary-General. 2014. "Secretary-General's Remarks to Security Council High-Level Summit on Foreign Terrorist Fighters." New York: United Nations. https://www.un.org/sg/en/content/sg/statement/2014-09-24/secretary-generals-remarks-security-council-high-level-summit.

van der Veen, A. Maurits. 2014. "The Power of Terrorism Frames: Responses to Non-Islamist Lone-Wolf Terrorism in Europe." In *Arguing Counterterrorism*, edited by Daniela Pisoiu, 92–110. New York: Routledge.

van der Veen, A. Maurits, and Erik Bleich. 2021a. "Atheism in US and UK Newspapers: Negativity about Non-Belief and Non-Believers." *Religions* 12: 291. https://doi.org/10.3390/rel12050291.

van der Veen, A. Maurits, and Erik Bleich. 2021b. "Automated Sentiment Analysis for the Social Sciences: A Domain-Independent, Lexicon-Based Approach." Williamsburg, VA: College of William & Mary.

Vargo, Chris J., and Lei Guo. 2017. "Networks, Big Data, and Intermedia Agenda Setting: An Analysis of Traditional, Partisan, and Emerging Online U.S. News." *Journalism & Mass Communication Quarterly* 94 (4): 1031–55. https://doi.org/10.1177/1077699016679976.

Vasterman, Peter, ed. 2018. *From Media Hype to Twitter Storm: News Explosions and Their Impact on Issues, Crises and Public Opinion*. Amsterdam: Amsterdam University Press.

Vliegenthart, Rens, and Conny Roggeband. 2007. "Framing Immigration and Integration: Relationships between Press and Parliament in the Netherlands." *International Communication Gazette* 69 (3): 295–319. https://doi.org/10.1177/1748048507076582.

Vu, Hong Tien, Lei Guo, and Maxwell E. McCombs. 2014. "Exploring 'the World Outside and the Pictures in Our Heads': A Network Agenda-Setting Study." *Journalism & Mass Communication Quarterly* 91 (4): 669–86. https://doi.org/10.1177/1077699014550090.

Vultee, Fred. 2009. "Jump Back Jack, Mohammed's Here: Fox News and the Construction of Islamic Peril." *Journalism Studies* 10 (5): 623–38. https://doi.org/10.1080/14616700902797333.

Walsh, Declan. 2016. "American Muslims and the Politics of Division." *New York Times*, August 11, 2016, sec. World. https://www.nytimes.com/2016/08/12/world/americas/abroad-american-muslims.html.

Weinberger, Joel, and Drew Westen. 2008. "RATS, We Should Have Used Clinton: Subliminal Priming in Political Campaigns." *Political Psychology* 29 (5): 631–51. https://doi.org/10.1111/j.1467-9221.2008.00658.x.

Whitaker, Brian. 2002. "Islam and the British Press after September 11." al-bab.com, June 20. https://al-bab.com/special-topics/islam-and-british-press-after-september-11.

Wilhoit, G. Cleveland, and David Weaver. 1983. "Foreign News Coverage in Two U.S. Wire Services: An Update." *Journal of Communication* 33 (2): 132–48. https://doi.org/10.1111/j.1460-2466.1983.tb02395.x.

Wilson, Theresa, Janyce Wiebe, and Paul Hoffmann. 2005. "Recognizing Contextual Polarity in Phrase-Level Sentiment Analysis." In *Proceedings of Human Language Technology Conference and Conference on Empirical Methods in Natural Language Processing, Vancouver, British Columbia*, 347–54. Stroudsburg, PA: Association for Computational Linguistics. https://www.aclweb.org/anthology/H05-1044.

Wimmer, Andreas. 2013. *Ethnic Boundary Making: Institutions, Power, Networks*. Oxford Studies in Culture and Politics. Oxford: Oxford University Press.

Yancey, George. 2010. "Who Has Religious Prejudice? Differing Sources of Anti-religious Animosity in the United States." *Review of Religious Research* 52 (2): 159–71.

Yazdiha, Hajar. 2020. "All the Muslims Fit to Print: Racial Frames as Mechanisms of Muslim Ethnoracial Formation in the *New York Times* from 1992 to 2010." *Sociology of Race and Ethnicity* 6 (4): 501–16. https://doi.org/10.1177/2332649220903747.

Young, Jock, and Stanley Cohen. 1973. *The Manufacture of News: Social Problems, Deviance and the Mass Media*. London: Constable.

Young, Lori, and Stuart N. Soroka. 2012. "Affective News: The Automated Coding of Sentiment in Political Texts." *Political Communication* 29 (2): 205–31. https://doi.org/10.1080/10584609.2012.671234.

Yu, Frederick T. C., and John Luter. 1964. "The Foreign Correspondent and His Work." *Columbia Journalism Review* 3 (1): 5–12.

Zhang, X. 2018. "Intermedia Agenda-Setting Effect in Corporate News: Examining the Influence of the *New York Times* and the *Wall Street Journal* on Local Newspapers." *Journal of Applied Journalism and Media Studies* 7 (2): 245–63. https://doi.org/10.1386/ajms.7.2.245_1.

Zolberg, Aristide R., and Litt Woon Long. 1999. "Why Islam Is Like Spanish: Cultural Incorporation in Europe and the United States." *Politics & Society* 27 (1): 5–38. https://doi.org/10.1177/0032329299027001002.

Index